GOOD COOKING
FOR TWO

LILY HAXWORTH WALLACE

GOOD COOKING FOR TWO

OVER 400 EASY RECIPES

DOVER PUBLICATIONS, INC.
NEW YORK

Published in Canada by General Publishing Company, Ltd.,
30 Lesmill Road, Don Mills, Toronto, Ontario.
Published in the United Kingdom by Constable and Company,
Ltd., 10 Orange Street, London WC2H 7EG.

This Dover edition, first published in 1984, is an unabridged
reprint of the edition originally published by M. Barrows &
Company, Inc., New York, in 1949 (the work originally appeared
in 1942).

Manufactured in the United States of America
Dover Publications, Inc., 31 East 2nd Street, Mineola, N.Y.
11501

Library of Congress Cataloging in Publication Data

Wallace, Lily Haxworth.
  Good cooking for two.

  Reprint. Originally published: Just for two cookbook. New
York : M. Barrows, 1949.
  Includes index.
  1. Cookery.   I. Title.
TX652.W24   1984   641.5'61   83-20529
ISBN 0-486-24608-6

CONTENTS

CONTENTS

FOREWORD

To the Bride and Groom
  To the Business Pals
    *To the Family Which Remains Two Throughout the
Years This Book Is Dedicated.* It is for YOU that it has
been planned. We have tried to make it helpful and interesting and to prove that meals for two need not be a chore
but a recurrent delight.

Of course there are going to be problems. It is quite an
art to provide adequate meals which will not overtax the
ability of the beginner, the time of the career girl or the
food budget of either. But they are all problems which can
be solved by careful planning and everyone knows that the
successful homemaker—be she expert or neophyte—*does*
plan. She plans her budget, she plans her menus, making
one thing fit in with another. It is like a kind of jigsaw
puzzle which when properly put together makes a perfect
picture. Everything depends on whether we make it a chore
or a game, there is endless worry in one, endless fun in
the other.

GOOD COOKING
FOR TWO

CHAPTER ONE

KITCHEN EQUIPMENT, MENUS AND PRESSURE COOKERY

An efficient kitchen is not necessarily elaborate but one in which maximum work can be done with minimum effort. Ideally, a kitchen should be built around its equipment, not vice versa, but most of us must take our kitchens as we find them and only rearrange, reassemble, or change colors to suit convenience and taste.

Ventilation and lighting are first considerations. Cross ventilation provides comfort and freedom from cooking odors. Where it is lacking, relatively inexpensive ventilating units are well worth considering since they pay for themselves over and over again. A central light (preferably indirect) plus additional outlets at the main work centers are essential.

The modern range with insulated oven and temperature control is both beautiful and efficient, but you can do a wonderful job even on an old range, if you provide yourself with a reliable oven thermometer. Keep the range spotlessly clean; wipe up spillage immediately. Use a damp cloth for cool surfaces, a dry paper towel for hot. When they are available, study and then follow carefully the manufacturer's directions for the use and care of your range and remember that your Public Service Company stands ready to check gas and electric equipment, if it doesn't give satisfactory service. Just give them a call.

If purchasing a new automatic refrigerator, select one

with freezer tray or cabinet for the home storage of quick-frozen foods. Follow the manufacturer's directions also on your refrigerator. Above all, keep it scrupulously clean. If automatic (electric, gas or oil operated) defrost regularly —about once a week in summer and once in two weeks in winter. A heavy deposit of ice lessens efficiency. Modern ice refrigerators are so well insulated that they need re-icing but once or twice a week. With this type the drain pipe must be flushed out with a solution of washing soda— 1 heaping tablespoon to a quart of water—once a week.

For safe storage of food the interior temperature of any refrigerator should never exceed 45-50 degrees F. You can check this by the use of a refrigerator thermometer.

Correct height for both sink and work table is vital to comfort. For a person of average height, that is about five and a half feet, the sink should be approximately thirty-five inches from the floor and the table top eight inches below the worker's elbow. Two sink drainboards are much more convenient than one and a built-in ventilated storage space most useful underneath them.

In cleaning the sink avoid harsh abrasives. Always use a strainer over the drain opening and scrape the dishes before stacking for washing to avoid clogging the drain with grease.

A kitchen cabinet is a wonderful convenience, either the permanent or the portable type that fits practically any space, any purse. Many cabinets may be matched up with smaller units for the storage of cleaning supplies and equipment.

A high stool or high chair should have a place in every kitchen. Dozens of jobs can be done just as well and with less effort sitting instead of standing. Tired feet and an aching back never yet made for efficiency in the kitchen.

SMALL EQUIPMENT

The following list forms a good working basis though many substitutions are possible. Good pastry has been rolled with a milk bottle instead of a rolling pin and many pieces of small equipment can be made to do double duty. Kitchen cabinets have storage containers, particularly for sugar, flour, and spices. They also have bread and meat boards.

FOR PREPARATION OF FOOD

Set of nested mixing bowls
2 measuring cups: 1 pyrex, 1 aluminum
Set of measuring spoons
2 tablespoons
2 teaspoons
1 slotted or perforated spoon
2 mixing spoons: 1 wooden, 1 metal
2 spatulas: 1 narrow, 1 broad
4 knives: 1 bread, 1 carving, 1 large utility, 1 paring
3 forks: long, medium, short
Rubber scraper
Grater and shredder
Fruit reamer

Can opener, preferably wall type
Scissors
Flour sifter (unless in cabinet)
Bread board (unless in cabinet)
Rolling pin
Combination cookie, doughnut, biscuit cutter
Spouted pitcher, 1 qt.
Apple corer
Bottle opener and corkscrew
Jar opener
2 strainers: 1 fine, 1 coarse mesh
Colander
Ladle
Potato masher

FOR TOP-OF-THE-RANGE COOKING

Double boiler, 1 qt.
2 saucepans with covers: 1 pt., ½ pt.
Tea kettle
Coffee
2 kettles with covers: 6 qt., 1 qt.

2 frying pans, preferably iron: 10 in., 5 in.
Top-of-the-range baker
Dutch oven
Pressure saucepan, 4 qt.

FOR OVEN COOKING

15 in. roasting pan with rack
2 cookie sheets
2 layer cake pans
1 pie plate

1 set muffin pans
2 casseroles: 1 qt., 1 pt.
1 wire cake cooler
Oven thermometer
Meat roasting thermometer

AT THE SINK

Dish drainer
Dish mop
Soap dish and shaker
Sink strainer
Rubber sink stopper
Spray for kitchen faucet

Dish pan or rubber sink mat
Brushes: bottle, percolator,
    vegetable, sink
Holder for steel wool
Rubber gloves

KITCHEN ESSENTIALS

Table (unless other work space)
Step stool
Bread and cake box
Vegetable bin
Set of covered refrigerator dishes
Refrigerator thermometer
Garbage pail
Clock

Waxed paper
2 trays: 18 in., 12 in.
16 towels: 8 dish, 8 glass
4 hand towels or paper toweling
    and holder
Oven cloths and holders
Metal waste basket

SUPPLEMENTARY LIST TO BE ADDED AS NEEDED OR DESIRED

Grapefruit knife
Egg slicer
Potato ricer
Vegetable ball cutters
Small funnel
Whisk egg beater
Tongs
Large jelly mold
Individual jelly molds
Mincer for parsley
Set of cutters
Pastry jagger
Extra pie plate

Pastry blender and cloth
Food chopper
Bread pan
Loaf cake pan
Tube cake pan
Storage canisters
Frying kettle and basket
Griddle
Scales
Match safe
Electric mixer or beater
Electric toaster
Electric waffle iron

A wall rack holding a ladle, fork, spatula, plain and perforated spoons is a useful article, also a knife rack.

CLEANING EQUIPMENT

Broom
Dustpan and brush
Dry mop
Wet mop
Whisk broom
Pail
Dust cloths

Carpet sweeper
Vacuum cleaner
Furniture polish
Polishing cloth
Silver polish
Chamois or silver polishing cloth
Floor waxer and polisher

PLANNING MENUS FOR A BALANCED DIET

Just as houses are built of wood, stone, bricks and mortar, so the human body is built by its intake of food. In each instance, materials must be carefully selected and properly combined. Every member of the human family needs:

Energy or Fuel Foods: Carbohydrates (starches and sugars) and fats: cereals, bread, potatoes, sugar (including honey and sirups), dried fruits, butter, cream, and other animal and vegetable fats.

Building and Repair Foods: Meats, poultry, fish, whole grain cereals, gelatin, milk, egg yolk, cheese, fruits, nuts, and vegetables, both fresh and dried—all rich in proteins and mineral salts. Children need these foods for growth; adults need them to replace tissues broken down by the wear and tear of living.

Protective and Regulating Foods: Milk, cheese, egg yolk, leafy vegetables, whole grains, meat and sea foods—all rich in minerals, such as calcium, iron, iodine, and phosphorus.

Water: To carry off waste through the skin and kidneys.

A balanced diet forms the basis of good health by building and repairing the body, maintaining it in good working order, and providing energy and vigor for work and play. Therefore include in each day's meals:

Milk. 3/4-1 qt. for a growing child; 1 qt. for an expectant or nursing mother; 1 pt. or more for other adults.

Leafy, Green or Yellow Vegetables: 1 or more generous servings.

Tomatoes, Oranges, Grapefruit or Any Raw Fruit or Vegetable Rich in Vitamin C. 1 or more servings.

Potatoes, Other Vegetables or Cooked Fruit: 2 or more servings.

Eggs: 1 a day, or at least 3 or 4 a week.

Lean Meat, Poultry, Fish: 1 or more servings.

Cereals and Breads: At least 2 servings of whole grain or enriched products.

Fats, Sweets: As needed to satisfy the appetite.

Water: 6 or more glasses.

To sum the matter up briefly, a balanced diet, that is one containing the necessary food elements as outlined, automatically supplies us with all the vitamins we need. Health cannot be maintained, nor can the body function properly, without these invisible welfare workers. No food provides all the vitamins. Some foods contain two or more, others perhaps only one. That is why a variety of food is essential to obtain an abundant supply.

BREAKFASTS

Most of us are creatures of habit and, for the majority, breakfast is a more or less standardized meal consisting merely of fruit, toast or rolls, and coffee. Never forget that coffee can make or mar any meal so be sure to have it hot and strong. (For Coffee, see page 294.)

On leisurely Sunday mornings, Saturdays, too, for five-day-a-week workers, splurge a bit as follows:

BREAKFAST MENUS

Orange Juice
Hot Cereal
Broiled Ham with Apple or Pineapple Slices
Drop Biscuits

Stewed Prunes or Prune Juice
Puffed Cereal
Creamed Dried Beef
Spoon Bread

Tomato Juice
Cold Cereal
Poached Eggs on Corned Beef Hash
Hot Rolls   Butter   Marmalade

Apple Sauce or Baked Apples
Sausages with Fried Corn Meal Mush
Melba Toast

Halved Grapefruit
Chicken Liver Omelet
Quick Coffee Cake   Tart Jam

Fresh Berries
Shredded Cereal
Bacon and Eggs
Popovers   Marmalade

Pineapple Juice
Crisp Bacon or Sausage Patties
Waffles or Griddle Cakes with Sirup

Sliced Peaches with or without Flaked Cereal
Fish Cakes or Broiled Salt Mackerel
Muffins

Chilled Honey Dew Melon with Lime or Lemon Wedges
Broiled Bacon and Tomatoes
Date Muffins

LUNCHES

A business woman is not interested in home lunches except at weekends, but the housewife should always prepare and enjoy an attractive midday meal. Leftovers may form the base for soup, salad, casserole or sandwich. Then there are bouillon cubes, eggs, cheese, cereals and fruits to have along with a favorite beverage—but make lunch interesting, serve it daintily.

Lunch with a guest calls for rather more preparation but even so needs little extra effort if planned in view of the last or the next night's dinner. After all, your friend is coming to enjoy YOU, not merely the food you serve.

LUNCH FOR ONE

Cup of Bouillon (cube)   Crackers
Pineapple and Banana Salad
Toasted Raisin Bread

French Toast with Minced Ham or Other Meat
Fruit   Cookies

Egg Salad Sandwich
Fruited Tapioca

Frizzled Dried Beef   Rye-Krisp
Raspberry Junket

Egg Baked in Crusty Roll
Fruit Salad

Lettuce or Romaine with Cottage Cheese Balls
Melba Toast   Stewed Dried Fruit

Bacon and Lettuce Sandwich
Sliced Banana   Hermits

Raw Vegetable Salad   Cheese Straws
Fruited Gelatin (or other left-over dessert)

LUNCH WITH A GUEST

Eggs Benedict
Oakland Salad   Cream Cheese Cookies

Cold Sliced Tongue
Asparagus Hollandaise
Hot Biscuits   Fruit Compote

Consommé Madrilene (canned)
Stuffed Tomato Salad
Hot Rolls   Pecan Tarts

Baked Eggs au Gratin
Tossed Green Salad
Bread Sticks   Coffee Jelly

Oysters Casino
Parkerhouse Rolls
Fruit Salad with Honey Cream Dressing

Individual Fish Soufflés
Whole Wheat Bread
Olives   Radishes
Lemon Tarts

Mushroom Soup
Tray of Assorted Sandwiches
Stuffed Celery   Apricot Whip

Lobster Cutlets   Green Peas
Saratoga Potatoes
Tiny Crusty Rolls
Mocha Custard

DINNER MENUS FOR EACH MONTH

FOR A WEEK IN JANUARY

Sunday

Vegetable Juice Cocktail
Broiled Chicken
Steamed Rice   Frenched Green Beans
Cranberry Sauce
Apricot Fluff

Monday

Tomato Juice
Roast Shoulder of Lamb
Baked Potatoes   Green Peas
Shredded Raw Carrot and Bean * Salad
Orange Shortcake

Tuesday

Savory Cole Slaw
Shepherd's Pie *
Creamed Carrots *
Hot Gingerbread with Whipped Cream

Wednesday

Apple Juice
Savory Meat Loaf
Scalloped Potatoes   Harvard Beets
Cottage Pudding

* Indicates use of left-overs.

Thursday

Clam Chowder (canned)   Pilot Crackers
Sliced Meat Loaf *   Mustard Pickles
Mixed Vegetable Salad   Cream Cheese Balls
Gingerbread * (reheated) with Apple Sauce

Friday

Boiled Fish   Oyster, Egg or Mushroom Sauce
Parsley Potatoes   Buttered Parsnips
Jewel Salad
Chocolate Éclairs

Saturday

Sauerkraut Juice
Broiled Fresh Spareribs
Hashed Brown Potatoes *   Buttered Spinach
Molded Gelatin with Fruit

These menus need not be followed exactly as given. Personal preferences can be catered to. But they show how to dovetail one meal in with another by the planned use of left-overs. The cold fragments of lamb provide another hot dinner dish in shepherd's pie; vegetables are utilized in subsequent salads; a whole package of gingerbread-mix bakes with the same fuel expenditure as a half, and provides a second dessert. Again, two main dishes are provided for in Savory Meat Loaf. If there is a "Market Special" on steak, you may want to substitute that hot on Wednesday, cold sliced on Thursday.

* Indicates use of left-overs.

FOR A WEEK IN FEBRUARY

Sunday
Chilled Pineapple Juice
Baked Ham
Southern Sweet Potatoes   Green Peas
Refrigerator Ice Cream   Cookies

Monday
Cream of Mushroom Soup (canned)
Cold Sliced Ham *
Baked Potatoes   Harvard Beets
Brown Betty

Tuesday
Veal Cutlet
Buttered Noodles   Stewed Tomatoes
Cole Slaw with Diced Beets *
Butterscotch Pudding (prepared)

Wednesday
Sauerkraut Juice
Baked Ham Croquettes *
Potatoes on the Half Shell
Creamed Carrots and Peas
Prune Whip

Thursday
Split Pea Soup (using ham bone) *
Hamburg Stuffed Eggplant
Scalloped Potatoes
Orange Salad with Cranberry Dressing

* Indicates use of left-overs.

Friday

Tomato Juice
Sea Food Casserole
Cabbage Salad * with Roquefort Dressing
Steamed Fig Pudding, Hard Sauce

Saturday

Vegetable Juice Cocktail
Baked Beans   Brown Bread
Cucumber Pickles
Coffee Bavarian

Baked ham for the small family? Yes, half a small ham, and though it must be used several times it may always appear in a new guise. On Friday, if the inexpensive sea food casserole may not be specially pleasing to the man of the family, his masculine taste is definitely catered to in the salad dressing and the pudding.

FOR A WEEK IN MARCH

Sunday

Chilled Fruit Nectar
Pot Roast with Onions and Carrots
Macaroni or Noodles
Lettuce   French Dressing
Grapenuts Mousse

Monday

Citrus Appetizer Salad
Sliced Pot Roast * (reheated) in Tomato Sauce
Stuffed Potatoes   Buttered Spinach
Devil's Food Cake (prepared mix)   Milk Frosting

* Indicates use of left-overs.

Tuesday

Breaded Shoulder Lamb Chops
Boiled Potatoes   Sautéed Eggplant
Romaine Mignonette Dressing
Devil's Food Squares * with Vanilla Sauce

Wednesday

Salmon in Rice Nests with Green Peas
Lettuce   Mayonnaise
Coconut Custard Pie

Thursday

Pineapple Juice
Ham Slice Baked in Milk
Mashed Potatoes   Buttered Cabbage
Cranberry Sauce
Apple Roly-poly

Friday

Baked Fish Fillets   Olive Sauce
Potato Puff   Sliced Beets
Cole Slaw *
Chocolate Pudding (prepared)

Saturday

Spaghetti with Tomato Sauce and Grated Cheese
Tossed Green Salad
Bread Sticks
Raspberry Junket   Molasses Cookies

* Indicates use of left-overs.

Sunday dinner as planned for this week means a real day of rest for the housekeeper. Pot roast is improved by being cooked a day ahead, so prepare it on Saturday. This is also a good time to substitute macaroni or noodles for the rather overworked potatoes. When making the devil's food cake, frost only half for the first service, then cut the remainder into squares and thoroughly mask with sauce. It is unlikely that it will be recognized as a left-over; call it chocolate squares if you like.

FOR A WEEK IN APRIL

Sunday

Cranberry Cocktail
Roast Lamb   Mint Sauce or Jelly
New Potatoes   Green Peas
Hot Apple Pie

Monday

Tomato Bisque   Croutons
Cold Roast Lamb *   Currant Jelly
Fried Raw Potatoes   Brussels Sprouts
Apple Pie * à la Mode

Tuesday

Chilled Tomato Juice
Swedish Meat Balls   Brown Gravy
Steamed Rice   Buttered Carrots
Cabinet Pudding   Wine Sauce

* Indicates use of left-overs.

Wednesday

Pineapple Juice
Vegetable Platter: Molded Spinach, Sliced
Carrots,* Diced Beets, Cauliflower, with Cheese Sauce
Upside-down Cake

Thursday

Apricot Nectar
Broiled Steak with Mushrooms
Baked Potatoes   New Asparagus
Fruited Gelatin

Friday

Vegetable Juice Cocktail
Cod Steak
Parsley Potatoes   Green Beans
Rhubarb Betty

Saturday

Chiffonade Salad Appetizer
Baked Hash of Steak,* Potatoes,* and Mushrooms
Tomato Catsup
Broccoli
Banana Cream Cake

Make use of the seasonal fruits as they come into market.
Rhubarb for instance is more abundant in April and is a
grand spring tonic. Remember having it when you were a
youngster? That vegetable platter on Wednesday night,
what a picture it can be and the vitamins you will store
up, especially if the vegetables are cooked quickly the

* Indicates use of left-overs.

waterless way. And a favorite dessert to top off with! Saturday's dinner gathers up all the fragments into a glorious dish of hash. Depend on it there will not be a scrap left!

FOR A WEEK IN MAY

Sunday

Pineapple Mint Cup
Roast Chicken   Corn Bread Stuffing
Steamed Rice   Carrots and Peas
Vanilla Ice Cream with Chocolate Sauce

Monday

Tomato Juice
Chicken Pie * with Vegetables * (biscuit crust)
Strawberry and Pineapple Salad
Brownies

Tuesday

Veal Cutlet   Tomato Sauce
Baked Potatoes   Brussels Sprouts
Junket with Fruit   Oatmeal Cookies

Wednesday

Oxtail Soup (canned)
Cheese Soufflé
Chef's Salad
Crusty Rolls
Butterscotch Pie

* Indicates use of left-overs.

Thursday

Vegetable Juice
Chopped Beef Patties with Glazed Apricots
Peas in Potato Nests
Individual Fruit Shortcakes

Friday

Broiled Fresh Mackerel with Lemon
Parsley Potatoes   Beet Greens
Lemon Chiffon Tart

Saturday

Broiled Grapefruit
Planked Lamb Chops Jardinière
Asparagus with Crumbs
Apricot Mousse   Cookies

Light the oven only for baked potatoes on Tuesday? No indeed, not while there are top-of-the-range ovens which bake potatoes, tomatoes, peppers, a small meat loaf, macaroni and cheese, as well as heating biscuits, muffins, rolls, etc., with a minimum consumption of fuel.

FOR A WEEK IN JUNE

Sunday

Cranberry Juice Cocktail
Mixed Grill
Broiled Tomatoes   Oven Frenched Potatoes
Strawberry Shortcake

Monday

Cream of Tomato Soup
Frankfurters   Mustard
Hot Potato Salad
Bread and Butter Sandwiches
Fruit Compote   Vanilla Cookies

Tuesday

Fried Scallops   Sauce Tartare
Creamed Parsley Potatoes
Mixed Vegetable Salad
Chocolate Pudding (prepared)

Wednesday

Lamb Stew (carrots, potatoes, onions)
Lettuce   Russian Dressing
Fig Pudding (canned)   Lemon Sauce

Thursday

Tomato Juice
Minute Steak   Watermelon Pickles
Cottage Fried Potatoes   Summer Squash
Cheese   Crackers

Friday

Clam Broth
Baked Shad or Mackerel   Sliced Cucumber
Scalloped Tomatoes   Mashed Potatoes
Rhubarb Pie

Saturday

Vegetable Juice Cocktail
Frizzled Ham
Corn Bread   Butter
Romaine   Chiffonade Dressing
Cottage Pudding   Fruit Sauce

With warmer weather, no one wants to spend unnecessary time in the kitchen; but that's no reason why meals
should suffer in attractiveness. There are any number of
quickly prepared dishes with which to tempt jaded appetites. With the exception of the lamb stew any of this
week's dinners can be prepared within the hour provided
some preliminary preparation is made during the day or
the night before.

FOR A WEEK IN JULY

Sunday

Chilled Apricot Nectar with Lemon
Broiled Tenderloin Steak
New Potatoes with Parsley
Asparagus with Brown Crumbs
Fresh Chilled Raspberries
Lady Fingers

Monday

Braised Shoulder Lamb Chops with Carrots and Onions
Mashed Potatoes   Lettuce   Savory French Dressing
Halved Melon

Tuesday
Jellied Clam Broth
Scandinavian Vegetable Plate
Angel Ice Cream Sandwiches

Wednesday
Vegetable Juice Cocktail
Roast Beef
Browned Potatoes   Cauliflower
Lime Gelatin with Pears

Thursday
Pineapple Juice
Cold Roast Beef *
Baked Potatoes   Corn-on-the-Cob
Bread Pudding with Fresh Fruit or Butterscotch Sauce

Friday
Chicken Gumbo (canned)
Fresh Crabmeat Salad   Saratoga Potatoes
Rolls   Butter
Apricot Upside-down Cake

Saturday
Tomato Juice
Hot Roast Beef Sandwiches *
Mashed Potatoes   Parsley Carrots
Upside-down Cake * (sliced and reheated)

Fruit's the thing in July and August! Luscious berries
are at their best, melons and peaches are beginning to
* Indicates use of left-overs.

come in, so there is a superabundance from which to select. Cut down a little on the meat, and increase your
vegetable and salad intake. For the sandwiches for Saturday night, if there are good slices of beef left, reheat them
in gravy, otherwise mince the meat and use in place of the
slices.

FOR A WEEK IN AUGUST

Sunday

Pineapple Juice
Chicken Maryland   Currant Jelly
Fresh Lima Beans
Peach Bavarian

Monday

Appetizer Salad
Round Steak in Casserole with Potato Balls
Corn * Custard
Peach Bavarian *

Tuesday

Tomato Juice
Planked Ham and Eggs with Duchesse Potatoes
and Green Peas
Hot Biscuits   Butter
Mixed Fruit Salad
Sponge Cup Cakes

Wednesday

Bouillon
Boiled Salmon   Parsley Sauce
Potatoes au Gratin   Green Beans
Blueberry Pie

* Indicates use of left-overs.

Thursday
Shrimp Cocktail
Stuffed Lamb Chops
Sautéed Eggplant   Minted Carrots
Fruited Tapioca

Friday
Chilled Tomato Juice
Salmon Croquettes
Creamed Potatoes   Wax Beans
Peach Shortcake

Saturday
Cup of Chowder   Crackers
Jellied Veal Loaf   Saratoga Potatoes
Mixed Vegetable Salad *
Rolls   Butter
Cream Pie

We often associate plank cookery only with steak or shad, but that is giving the plank too easy a time of it. One may plank pork or lamb chops, ham, bacon and eggs, sausage patties, fat little fillets of fish, even the lowly hamburger.

FOR A WEEK IN SEPTEMBER

Sunday
Avocado and Orange Cocktail
Roast Duck   Sage and Onion Stuffing
Mashed Potatoes   Green Peas
Apple Sauce
Milk Sherbet

* Indicates use of left-overs.

Monday

Cream of Celery Soup (canned)
Cold Duck *   Potato Patties *
Orange Salad
Apple Dumplings Baked in Sirup

Tuesday

Boiled Smoked Tongue   Raisin Sauce
Buttered Spinach   Corn Custard
Plum Cobbler

Wednesday

Cream of Corn Soup *
Cold Tongue *   Sliced Tomatoes
Potato Salad
Rolls
Quick Peach Cake

Thursday

Savory Meat Loaf
Mashed Turnips   Creole Tomatoes
Baked Ginger Pears   Cookies

Friday

Vegetable Cocktail
Baked Halibut with Oyster Sauce
Potatoes on Half Shell   Peas and Carrots
Black Cap Pudding

* Indicates use of left-overs.

Saturday

Sliced Meat Loaf *
Hashed Brown Potatoes
Baked Acorn Squash
Apple Fritters   Lemon Sauce

Oysters R in season; rosy apples, plums, and Concord grapes with their velvety sheen and fragrant aroma all remind us of the coming harvest. Make the most of these good things while they are here. Even mature ears of corn will be good for custard and cream soup. This month you will not mind heating the kitchen up a little for baking on the cooler nights. That is why baked ginger pears and peach cake and meat loaf are now on the menu. Homey things, but, oh so good!

FOR A WEEK IN OCTOBER

Sunday

Chilled Cranberry Juice
Roast Beef   Yorkshire Pudding
Franconia Potatoes   Broccoli
Celery Hearts
Fruited Gelatin   Loaf Cake

Monday

Tomato Bouillon
Cold Roast Beef *   Mustard Pickles
Lyonnaise Potatoes *   Stewed Celery *
Loaf Cake Slices * (heated) with Maple Nut Sauce

* Indicates use of left-overs.

Tuesday

Vegetable Soup (canned)
Roast Beef Hash *
Buttered Beets
Chocolate Soufflé

Wednesday

Raw Carrot and Apple Salad
Tripe with Onions
Baked Potatoes
Jam Roly-poly

Thursday

Pork Chops Apple Sauce
Mashed Sweet Potatoes Green Beans
Romaine French Dressing
Tapioca Cream

Friday

Fillets of Haddock Cheese Sauce
Boiled Potatoes
Mixed Vegetable Salad *
Nut-stuffed Baked Apples

Saturday

Tomato Juice
Sizzle Platter: Lamb Patties, Onion Rings,
Bananas, Duchesse Potatoes, and
Spinach Timbales
Apricot Lime Dessert

* Indicates use of left-overs.

October makes us think of apples, cheese, nuts, and hob-goblins; the first two being of the utmost importance. Cheese is so rich in protein that it may well appear in any number of meals, especially when the price of meat mounts sky high. Highly concentrated, it combines marvelously with such bland foods as vegetables, rice, and macaroni; it is an excellent addition to eggs; and it turns a simple sauce into one of nutrition and fragrance.

FOR A WEEK IN NOVEMBER

Sunday

Mixed Fruit Cup
Chicken Fricassee with Dumplings or Rice
Buttered Asparagus (canned)
Celery Hearts
Frozen Pudding

Monday

Chicken Fricassee *
Potatoes on Half Shell   Baked Hubbard Squash
Shredded Lettuce   Mignonette Dressing
Apple Pudding

Tuesday

Onion Soup (canned)
Baked Stuffed Liver
Baked Noodles with Tomatoes and Green Peppers
Combination Fruit Salad
Sponge Cup Cakes

* Indicates use of left-overs.

Wednesday

Tomato Juice with Lemon
Corned Beef with Carrots, Potatoes, and Turnips
Fruit Betty

Thursday

Pea Soup (canned)
Cold Corned Beef * with Vegetable Hash *
Mustard Pickles
Steamed Ginger Pudding   Foamy Sauce

Friday

Fried Panfish   Lemon
Boiled Potatoes   Hot Buttered Beets
Shredded Cabbage   Roquefort Dressing
Cranberry Pie

Saturday

Black Bean Soup (canned)
Corned Beef Hash *   Pickled Beets *
Dessert Omelet

In these modern days we seem to have gotten away from some of the good old-fashioned hearty desserts such as apple pudding, cranberry pie, fruit betty, and steamed ginger pudding. Each one of them will make the head of the family admit that you are just as good a cook as his mother ever was, and that is high praise from any man! They are simple things to make, and are full of the kind of nourishment we need in cold weather. They are surely worth the little effort they take to produce.

* Indicates use of left-overs.

FOR A WEEK IN DECEMBER

Sunday

Apple Juice
Roast Loin of Pork   Cranberry Orange Relish
Baked Sweet Potatoes   Mashed Turnips
Pumpkin Pie

Monday

Consommé Madrilene
Cold Roast Pork *   India Relish
Sweet Potato Puffs *   Succotash (canned)
Cottage Pudding

Tuesday

Fruit Juice Cocktail
Baked Round Steak Creole
Oven Steamed Rice   Hot Cabbage Slaw
Gingerbread with Cheese

Wednesday

Casserole of Liver and Bacon
Baked Hubbard Squash
Lettuce and Green Pepper Salad
Hot Gingerbread Squares * with
Molasses Whipped Cream Sauce

Thursday

Veal Pot Pie
Carrots and Peas
Shredded Lettuce   Russian Dressing
Charlotte Russe

* Indicates use of left-overs.

Friday

Fish Chowder   Pilot Crackers
Tossed Green Salad
Mince Pie   Cheese

Saturday

Bouillon
Individual Meat Rolls with Mushroom Sauce
Pickled Peaches
Asparagus Tips (canned)   Vinaigrette Dressing
Peppermint Mousse

That fish chowder main course (Friday) brings memories of the best fish chowder your author ever ate; but the fish had probably been caught that morning and the potatoes were home grown! It couldn't be December without mince pie. In England, during the week between Christmas and the New Year everyone is expected to eat twelve mince pies, each one insuring a happy month in the year to come. Fortunately, English mince pies are made in tiny individual pans, otherwise there might be a hurry call for the doctor, which would be a tragic ending to our year's menus!

ENTERTAINING DURING THE YEAR

January—New Year's Eve Buffet

Hot Bouillon in Cups
Cold Sliced Turkey, Chicken, and Ham
Cranberry Jelly
Mixed Vegetable Salad
Buttered Rolls

* Indicates use of left-overs.

Olives   Pickles
Fruit Cake   Petits Fours
Coffee   Punch

February—Washington's Birthday Dinner

Cream of Corn Soup, Toast Strips
Baked Virginia Ham, Raisin Sauce
Grilled Sweet Potatoes
Buttered Onions
Watermelon Pickle   Celery
Washington Pie or Frozen Cherry Custard
Coffee

March—St. Patrick's Supper

Oyster Bisque with Parsley
Cold Sliced Tongue
Potato and Green Pepper Salad
Pickles
Shamrock Biscuits   Butter
Pistachio Ice Cream
Green-frosted Cup Cakes
Tea
Green Mints

April—Easter Morn Brunch

Chilled Grapejuice
French Omelet Garnished with Thin Slices Broiled Ham
and Pineapple
Muffins or Popovers   Butter
Conserve   Jelly
Coffee

May—Luncheon for the Nominating Committee

Consommé   Crackers
Creamed Sweetbreads or Sweetbread Patties
Saratoga Potatoes
Pickles   Olives
Tiny Hot Buttered Rolls
Endive with Pimiento Dressing
Butterscotch Parfait
White Cake
Coffee

June—Refreshments after the Game

Frozen Fruit Salad
Potato Flour Sponge Cake
Hot and Iced Tea
Spiced and Salted Nuts

July—Independence Day Luncheon

Crabflake or Shrimp Appetizer
Spinach Ring with Creamed Chicken and Mushrooms
Finger Rolls   Butter
Raspberry Shortcake
Coffee   Tea

August—Porch Supper

Chilled Fruit Juice
Combination Meat and Vegetable Platter
Toasted Buttered French Bread
Upside-down Cake
Coffee

September—Labor Day Picnic

Thermos Jug of Hot Cream Soup
Spiced Ham or Meat Loaf
Potato Salad   Small Whole Tomatoes
Bread and Butter Sandwiches
Gingerbread with Cream Cheese Filling (carried in pan in
which baked)
Campfire Coffee

October—Old-Fashioned Refreshments for Hallowe'en

Spicy Baked Beans
Brown Bread   Butter
Cole Slaw
Apple Pie   Cheese   Doughnuts
Coffee

November—Thanksgiving Dinner

Fruit Juice Cocktail with Crackers
(served in living-room)
Roast Hen Turkey   Chestnut Stuffing
Mashed Potatoes   Buttered Onions
Cranberry Sauce
Pickles   Olives
Mince Pie (prepared mincemeat)
Coffee   Cider

December—Company Supper during Christmas Week

Tomato Juice with Horseradish
Scalloped Oysters
Whole or Cracked Wheat Bread and Butter
Dill Pickles

Tossed Green Salad
Jellied Plum Pudding with
Custard Sauce
Coffee

SUNDAY NIGHT SUPPERS

Scalloped Oysters
Hot Rolls
Celery   Olives   Pickles
Honeyed Ambrosia   Cookies

Tomato Juice
Spicy Baked Beans   Chili Sauce
Brown Bread
Delmonico Apple Pudding

Chicken à la King on Hot Waffles
Fruit Compote   Jumbles

Hot Bouillon
Assorted Cold Cuts   Stuffed Celery
String Bean Salad, Chili Dressing
Melba Toast
Individual Fruit Shortcakes

Crabmeat Mousse   Saratoga Potatoes
Crusty Rolls   Butter
Olives
Golden Gate Tarts

Molded Salmon Salad, Cucumber Garnish
Hot Biscuits
Chantilly Mousse   Feather Spice Cake

Consommé, Hot or Jellied
Lobster Club Sandwiches
Boston Cream Pie

Individual Supper Salads   Thousand Island Dressing
Hot Rolls
Halved Melon with Vanilla Ice Cream

STAG MEALS—WHEN HE AND HIS CRONIES GET TOGETHER

Dinners

Onion Soup
Thick Broiled Steak
Maître d'Hôtel Butter
Baked Potatoes   Broiled Tomato Halves
Olives   Pickles
Tiny Hot Rolls
Fruit Shortcake

Sea Food Cocktail
Rare Roast Beef   Dish Gravy
Horseradish
Potatoes Browned in the Pan
Green Peas
Apple Pie with Cheese *or*
Apple Dumplings in Sirup

Chilled Apple Juice
Broiled or Baked Tenderized Ham with
Garnish of Pineapple Slices
Southern Sweet Potatoes   Lima Beans
Endive   French Dressing
Crackers   Cheese

Suppers

Clam or Fish Chowder
Pilot Crackers
Mixed Green Salad Bowl
Assortment of Breads
Upside-down Pineapple Cake

Cup of Oyster Stew
Cold Sliced Turkey and Ham
Peas and Carrots
Raised Biscuits
Watermelon Pickle
Boston Cream Pie

Chilled Tomato Cocktails
Cold Cuts
Potato or Mixed Vegetable Salad
Hot Buttered Rolls
Ripe Olives
Cheese Tray

Broiled or Baked Sandwiches
Dill Pickles
Black Chocolate Cake

And always coffee, hot, strong and abundant.

"POT LUCK" OR EMERGENCY MENUS

Enviable indeed is the reputation of the young home maker who, with no misgivings, can suggest that her friends stay and take "pot luck," well knowing that she can rise to the occasion, and without apparent effort serve an attractive meal.

Dinners

Chicken Gumbo (canned)
Salted Crackers
Veal Loaf (canned)
Hashed Brown Potatoes   Harvard Beets
Molded Spinach Salad
Fruit   Cookies

Onion Soup (canned) or Purée Mongole Croutons
Broiled Rib Lamb Chops with Bacon Strips
and Broiled Bananas
Potatoes on Half Shell   Canned Corn
Cole Slaw with Green Pepper
Gingerbread or Fig Pudding

Clam Chowder (canned)
Crackers
Grilled Ham (canned or cooked)
Grilled Sweet Potatoes   Green Peas
Melba Peaches (canned)
Cookies

Pea Soup (canned)
Cold Sliced Tongue (canned)
Creamed Potatoes with Parsley
Spinach with Hard-cooked Egg
Sliced Cucumber Pickles
Toasted Crackers   Cheese

Suppers

Chilled Tomato Juice
Mushroom Omelet
Melba Toast or Rye-Krisp

Asparagus Tip Salad, Pimiento Dressing
Ambrosia   Cookies

Clam Juice Cocktail
Corned Beef Hash Patties with or without
Poached Eggs
Chili Sauce   India Relish
Biscuits   Butter
Fruit Salad

Sauerkraut Juice
Stuffed Frankfurters
Shoestring Potatoes   Diced Buttered Beets
Baked Apples (canned)
or Apple Sauce

Bouillon (cubes or canned)
Crabmeat à la King or Crabmeat Salad
Whole Wheat Bread and Butter Sandwiches
Biscuit Shortcake with Canned or Stewed Fruit

An emergency meal does not necessarily imply planning that meal from scratch. Consider the third dinner menu above as an example. The meal as planned for two may have been pea soup (canned), broiled rib chops (two per person), baked potatoes, corn, cole slaw, and gingerbread squares. The soup is easily stretched by combining with a can of tomato soup, thus doubling its bulk and adding individuality. If a lighter soup is preferred, substitute onion soup, saving the heavier pea soup for another day. No one can stretch four lamb chops to make eight, but the bacon strips and broiled bananas make them look more and go further. The same applies to the potatoes; one each was originally allowed but on the half shell two will serve four.

DEEP FREEZING

The busy homemaker finds frozen foods real time savers. Remember though that *home* freezing is only for those who own a home freezer cabinet or live near a community deep-freeze locker.

Foods which have been properly stored by the deep-freeze method are both safe and delicious, retaining practically all color, flavor and food value. Almost all fruits and vegetables, poultry and meats, can be frozen for future use. The method is very simple but a few things *must* be remembered.

1. Freeze promptly, as soon after harvesting as possible.
2. Use only first quality products.
3. Pick fruits and vegetables at the point at which they are best for eating. Avoid under- and overripe products.
4. Avoid overfilling containers. Some fruits expand when frozen, others crush readily. In either case if packed too tightly containers may burst.

To Prepare Vegetables for Deep Freezing

Wash; prepare as for the table; blanch in boiling water or steam to set color and prevent further ripening; cool quickly by dipping into cold water; pack immediately; seal and freeze promptly.

To Prepare Fruits for Deep Freezing

Gather preferably in the early morning, picking only what can be handled promptly. Prepare exactly as for table service, wash but do not blanch. Remove stems of berries after washing. Pack fruits in dry sugar or cold sirup. To avoid darkening of peeled fruits, place them immediately in an acid bath (1½ tbsps. lemon juice to 2 qts. water). Fruits may be sliced right into cartons, sweetened, sealed and frozen without delay.

Packaging

Containers for fruits and vegetables must have a tight seal and be absolutely safe from leakage. The more nearly moisture- and vaporproof the container, the better the products. Leave ¼ in. space at top for possible expansion during freezing.

Freezing

It cannot be emphasized too strongly that the filled cartons be frozen promptly. If they cannot be transported to a community locker immediately after packing place them in the home refrigerator in the interim, but never for more than two or three hours. The shorter the time between picking and freezing, the better the results.

Never take from the locker or deep-freeze cabinet more packages than can be promptly utilized. Once they are brought into the home kitchen cook or serve them as soon as possible. All frozen food deteriorates rapidly after thawing, losing flavor, texture and nutritive value. Thaw fruit in the home refrigerator, leaving it in container until time of serving. It is unnecessary to thaw vegetables before cooking; transfer them immediately from container to saucepan.

PRESSURE COOKERY
(See Timetable, page 180)

There are many pressure saucepans on the market all differing slightly, especially in the method of closure, all, however, operating practically alike. Follow closely the directions and recipes which come with YOUR pressure saucepan.

Pressure builds up only after all air has been exhausted, this being indicated by a steady flow of live steam from the air vent in the cover at which time the pressure weight or gauge is set in place. With a pressure of 15 pounds there is a temperature of 250 degrees F., far above that of boiling (212 degrees F.) as reached in an ordinary saucepan. This high temperature is the reason food can be cooked in so much less time than by usual methods and come out with richer flavor, better color, greater retention of nutrients and less shrinkage.

BASIC STEPS

1. Place prepared food with indicated amount of liquid in saucepan.
2. Lock cover on, set over heat and allow air to exhaust.
3. Set pressure weight in place and begin to count cooking time *only* when cooking point is indicated.
4. Cool as directed. Never attempt to open saucepan until pressure is completely off.

Several foods can be cooked in a pressure saucepan at one time provided all of them need the same cooking time. If they require different times, they *may* be cooked together. The one needing longest cooking is started first. The pan is then cooled, opened and the additional short-time foods added. Pressure must again be brought to the cooking point.

A FEW DOS AND DON'TS

Keep pressure saucepan spotlessly clean, paying particular attention to the vent opening.

Use only the amount of liquid specified in recipe.

Avoid overfilling the saucepan.

Keep pressure steady. If it fluctuates the food will not be cooked in the time indicated.

Don't limit the use of your pressure saucepan to meats and vegetables. Cereals, fruits, puddings, brown bread and fruit cakes also adapt themselves wonderfully to this new method and the cooking time is so short it seems unbelievable.

CHAPTER TWO

MARKETING TIPS

No one person can lay down hard and fast rules as to how, when, or where another shall do her household marketing. The woman whose time is her own should try to get out early in the morning, when there is a wider choice of perishables and everything is at its freshest and best. The business housekeeper must perforce do her marketing on the way home from work, although she can often buy for two or three days at once, thus saving time and energy. Staples, dry groceries, cereals, etc., can be left to weekend buying when time is less limited.

The Store: The type of store selected depends primarily on where one lives. In a city, there is every type from which to choose. Even in small communities we find chain stores with lower prices because their purchasing is done in enormous quantities with large discounts, and they can pass these savings on to the consumer.

Marketing Personally or by Telephone: When marketing personally we can see just what we are getting, what seasonal specials are available, and we can take advantage of many good buys made possible by a superabundance of supply with consequently lower prices.

Marketing by telephone has the advantage of saving time and energy, provided we know what we want, trade at a reliable store, and talk with a clerk familiar with our needs.

Buying for Cash: Our advice is definitely for cash buying, because a housekeeper may shop where she chooses and take advantage of sales and thus often effect considerable saving. When paying cash, one keeps a closer check on buying, and is more apt to exercise good judgment and economy than when payment is deferred until the end of the week or month.

BUYING STAPLES

Cereals: Buy in variety both ready-to-eat cereals and those needing cooking; don't overlook bran with its valuable mild laxative qualities.

Flour: Wheat (white) flour includes both all-purpose and cake or pastry flours. The first is obtainable in various-sized containers from two and a half pounds up. Purchase in small or large amounts according to your storage facilities. Cake or pastry flour comes in small convenient cartons.

The various whole grain flours do not keep well, so buy only in small quantities.

There are special blends, biscuit mixes, self-rising flours, and special blended mixes for griddle-cakes, muffins, etc.; all very convenient, especially when time-saving is important.

All flour is sensitive to moisture and must be kept in a cool dry place.

Coffee: It is as dangerous to recommend a coffee as to recommend a doctor. The main thing is to buy the brand you enjoy most, not more than a week's supply at a time, ground to suit your type of coffee-maker.

Tea: Buy the brand you like, not more than a quarter

or a half pound at a time. Tea balls are excellent and convenient.

Cocoa: Good for a change of beverage, especially in cold weather. Buy in quarter or half pound cans.

Sugar: Buy standard granulated sugar in five or ten pound lots as there is a slight cash saving, to say nothing of the convenience of having a reserve supply. Keep on hand one package each of brown, confectioner's, powdered, and cube sugar.

Baking Powder: This is classified as a phosphate or a tartrate powder, depending on the acid ingredient. Phosphate (combination) powders act more slowly than tartrate (single action) powders and when moistened yield only a portion of their gas, the remainder being liberated by heat during the baking. The phosphates are also known as double action powders.

Baking Soda: Use with sour milk or cream, one-half teaspoon to each cup of liquid.

Cream of Tartar: Used with baking soda.

Yeast: A slow-working leavening agent for raised doughs. Buy compressed yeast only as needed; dry yeast (now available also in quick-working form) in small packages. Store all leavening agents in tightly covered containers.

Shortening: May be liquid or solid, animal or vegetable. Buy preferably in small quantities. Store in cool place.

Salad Dressings: Every type is available in both small and large containers. Some are rather highly seasoned, others bland in flavor. Store in cool dry place.

Dried Fruits: These include apricots, peaches, figs, raisins, currants, dates, prunes, etc. All come in small convenient packages. After opening, store in covered containers to avoid drying out.

Packaged Desserts and Mixes: The list of these, puddings, jellies, cake, gingerbread and frosting mixes, etc., is too long to enumerate here. They are of special value to the business housekeeper and the small family, being convenient, wholesome, and quickly prepared.

Household Supplies: Keep on hand an assortment of toilet and household supplies—soaps in cake, powder, and flake form; a good fine abrasive; household ammonia; germicide and deodorant—replenishing as needed. Other essential supplies include waxed paper and paper towels of various types.

BUYING DAIRY PRODUCTS

The importance of dairy products is evidenced by the fact that budget experts concede twenty per cent of each expended food dollar to this vital group.

Milk: Learn what grades are available; then select the one best suited to your individual needs. Buy fresh each day or arrange for daily delivery. Keep covered in the coldest part of the refrigerator. One or two cans of irradiated evaporated milk should always be kept on hand.

Butter: This comes in print, roll, and tub. Buy no more than a week's supply. Keep covered in the refrigerator, away from strong odors.

Eggs: Eggs are classed as "fresh" and "cold storage"; "fresh" refers to any egg which has not been held in storage. Generally speaking, eggs offered for sale are graded: the freshest, largest size, and highest quality being "fancy" or Grade A. Buy either brown or white eggs, the color of the shell does not influence the flavor of the egg. Store uncovered in the refrigerator. Do not buy more than a week's supply at a time.

Cheese: There are literally hundreds of varieties of cheese, that highly concentrated food which most of us

use as an accessory rather than as an actual food. It is, however, an excellent meat or fish substitute, especially when
combined with such starchy bulky foods as macaroni, rice,
or bread. Wrap cheese lightly in waxed paper and keep in
a cool place. Do not place in a tightly covered container as
this induces the growth of mold.

Cream: There are two grades of cream from which to
choose: heavy or whipping cream, and light, sometimes
called coffee cream, the two being graded according to
their butter-fat content. Keep covered in the coldest part
of the refrigerator.

BUYING FRESH FRUITS AND VEGETABLES

Buy such perishable fruits and vegetables as peaches,
strawberries and raspberries, peas, and corn on the cob
from day to day. Citrus fruits, firm apples, potatoes, and
onions, for example, may be bought weekly.

In buying perishables the extra cost of the higher grade
product may be money well spent because lower priced
items are apt to be less perfect, and a very little waste soon
balances the difference in cost.

There is a definite trend toward buying vegetables and
fruits by weight rather than by measure or count. A pound
is always a pound whether one is buying lamb chops or
lettuce. A twelve-cent head of lettuce may be larger in one
store, smaller in another, whereas a pound of lettuce
would always be a pound; a dozen bananas might be large
or small, but a pound of bananas would always be a
pound.

Remember always, that fresh fruits and vegetables are
apt to be at their best when most abundant therefore low-
est in price.

FRESH FRUITS

Apples: Select firm unbruised fruit. Delicious, Golden, Delaware, and Snow are good for eating; Greenings for pies or apple sauce; Rome Beauties are good bakers; Baldwin, Macintosh, Winesap, and Northern Spy for all purposes. Store in cool dry place; if possible keeping separate from each other. 2 pounds cooking apples make one 9-inch pie or approximately 3 cups apple sauce.

Avocados: Select smooth-skinned variety. Handle carefully as they bruise easily. Store in cool dry place. Use promptly after cutting.

Bananas: Select golden fruit freckled with brown for eating; slightly less ripe fruit for cooking. Once fully ripened, bananas decay rapidly. Never refrigerate. 3 bananas average 1 pound.

Berries: Select fully ripened dry fruit. Look over carefully and remove any spoiled ones. Do not wash until just before using. All small fruits of berry type are very perishable. 1 box averages 4 to 5 servings.

Citrus Fruits: All citrus fruits should be heavy for their size, this indicating a higher percentage of juice. Most citrus fruits are graded according to size.

Grapefruit: Select firm, ripe, thin-skinned fruit. Avoid pointed grapefruit as apt to be thick skinned and scant in juice. Best during cool months. Store in cool dry place.

Lemons: Select bright-colored firm fruit with oily fine-textured skins. Dull leathery looking lemons indicate age. Store in refrigerator.

Limes: May be green, yellow, or greenish-yellow. More tart than lemons. Spoil easily, so buy only in small quantities. Store in refrigerator.

Oranges: Select Valencia type (California or Florida) for juice, navels for slicing and for salads. Store in cool place.

Tangerines: Season usually limited to several weeks during winter. Select those of deep color and heavy for size. Store in cool dry place.

Cranberries: A cool weather fruit. Select firm well-colored berries, avoiding bruised or over-ripe ones. ½ pound makes about 2 cups sauce or jelly.

Grapes: Wide variety. Select firm-fleshed, even-colored fruit of whatever type. Muscats, small Thompson seedless, and Niagara have greenish white skins; Tokay and Delaware, reddish; Concord, blue; Catawba, purplish red. Grapes do not keep well, so buy only as needed.

Melons: Divided roughly into two groups: smooth-skinned, as honeydew, Persian, Casaba; netted, as muskmelon or cantaloupe. Fragrance is the surest guide to ripeness. The common thumb-pressure test may be misleading (other people have thumbs too!). Select fruit free from moist depressions which indicate over-ripeness. Refrigerate only long enough to thoroughly chill, preferably wrapping in waxed paper to avoid imparting odors to other foods with consequent disastrous results.

Watermelons: Difficult to test for ripeness without plugging. May be deep or light colored, oblong or round. Sometimes sold in sections. Trend is toward growing small-sized watermelons. Require long chilling (many dealers will chill for you in their refrigerators). If cut, cover all cut surfaces with waxed paper.

Peaches: Select firm yet tender fruit. Freestone or clingstone, that is, pit readily freed from, or clinging to flesh. Either may be white or yellow fleshed. Very perishable, easily bruised. Buy only for prompt use. 1 pound equals 4 to 7 peaches yielding approximately 2 cups of fruit when sliced.

Pears: Select, preferably, slightly under-ripe fruit with smooth unbroken skin, allowing to ripen at room temperature. Very perishable and easily bruised. Early varieties usually sweet and juicy, russet pears (winter) much firmer. 1 pound equals 3 to 4 medium-sized.

Pineapple: Select fruit heavy for size, avoid bruises. Test for ripeness by fragrance, also by pulling out a spine which should come out easily. With ripe fruit, crown can be twisted off before chilling (whole) in refrigerator. 1 medium-size equals about 3 cups shredded fruit.

Rhubarb: Really a vegetable stalk used as a fruit. Hot house type, bright pink-colored stalks; garden rhu, barb, red and green stalks. 1 pound equals about 4 stalks.

FRESH VEGETABLES

Artichokes: French or Globe. Select small green ones, as they are tenderer and better flavored. Buy only as needed, allowing one to a portion. The Jerusalem artichoke is a knobby, potato-like tuber of brownish color and distinctive individual flavor. 1 pound equals 3 or 4.

Asparagus: Two varieties, green and white. Look for tightly closed tips and tender stalks. Buy only as needed. Store in refrigerator until ready to use. Sold by bunch or pound. 1 pound equals approximately 12 to 15 stalks.

Beans:
  Green or Yellow (Wax): Select slender, smooth, crisp

beans which snap easily when bent over. Buy only as needed. ½ pound serves 2.

Lima Beans: Choose those having small fresh-looking pods. 1 pound serves 2. (Sometimes one can buy shelled limas.)

Shell Beans: Several varieties, sometimes bought in pod for shelling, sometimes sold shelled. Select those having clear crisp appearance. Buy only for immediate use. ½ pound shelled serves 2.

Beets: Winter beets are sold by the pound, keep well, and need long cooking. Store in cool dry place. Spring and summer beets, sold by the bunch, are smaller and more tender. Use tops as greens for one meal, roots for another. 1 pound or 1 bunch beets equals 3 to 4 servings.

Cabbage Family:

Green: Select firm heavy heads, discard discolored outer leaves. Keep in cool place. If cut, wrap remainder and store in refrigerator.

Red: Select and treat same as green cabbage.

Broccoli: Should be dark green and firm. Use both flower and tender stem. Sold by bunch or pound. 1 pound serves 2.

Brussels Sprouts: Should be crisp and green. Need very thorough washing and soaking in salted water. Sold by box or pound. 1 pound serves 4 to 5..

Carrots: Buy, preferably, slender, bunched carrots with tops, though in some markets in winter only topped carrots are available. Select firm, smooth, fresh-colored, and even-sized. Store in cool dry place. Chill and crisp for eating raw. 1 pound equals 5 to 6 medium-sized.

Cauliflower: Select for compact shape and creamy color. Surrounding leaf stalks should be bright green. Buy only for immediate use. Needs thorough cleansing.

Heads vary materially in size, 1 small one serves 2.
Celery: Select with crisp brittle stalks, free from rusty discoloration and with green unwilted leaves. Sometimes celery hearts are offered for sale, but whole bunch provides outer stalks for cooking plus hearts for serving. Store in refrigerator in cellophane bag, damp cloth, or waxed paper.
Corn: Two varieties, early white, and later, yellow. Look for fresh green husks and golden-to-brown silk. Strip back husks and examine for signs of worms. Milk should exude on puncturing kernels. To store, remove outer husks but retain thin inner layer until cooking time. Buy only for immediate use. When serving on cob, number of ears needed depends on individual appetites. Approximately 3 to 4 ears equal 1 cup corn cut from cob.
Cucumber: Should be slender, straight, smooth, firm, green, and heavy for size. Shriveling and yellowishness indicate age and pithiness. Wash and crisp in refrigerator. 1 seven ounce cucumber equals 1 cup sliced.
Eggplant: Select firm, smooth, glossy, and medium-sized. Large heavy eggplants apt to be pithy, dry, and bitter. Store in dry place. Unused portion should not be pared but wrapped in wax paper and placed in refrigerator. 1 pound equals approximately 8 slices for frying or 3 cups diced.
Greens: Chard, Spinach, Beet Tops, Dandelion, etc.: Buy by weight, only enough for immediate service. Store in refrigerator; do not wash until ready to use. All apt to be sandy, therefore need very thorough cleansing. 1 pound spinach equals 2 small portions. 1 pound uncooked greens, other than spinach, equals approximately 3 cups cooked.

Salad Greens: Lettuce, Romaine, Chicory, Escarole, Watercress, etc. Select crisp fresh-looking greens, avoid wilted discolored ones. Head lettuce preferable to leaf; select firm heavy heads. Wash thoroughly. Store in covered container in refrigerator. To crisp quickly, place in ice water.

Mushrooms: Select creamy or white-skinned, firm, moist mushrooms. Avoid those having withered or spotted appearance. Store in refrigerator in tightly closed container, but use promptly. 1 pound serves 2 generously as main dish.

Onion Family: Two main classes: sweet onions, Bermuda or Spanish; cooking onions, white, red, or yellow, more pungent than the former. Select firm, brittle-skinned onions, choosing colors according to taste preference. Do not refrigerate. Number per pound varies materially according to size.

    Other members of the onion family include:

    Leeks: Mild flavored, good for soups, stews, creaming.

    Scallions: Usually eaten raw, sold by bunch.

    Shallots: Stronger than onion, but more mellow in flavor. Used in cooking and pickles.

    Chives: Bright, grasslike, green blade, the mildest member of the family.

    Garlic: Bulb made up of many highly flavored "cloves" or toes.

Parsley: Should be fresh and green. Use in cooking and as a garnish. Sold by bunch or loose.

Parsnips: Sweetish fall and winter vegetable of distinctive flavor, usually sold by the pound. Choose those which are firm, straight, smooth, and small; large ones apt to be strong flavored and pithy. 4 roots equal 1 pound, or about 2½ cups cooked.

Peas: Select bright, green, crisp, reasonably well-filled pods. Buy only as needed. Do not shell until ready to cook, and cook a few pods with the peas. 1 pound serves 2.

Potatoes: White: Choose those of uniform shape and size, avoiding sprouts, deep-seated eyes, and green spots. Store in dark cool, well-ventilated place. Approximately 3 to 4 per pound; about 2½ cups diced raw or 2 generous cups mashed.

Large Idaho potatoes are specially good for baking.

Sweet: Two general types—light-colored, or deeper yellow. Either may be dry or moist. Readily bruise and spoil, therefore buy only for immediate use. Do not refrigerate. Vary greatly in size. 1 pound approximately 3 medium.

Squash: Summer: Crookneck—yellow or white with "crooked neck" now being scientifically treated to straighten. Marrow—dark green, with light stripes; for slicing and frying. Pattypan—white, cup-shaped, with scalloped edge. Sold either by pound or unit. 1½ pounds serves 2. Select firm, with no moldy or brown spots.

Winter: Hubbard—orange or green; keeps well. Cover any cut surface with waxed paper and store in refrigerator. Yields about 1 cup, mashed, for each pound weight. Acorn—similar to Hubbard; bakes well. Small size. ½ or 1 per portion.

Tomatoes: Really a fruit used as a vegetable. Select those of bright red color and smooth, even shape; avoid those having cracks or dark spots. Wash thoroughly, dry, store in refrigerator. Serve generously raw or cooked. 1 pound equals about 4 average-sized.

Turnips: Two types, white and yellow. Select smooth even-shaped roots, heavy for size; avoid softness or wrinkles. (Turnip tops make good greens.) Keep well in cool dry place. 1 pound equals 3 to 4 good-sized white, about 2 cups cooked.

Yellow (Rutabaga or Swedish): 1 pound yields about 1¾ cups mashed.

MARKETING FOR MEAT

Meat from large packing-houses having national distribution is rigorously inspected by federal authorities; while in many instances state and city regulations also provide for careful inspection of local produce. Look for this stamp of approval, which indicates that the meat you buy has been inspected. Inspection spells safety; it is your guarantee of good wholesome meat.

Tenderness and Flavor: Generally speaking, the choicest (tenderest) cuts of meat lie in the region of the "saddle," the meat on both sides of the backbone, where the saddle would be placed on a horse. In cutting for market, carcasses are divided lengthwise through the center, then subdivided into various crosswise cuts; this crosswise cutting varies slightly in different localities. Meat from the hindquarter is choicer than that from the forequarter, leg of lamb as opposed to shoulder, or ham (hind) as opposed to shoulder (fore) of pork.

Although certain cuts are often referred to as less choice, this does not necessarily mean that they are less nutritive. The toughness of these cheaper cuts is due to the fact that they are those parts which have received most exercise in life, and, being toughened, must be tendered or softened by long, slow, moist cooking, as stewing or braising. The more costly and most tender porterhouse and tenderloin steaks, or loin chops, for instance, need only brief cooking, preferably broiling by quick clear heat.

Flavor is another consideration, and this, as well as the tenderness of meat, depends largely on two factors: the high or low grade animal from which the meat was cut, and the length of time it has been tendered and mellowed by proper refrigerated hanging.

Characteristics of Good Meat: Good beef is firm and fine grained in texture with a fair amount of creamy fat, the lean also being flecked with fat. Poor beef is coarser grained, looser in texture, and the lean lacks rich fatty particles.

Good veal has firm, rather white fat and light pinkish lean. It is close grained, less firm in texture, and more gelatinous than beef.

The fat of lamb is both firmer and whiter than that of beef, and the lean is also lighter in color. The bone of good lamb, when cut through, shows a red juiciness with slightly porous texture. As the animal matures, the juices recede from the bone, leaving it brittle and white.

Pork is somewhat similar in color to veal, is close grained, and should possess a fair amount of soft fat in proportion to lean. Bacon should have a smooth skin, firm texture, and be streaked with lean and fat.

Do not overlook the food value of hearts, kidneys, brains, tongue, and liver. These, especially liver, are excellent sources of minerals and vitamins. Veal (or calf's) liver is considered the most delicate, but liver from any of the meat animals may be used. Be sure that it has a bright fresh color.

The advice of a reliable butcher is most valuable to the novice. He can give you the best and most helpful information regarding grade, quality, and type of meat to buy for your particular purpose.

CUTS OF MEAT	HOW TO COOK	HOW MUCH TO BUY FOR TWO (*Roasts allow 2 to 3 meals*)

Beef—Always in Season

Choice Cuts

Prime Ribs	Roast, standing, bones retained rolled, bones removed, meat rolled and tied	2 ribs (have thin end cut off for braising)

Steaks

Porterhouse or T-Bone	Broil or pan-broil	1 steak about 1 inch thick
Club	Broil or pan-broil	2 individual steaks
Tenderloin (Filet Mignon)	Choicest and most tender steak, also most expensive; sometimes served as roast	2 individual steaks; for roast, 2-2½ lbs.

Less Choice Cuts

Rump and Round	Solid meat, good for pot roasts, stewing, braising, and casserole cooking	3 lbs. for pot roast
		1 lb. for stewing
	Chopped, for meat loaf, meat balls, etc.	½ to ¾ lb.
Chuck or Blade	Pot roast or braise	3 lbs.
Shin and Neck	Stew or soup	1-2 lbs.
Flank	Braise, stew, or stuff and bake	1 steak, about 1½ lbs. (2 meals)
Brisket and Plate (usually corned)	Simmer	3-3½ lbs.

Veal—Best in Spring and Early Summer

Choice Cuts

Leg, solid meat	Use thick slice for roasting	2½ lbs.
	Thin slice (pounded) for cutlet	1 lb. (2 meals)
Loin and Rack	Roast	2-2½ lbs.
	Chops	2 or ?

CUTS OF MEAT	HOW TO COOK	HOW MUCH TO BUY FOR TWO *(Roasts allow 2 to 3 meals)*

Less Choice Cuts

Breast	Stuff and roast	1 breast
Breast, shoulder, neck	Stew or casserole	1½ lbs.
Knuckle	Veal loaf, jellied veal, or stew	2 lbs. (2 meals)

Lamb—At Its Best in Summer and Fall

Choice Cuts

Leg	Roast (for company)	4½-5 lbs. Have chops cut off for separate service. Some butchers will sell a half leg
Chops: Loin	Broil or pan-broil (3 or 4 chops undivided, but with bone well cracked, make good small roast)	2-4 chops. About 2 lbs. for roast
Rib	Smaller chops than loin; also good roasted undivided, but with bone well cracked	4 chops. About 2 lbs. for roast

Less Choice Cuts

Shoulder	Roast (may be boned and stuffed)	3 lbs.
	Stew or braise	1-1½ lbs.
Shoulder Chops	Sauté or braise	2-3 chops

Pork—Best in Cold Months

Fresh

Loin, Center Cut	Roast	2-2½ lbs.
End Cut	Roast (more bony)	3-3½ lbs.
Shoulder	Roast	Buy half, 2-3 lbs.
Chops: Loin or Rib	Sauté	2-4
Shoulder	Sauté or Braise	2-4
Spareribs	Broil or roast	2 lbs.

CUTS OF MEAT	HOW TO COOK	HOW MUCH TO BUY FOR TWO (Roasts allow 2 to 3 meals)
Fresh		
Tenderloin	Stuff and roast, or have Frenched and sauté	1
Ham (Smoked)	Boil, finish by baking Tenderized hams may now be baked without previous boiling	Buy small half ham
Slice of Ham (Center Cut)	Bake, broil, fry	1 slice, ¾ inch
Bacon	Broil or pan-fry	4-6 slices
Spareribs (Corned)	Boil with sauerkraut	1½-2 lbs.

MARKETING FOR POULTRY

The food value of poultry does not differ materially from that of other meats. In most instances the fat lies immediately under the skin, goose being a notable exception. It is because of this general lack of fat in the flesh itself that poultry, generally speaking, is more readily digested than meat.

Select birds having plump breasts, soft feet, smooth legs and skins. A young bird is apt to show many pin feathers; long hairs denote greater maturity.

Broilers range in weight from twelve ounces to two and a half pounds, the smallest being termed squab broilers. Aside from size, the distinguishing features are that the tip of the breastbone is very soft and pliable, really gristle rather than bone; the skin smooth, soft, and clear; legs and feet soft; and tendons almost negligible.

Fryers weigh from two to three pounds, and have the same general characteristics as broilers.

Roasting chickens weigh from three and a half to five

pounds. Judge quality by pliability of breastbone tip, smoothness of legs, and general clearness of skin. At this stage, the tendons have begun to develop.

Capons (unsexed males) are larger and plumper (six to ten pounds) than roasting chickens; they are well flavored, and cost more per pound.

Fricassee or soup fowls are older birds, weighing from four to six pounds. The flesh is coarser, tendons more fully developed, feet larger and rougher, breastbone tip firm, almost hard.

A good turkey has a plump, full breast, pliable smooth legs, soft spurs, and short neck. Ten to twelve pounds is considered an ideal weight.

Neither duck nor goose should be more than a year old. The young of both species have soft feet and tender wing tips. They should be plump and heavy in proportion to their general size. The windpipes of young birds yield readily when pressed with finger and thumb. Ducks average three to five pounds, while geese weigh eight to ten pounds.

Young pigeons may be broiled, also roasted with or without stuffing; older birds are good braised or as pigeon pie. Squab (pigeons approximately four weeks old) may be roasted or broiled. As these young birds have never exercised, their flesh is exceedingly tender.

The best season for broilers and fryers is in the late spring and summer. So-called milk-fed and early spring chickens come into market early in July; capons and roasting chickens, though purchased the year round, are assumed to be especially good in the fall. Turkey has been considered a winter bird, but is now being marketed over an extended period. Duck and goose are at their best from June to January.

A broiler, unless very small, will serve two; a fryer, two

to four; a roasting chicken, fowl, or capon, four to six; duck, two to four; goose, or turkey of twelve pounds, six to eight generously.

In many large cities it is now possible to buy any desired portion of a dressed chicken, breast, leg, or wing, or even backs for soup. This is a great convenience for the small family.

MARKETING FOR FISH

No food is more abundant than fish; ocean, lake, river, and stream abound in it. The iodine content of fish is an important food constituent, and its absence from the diet may prove disastrous unless supplied in some other way.

Freshness in fish is indicated by bright red gills, clear eyes and scales, and firm elastic flesh. Generally speaking, one pound of solid fish will serve three; but with fish having a large percentage of waste skin, bone, and trimmings (although these can be utilized in the making of stock for soups and sauces) a more generous weight must be purchased.

FISH	HOW MUCH TO BUY FOR TWO	HOW TO COOK
Bluefish	Small	Bake or broil
Small Panfish:	1 to a portion	Fry or sauté
Butterfish		
Porgies		
Sea bass		
Perch, etc.		
Smelts	1 lb.	Fry
Fillets:	½-¾ lb.	Broil, bake, sauté, fry
Flounder		
Sole		
Haddock		

FISH	HOW MUCH TO BUY FOR TWO	HOW TO COOK
Cod *	2 medium steaks	Fry, broil, bake
	¾-1 lb. solid cut	Boil
Salmon *	2 medium steaks	Broil
	1½ lbs.	Boil
Halibut *	¾-1 lb.	Bake, boil, sauté
Mackerel	1 small	Broil, bake, fry
Oysters	12-15	Raw, stew, fry, broil
and Clams		
Lobster	2 small or 1 large	Boil, broil, bake
Crabmeat	½ lb.	Salad, cream, Newburg
Shrimps	1 lb.	Boil for salad, cream, curry
Scallops	¾ lb.	Broil, fry, sauté

CANNED FOODS

Foods intended for canning are selected because of their high quality and no homemaker can afford to overlook their value, convenience and variety. Canned foods are just the same fresh foods we eat every day, carefully grown, taken at perfection's peak, promptly canned (usually at the point of production,) sealed and sterilized, always under the closest supervision regarding temperature and duration of processing. These precautions ensure destruction of harmful organisms without affecting flavor, food value or vitamins.

Canned foods are convenient, offering wide variety for year-round meals; convenient too, because with all bulky waste eliminated, they require little storage space in the home. They are timesavers because all cleansing and pre-

* Left-over boiled fish may be creamed and used for patties or salad.

liminary cooking (sometimes the entire cooking) has been done at the cannery.

Canned products are economical. Every bit of food in the can is edible. Informative labels have put an end to blind buying. Today's labels are designed to give all essential facts relating to the product so that the buyer may purchase confidently and intelligently for her specific needs. Fruits, for instance, are available in rich heavy sirup to serve as they are, or in light sirup to use for purées or in the making of desserts. Vegetables also come in varying grades for varying uses. Meats, fish and poultry are boned and trimmed, replete with nutritive value, packed at their flavor peak and in convenient sizes as well as different grades to meet every need.

Canned foods keep without refrigeration. Yet they are ready for instant use though not necessarily just as taken from the can. The alert modern homemaker flavors, seasons and skillfully combines canned foods to suit her family's preferences.

Remember there is a size and a grade of canned food for every need and, incidentally, the small sizes are ideal just for two.

CAPACITY OF VARIOUS SIZED CANS IN GENERAL USE

Number of Can	Capacity in Cupfuls
8 oz.	1 cup
No. 1 (picnic)	1¼ cups
No. 300	1¾ cups
No. 1, Tall	2 cups
No. 2	2½ cups
No. 2½	3½ cups
No. 3	4 cups

QUICK-FROZEN FOODS

The value and convenience of quick-frozen foods is beyond question. Nowadays it is difficult even to consider housekeeping without them, especially where time is at a premium. To the original uncooked vegetables, fruits, fish, meat and poultry, have been added such specialties as frozen concentrated fruit juices, prepared entrées, such as Lobster Newburg or Chicken à la King, such cooked meats as fried and roast chicken or pot roast, and a host of other main dishes. There are also quick-frozen doughs for the speedy baking of rolls and breads, muffins and pies—yes, you can even buy entire quick-frozen plate meals all ready for heating and serving.

Certain precautions must be observed with quick-frozen foods. First they must be *kept* frozen until time for use. They cannot be defrosted then refrozen. That means that in the home they must be stored either in the freezer drawer or freezing unit of your refrigerator.

Most quick-frozen foods come in units designed to serve four. For two cut the package in half, immediately rewrap and replace the unused portion (still frozen) in the freezing unit; or, alternatively, cook the entire contents of the package and store any left-over. Never attempt to refreeze a frozen product which has once been thawed. Your refrigerator can never equal the intense cold of the quick-freezing machines.

Many quick-frozen foods, vegetables for example, need no defrosting but can be plunged right into the salted, boiling water as they come from the package. Most of us, however, prefer to defrost poultry, meats and fish before cooking. This will take several hours in the storage part of your refrigerator, or at least three hours at room temperature. Never defrost frozen foods by immersion in water. This lessens flavor and food value.

YOUR FIRST MARKETING

Now you're off on the big adventure! A home and a kitchen of your own, where you can have fun and cook the foods *you* like, the way *you* like them. It is a dream realized but it has a serious side. It is *your* problem, *your* responsibility. Before you can prepare that very first meal you must buy supplies. So to market, to market! Here's your first list to start you off in the right direction, your stock of supplies being built up gradually by the addition of many other items which you will need to individualize your meals and make them to your (and his) taste.

FOR YOUR FIRST MEAL

Savory Meat Loaf
Baked Potatoes   Buttered Peas
Lettuce with French Dressing
Vanilla Ice Cream with Chocolate Sauce

Meat—1 lb. chopped beef
   1 thin 2-inch slice salt pork
Potatoes—2 Maine or Idaho
Peas—1 pkg., frozen
Tomatoes—1 can, 8 ozs.
Lettuce—1 head
Ice Cream—1 pt. pkg., vanilla
Coffee—1 lb.
Tea—¼ lb. (or 1 small pkg. tea
   balls)
Sugar—5 lbs.
Bread—1 loaf and (or) ½ doz. rolls
Butter or Margarine—1 lb.
Chocolate, unsweetened—½ lb. pkg.
Eggs—1 doz. (brown or white)
Cheese—¼ lb. sharp type
Milk—1 qt. fresh, 3 small cans
   evaporated
Bacon—½ lb.
Cereal—1 pkg. to cook
   1 pkg. ready-to-eat
Flour—5 lbs. all purpose
   1¼ lb. pkg. cake or pastry
Baking Powder—1 can, 8 ozs.
Vegetable shortening—1 lb. can
Salt—1 pkg.
Pepper, paprika—1 small can each

Spices—cinnamon and nutmeg,
   1 small can each
Vanilla Extract—1½ ozs. bottle
Crackers—1 pkg. sweet
   1 pkg. plain, salted
Prunes—1 lb.
Oranges—6
Lemons—3
Mayonnaise dressing—½ pt. jar
French dressing—½ pt. bottle
Vinegar (cider)—1 pt.
Packaged desserts—2 gelatin,
   2 pudding
Canned soups—3 cans
Canned vegetables—3 cans, No. 1
Canned fruits—3 cans, No. 1
Canned juices—tomato, vegetable
   and fruit, 1 can each No. 1, tall
Waxed paper—1 pkg.
Paper towels—1 roll
Toilet tissue—3 rolls
Soap for kitchen—3 cakes
Soap for bath—3 cakes
Toilet soap—3 cakes
Soap chips—1 pkg.
Cleaning powder—2 cans
Silver polish—1 small jar

THE EMERGENCY SHELF

Keep in one place a few emergency foods which, supplemented by current staples, can be quickly turned into meals. Keep there also two or three menus (see pages 36 and 37) built around these same foods. But do not keep the same foods on hand week after week; make use of them occasionally in regular home meals. Then replace. *Soups*: Can each cream soup, bouillon and chowder. Package bouillon cubes. *Main Course:* Can each salmon, tuna, ready-to-cook fish cakes, roe, kippered herring, lobster, crabmeat and shrimp. Corned beef hash, meat loaf, chicken, tongue. Macaroni and cheese, Spaghetti Italienne, asparagus, corn, beets. *Relishes:* Jar each olives, pickles, catsup, cranberry sauce, potted meat and pâté (for canapés) jam, jelly or conserve. *Bread and Cake Mixes:* Package each, muffins, rolls, biscuits, gingerbread: Can each, brown bread and date bread. Packages, plain and sweet crackers. *Desserts:* Two packages each, gelatin, pudding, pie, ice cream mixes. Assorted canned fruits, fruit puddings. *Beverages*: Soluble coffee, milk, (canned and powdered), mineral water, ginger ale.

SEASONINGS AND FLAVORINGS

Don't be just a "pepper and salt cook"! A good cook is known by her seasonings and her skillful blending of flavors—an art which lies within the grasp of everyone. Even the corner grocery can provide us with those magic jars and bottles of spices, table sauces, herbs, extracts, etc., which stand ready and waiting for the command to do their bit in the home kitchen.

All seasonings should be used with discretion, so guard

against *over* as well as *under* seasoning; use enough, but always let subtlety be your guide.

A word of caution as to the keeping of spices, seasonings, and flavorings: store them in tightly covered containers to conserve flavor and aroma, and, above all else, don't keep them too long. They are temperamental, so buy in the smallest quantities possible and replenish often.

To start you off in the right direction, here's a list of spices, herbs, and flavorings in most common use.

HOW TO USE SPICES

Allspice: A single spice despite its name. In savory cooking generally, also in pickling.

Cloves: Dried flower buds of clove tree, strong flavored. Whole, particularly good inserted in fat of baking ham; in beef stews; to stud lemon slices for tea. Also available ground.

Curry Powder: A combination of ground seeds and spices of distinctive flavor. Curry sauce for meat, fish, or eggs; in certain vegetable dishes; cream soups; with shellfish.

Ginger: A root, green or dried; ground or whole. Cakes, puddings, pumpkin and squash pie, conserves, pickles.

Mace: Rust-colored covering of nutmeg, in blade form, also ground. Preserves, pickles, fish sauces, etc.

Mixed Whole Spices: Sold as an assortment. In soups, stews, gravies, pickles, preserves.

Mustard: Bright yellow, pungent, powdered seed of mustard plant. Meat accompaniment, salad dressings, sauces, and cheese dishes.

Nutmeg: Kernel of fruit of nutmeg tree, strong flavored and oily. Baked foods, canned fish dishes, spinach, topping of eggnogs, custards, etc.

HOW TO USE HERBS

Basil: Especially in vegetable cookery and salads.

Bay Leaves: Soups, stews, sauces, and meat cookery.

Marjoram: Stuffings, meat, and meat substitute dishes.

Mint: Sauce or jelly especially for lamb; cook with peas or new potatoes; good in fruit punches and iced tea.

Parsley: Sauces, salads, meat and fish cookery, also as garnish. Most popular of all herbs.

Sage: Stuffings, meat, and meat substitute dishes.

Summer Savory: Meat and soup cookery.

Tarragon: To flavor vinegar, also in salads and savory dishes.

Thyme: Stuffings, meat, and meat substitute dishes.

MISCELLANEOUS SAVORY FLAVORERS

Capers: Flower buds of low shrub, used in salads and sauces.

Horseradish: Pungent fleshy root, grated or scraped; especially good with cold roast beef, fish, or shellfish.

Mushrooms: Rich delicately flavored fungus; good in most savory cooking.

Onions: See page 52 for the Onion Family.

There are many commercial labor-saving flavorers, both in liquid and powdered form, for coloring, seasoning, and for thickening gravies and sauces. Use according to directions on container.

Of sauces, both for kitchen and table use, perhaps the best known is Worcestershire sauce. But don't overlook mushroom, walnut, tabasco, and chili sauces, or tomato catsup—to mention but a few.

Flavoring Extracts: Good flavorings are distinguished by their fine aroma and delicate flavor. They are produced

from vegetables, spices, fruits, flowers, and nuts from which
the essential oils are extracted, and their flavoring principles held in solution by means of pure alcohol. Those in
most common use for cakes and desserts are vanilla, almond, and lemon; for savory dishes, celery, garlic, and
onions.

TERMS DERIVED FROM FRENCH COOKERY

À la créole. With tomatoes, onions and peppers or pimien-
tos.

Au gratin. With browned crumbs and usually cheese.

Au jus. With its own natural gravy.

À la lyonnaise. With parsley and onions.

Au naturel. Plain, simple.

Bisque. A rich shellfish, bird or game soup, also a cream
soup thickened with a purée, usually of tomato. A rich
frozen ice cream made with powdered nuts or macaroons.

Crêpe. Light delicate pancake.

Compote. Fruits cooked in sirup.

Jardinière. A preparation of mixed vegetables stewed in a
sauce with savory herbs.

Julienne. Vegetables cut into matchlike strips, also a clear
soup with thin strips of vegetables.

Macédoine. A mixture of vegetables or fruits.

Maître d'hôtel. Literally steward or master of the hotel.
Applied to a sauce of creamed butter, parsley, onion
and lemon juice.

Piquant. Highly seasoned.

Soufflé. Literally "puffed up." A dish made light with eggs,
the whites stiffly beaten.

CHAPTER THREE

MEASUREMENTS AND METHODS

All recipes in this book are based on level measurements. Level means all that a cup or a spoon will hold when lightly filled, and then leveled off with the straight edge of a knife. To measure a half spoonful, fill as for level measurement, then divide lengthwise; for a quarter spoonful, divide again crosswise, a little back of center. The use of a set of measuring spoons insures absolute accuracy.

Standard glass or metal measuring cups are clearly marked to indicate halves, thirds, and quarters. Provide two, one (preferably lipped) for liquid, the other for dry ingredients. Measures of various small sizes are also available in plastic. Half pint, pint, and quart measures of heat-proof glass have the markings clearly indicated in red.

HOW TO MEASURE

Flour. Always sift once before measuring; fill cup lightly, using spoon; never pack; level off top with straight edge of knife. The coarser flours, bran, Graham, and whole wheat, are not sifted.

Sugar. Fill cup with granulated sugar, then level off as with flour. Pack brown sugar firmly down into the cup. Sift powdered sugar and confectioners' sugar if lumpy, then measure like granulated.

Baking Powder. Dip measuring spoon into can, fill, then level off with straight edge of knife, or use guide in can. Dry spices, baking soda, cornstarch, cream of tartar, etc., are similarly measured, but may need sifting before measuring.

Shortening. For full cupfuls, pack solidly in cup, and level off. For a half cup, half fill cup with water; add shortening to bring water up to cup level; then drain off water. This method of measuring shortening may be used for any fraction of a cup, one-third, one-half, three-fourths. Spoonfuls of shortening are measured level full.

If one remembers that 1 pound of butter or other shortening measures 2 cups, that 1/4 pound of print butter equals 1/2 cup, and that 1 ounce equals 2 tablespoons, accurate measuring will be materially simplified.

TABLE OF EQUIVALENTS

1 tablespoon cornstarch when used for thickening equals 2 tablespoons flour.

1/2 cup irradiated evaporated milk and 1/2 cup water equals 1 cup sweet milk.

1 cup sour milk plus 1/2 teaspoon baking soda equals 1 cup sweet milk.

1 cup skim milk plus 2 teaspoons added fat equals 1 cup whole milk.

1 cup sweet milk plus 1 tablespoon lemon juice or mild vinegar equals 1 cup sour milk.

1/4 cup cocoa plus 1 1/2 teaspoons shortening equals 1 square (ounce) chocolate.

7/8 cup all-purpose flour plus 2 tablespoons cornstarch equals 1 cup cake or pastry flour. (This, however, will make a slightly drier cake than if cake or pastry flour is used.)

1/2 cup firmly packed brown sugar, or 3/4 cup honey, or

1½ cups molasses, or 2 cups corn sirup, or 1½ cups maple sirup equals 1 cup granulated sugar in sweetening power.

When honey, molasses, or sirups are used in place of sugar, additional liquid is also added. The quantity of liquid originally called for in the recipe must therefore be decreased approximately ¼ cup for each cup of honey, molasses, or sirup used.

TABLES OF WEIGHTS AND MEASURES

4 ounces equals ¼ pound.
16 ounces equals 1 pound.
Dash equals less than ⅛ teaspoon.
60 drops equals 1 teaspoon.
3 teaspoons equals 1 tablespoon.
4 tablespoons equals ¼ cup.
5⅓ tablespoons equals ⅓ cup.
8 tablespoons equals ½ cup.
1 gill equals ½ cup.
2 cups equals 1 pint.
2 pints equals 1 quart.
4 quarts equals 1 gallon.
8 quarts equals 1 peck.

FOOD	UNIT	APPROXIMATE EQUIVALENT IN MEASURE
Apples	1 pound	3 medium
Bread Crumbs		
Soft	2½-3 half-inch slices	1 cup
Dry	5-6 half-inch slices	1 cup
Butter	1 pound	2 cups
	1 ounce	2 tablespoons
Cheese		
American	½ pound	2-2½ cups grated
Cream	3 ounces	Scant 7 tablespoons
Chocolate	1 ounce	1 square

FOOD	UNIT	APPROXIMATE EQUIVALENT IN MEASURE
Coconut, Shredded	1 pound	5 cups
Corn meal	1 pound	3 cups
Eggs	1 medium	2 ounces
	8-10 medium	1 pound
	8-10 whites	1 cup
	12-14 yolks	1 cup
Flour		
All-purpose, sifted	1 pound	4 cups
Cake flour, sifted	1 pound	4½ cups
Graham or whole wheat	1 pound	3½ cups
Fruits, Dried		
Apricots	1 pound	3-3½ cups cooked
Dates	1 pound	About 3 cups chopped
Figs	1 pound	2 2/3-3 cups chopped
Prunes	1 pound	About 4 cups cooked
Raisins, Seeded	1-15 oz. pkge.	3¼ cups
Seedless	1-15 oz. pkge.	3 cups
Lemon	1 medium	3 tablespoons juice
		1½ teaspoons grated rind
Marshmallows	¼ pound	16 marshmallows
Nuts in Shell		
Almonds, Peanuts, Pecans, Walnuts	1 pound	2 cups nut meats
Chopped nut meats	½ pound	2 cups
Brazil nut meats	1 cup	1 cup ground or sliced
Orange	1 medium	½ cup juice
		1 tablespoon grated rind
Rice	1 pound	2 cups
	½ cup raw (¼ lb.)	2 cups cooked
Potatoes		
White	1 pound	3 medium
Sweet	1 pound	About 3 medium
Sugar		
Granulated	1 pound	2-2¼ cups
Powdered	1 pound	2½ cups
Confectioners'	1 pound	3½ cups
Brown	1 pound	2 cups solidly packed
Tomatoes	1 pound	3-4 medium

DEEP FAT OR FRENCH FRYING

Deep fat or French frying is the method used for cooking food by complete immersion in a large quantity of heated fat. If properly done at the correct temperature, there is no greasiness, no absorption of fat, and the appearance of food fried in this manner is attractive and tempting. On the other hand, if carelessly or imperfectly done it is perhaps one of the least desirable of cooking methods.

Equipment for Deep Fat Frying: A heavy kettle, preferably with straight sides, large enough to hold sufficient fat to completely cover the food to be cooked.

A wire frying basket, in which the food is placed for ready immersion into the fat and easy removal from it, unless one wishes to go fishing for each portion of food as it is done. (A perforated spoon or skimmer may replace the basket but is neither as efficient nor as easy to handle.)

A frying thermometer on which the various temperatures needed for the different types of food are clearly indicated.

Absorbent paper on which to drain food after frying.

The Fat: Despite the fact that the use of a large amount of fat is suggested, this method of frying is *not* extravagant because the same fat is used over and over again.

Select whatever type of fat you prefer, animal or vegetable, liquid or solid; but be sure to heat it to the proper temperature.

When frying is completed, and fat cool enough to handle, strain through fine cheesecloth to eliminate any crumbs or bits of food which may have fallen into it.

When frying such floury mixtures as doughnuts, the fat will appear slightly cloudy, but a few slices of raw potato, subsequently cooked in it, quickly clear it.

Keep fat covered in a cool place between usings.

The Process of Egging and Bread Crumbing: To attain the much-desired crisp, golden-brown surface, see that any food to be fried is thoroughly dry when immersed in the fat. This is one good reason for egging and bread crumbing. Break an egg onto a plate, beat just enough to blend thoroughly yolk and white, but not enough to make them frothy. Add a tablespoon of water, then lay the food (fish, croquettes, or whatever you have) in the plate, and completely cover with the egg, preferably using a small brush to apply it. Lift out with a spatula, letting excess egg drain back into the plate; then turn (upside down) into crumbs (use plenty of these) which you have ready on a piece of kitchen paper. Cover completely with crumbs, lift up and carefully shake off any loose ones lest they fall into the fat and burn. If desired, season the crumbs with salt and pepper.

With very moist foods, such as oysters or clams, first pat dry in a soft cloth, then dip into crumbs, next into egg and again into crumbs, or they may be egged and crumbed twice. This last, however, makes a rather heavy surface coating.

Bread crumbs are preferable to cracker crumbs, the latter being apt to absorb grease. Any left-over crumbs should be sifted, dried if necessary, and stored for future use. Remember that for variety of appearance, crushed flaked, or shredded cereal, or fine-grain uncooked cereal, may be substituted for bread crumbs, and, with sweet croquettes, cake crumbs may be called into service.

After egging and crumbing lay a few portions of food in the wire frying basket and immerse *gently* in the fat which has been preheated to the correct temperature. Don't try to fry too much at one time. With croquettes, for example, two fryings of three croquettes each will give better results than trying to cook all at once, for obviously putting a quantity of cold food into the fat lowers the temperature unduly.

TIME AND TEMPERATURE CHART FOR DEEP FAT OR FRENCH
FRYING

FOOD	TEMPERATURE OF FAT (Fahrenheit)	TIME OF COOKING (Minutes)
Doughnuts, crullers, fritters, and un-cooked mixtures generally	360°-375°	2-5
Fish cakes, croquettes, and cooked mixtures generally	375°-390°	2-5
Fillets: flounder, sole, haddock	375°-390°	3-6
Small fish, smelts, etc.	375°-390°	2-5
Oysters, clams, scallops	375°-390°	2-5
Crabs (soft-shell)	360°-375°	3-5
Onion rings	380°	2-4
Potatoes: French Fried, Julienne, or shoestring	375°-390°	4-8
Eggplant	380°	2-4
Timbale cases	375°	1-1½

The Bread Test: If a frying thermometer is not available, drop an inch cube of bread into the frying fat. For cooked mixtures this should become golden brown in forty seconds, for uncooked mixtures it should brown in sixty seconds.

COOKING METHODS AND PROCESSES

Bake: To cook (by dry heat) in the oven. Temperatures may vary considerably. The same process is termed "roast" when applied to meat.

Barbecue: To roast meat by direct heat, basting frequently with highly seasoned sauce.

Bard: To envelop meat in or cover with a blanket of thin slices of fat salt pork or bacon, to enrich and moisten.

Baste: To moisten cooking meat or poultry by periodically pouring over it small amounts of liquid, usually fat or juice from the roasting pan.

Beat: To mix with a vigorous rotary motion with spoon, whisk, or electric mixer, to insure smoothness or to incorporate air.

Blanch: To dip briefly into boiling water to loosen skin, reduce strong flavor, or to whiten.

Boil: To cook in liquid at boiling temperature—212° F. at sea level. Decrease 1° F. for every 500 feet elevation. (See also Parboil.)

Braise: To brown meat or vegetables in a little hot fat, then to cook slowly (covered), with very little added liquid, in oven or on top of range.

Broil or Grill: To cook under (or over) strong direct heat. (See also Pan Broil.)

Caramelize: To melt sugar very slowly over low fire until it liquefies and turns brownish.

Chop: To cut into small pieces, using sharp knife or chopper.

Cream: To soften and blend ingredients (usually shortening and sugar, or shortening and flour) by working with back of spoon or in electric mixer.

Crisp: To restore texture: as of dry cereals, by heating in oven; or of vegetables, by soaking in ice water.

Cube or Dice: To cut into small square pieces.

Cut in: Blending cold shortening with flour by means of a wire blender, or two knife blades.

Dot: To scatter or distribute small bits, as butter or herbs, over surface of food.

Dredge: To coat with dry ingredients, as flour or sugar.

Dust: To sprinkle more lightly than in dredging.

Fold: To incorporate such ingredients as stiffly beaten egg whites, whipped cream, or sugar into a mixture with a gentle cutting and "over and over" motion.

Fricassee: A combination of sautéing and stewing, used chiefly for meat and poultry.

Fry: To cook in hot fat.

Deep Fat or French Fry: Use sufficient fat to completely cover the food.

Shallow Fry: Use only enough fat to partially cover the food.

Sauté or Pan Fry: Use only a small amount of fat.

Garnish: To decorate.

Grill: (See Broil.)

Knead: To work and press doughs with hands or mechanical mixer.

Lard: To draw very narrow fat strips of salt pork through lean meat with larding needle made for the purpose.

Lardoon: Fat strips used in larding.

Marinate: To flavor, moisten, and season by combining with and allowing to stand in a marinade, that is, an oil-acid mixture.

Mask: To completely cover, usually with mayonnaise or other sauce.

Mince: To cut or chop very fine.

Pan Broil: To cook on top of range in very slightly greased pan.

Parboil: To partially cook food, usually meat or vegetables in water or stock.

Pare or Peel: To remove rind or skin.

Poach: To cook briefly in hot liquid just below boiling point.

Purée: Cooked food pressed through sieve; also thick soup.

Scald: To bring liquid, usually milk, almost to boiling point.

Sear: To brown surface of meat by a quick application of intense dry heat.

Shred: To cut or tear into narrow strips.

Sift: To restore lightness, and sometimes to blend, two or more dry ingredients by passing through a sieve.

Simmer: To cook for a more or less extended period just below boiling point.

Skewer: To fasten with metal or wooden skewers or pins to preserve shape.

Steam: To cook in or by steam.

Stew: To cook gently for a long period in a moderate amount of liquid.

Stir: To blend ingredients, usually with spoon, but without beating.

Toast: To brown surface by direct heat.

Truss: To skewer or tie poultry or game to preserve shape while cooking.

Try Out: To cook until fat separates from solid tissue, leaving it crisp and brown. Usually applied to bacon or fat pork.

Whip: To beat with rapid motion to incorporate all possible air.

OVEN TEMPERATURES

Slow	250°-350° F.
Moderate	350°-400° F.
Hot	400°-450° F.
Very Hot	450°-500° F.

Modern ovens are equipped with thermostatic control. Set the regulator at the temperature desired before lighting the oven. Occasionally thermostats may need adjustment, which should be made by the regular dealer. Use a portable oven thermometer where an oven has no built-in regulator.

TIPS AND TIMESAVERS

When beating cream or eggs, keep bowl steady. Work quietly by placing folded towel under it.

To slice print butter evenly, cut with a knife blade dipped in boiling water.

To soften hardened brown sugar, place in cool oven until heated through. Store in tightly covered container in refrigerator.

Sift flour on paper towel to save washing a bowl.

To coat food with seasoned flour or with sugar, place in paper bag containing the coating.

Peel onions under cold water to avoid tears.

When only a little onion juice is needed, cut a slice from base of onion and scrape cut surface with tip of teaspoon.

To avoid discoloration of peeled fruits, especially apples, sprinkle with lemon juice.

To skin tomatoes, impale on fork, scald, then plunge into cold water; or hold over open flame to blister skin before peeling.

Wipe grease from surface of frying pans or broilers with soft paper before washing.

Rinse greasy or sugary utensils with scalding water before washing. Rinse other utensils, especially those used for eggs or flour mixtures, first with cold water.

Should meat or fat take fire when broiling under flame, close broiler door and immediately turn off heat. Should fire persist, smother flame with salt.

Keep a tube of burn emollient in kitchen for emergencies.

CHAPTER FOUR

BREADS

Always sift flour once before measuring.
All measurements are level.

BAKING POWDER BISCUITS

1 cup sifted flour	2 tablespoons shortening
1 teaspoon baking powder	Scant ½ cup milk
¼ teaspoon salt	

Sift dry ingredients thoroughly and add shortening, cutting it in with two knives, working it in with a fork, or
using a pastry blender. Add liquid to make a soft dough.
Turn onto floured board, and toss and work lightly with
fingers to insure a smooth surface. Roll out one-half to
three-fourths inch thick, cut with biscuit cutter and bake
on flat greased baking pan in hot oven, 450° F., about
twelve minutes.

Biscuit Pointers

If biscuits are to be light and tender, dough must be
quite soft.

A little kneading makes for smoothness and good texture
but it *must* be little and done quickly.

Use as little flour as possible on the board.

For crusty biscuits, place a little apart on baking pan;
for very soft ones set close together.

Biscuit dough may be made up ahead, cut out, and kept in the refrigerator for several hours before baking, in which case brush with melted butter to prevent a crust forming, and keep biscuits well covered. Let stand at room temperature half an hour before baking.

For Sour Milk or Buttermilk Biscuits, add $\frac{1}{8}$ teaspoon baking soda to dry ingredients when sifting, and moisten with sour milk (or buttermilk) in place of sweet.

For Graham or Whole Wheat Biscuits, substitute Graham or whole wheat flour for white. This may be sifted to make it light, but replace any bran that remains in the sifter. These flours need more moisture, therefore increase amount of milk used.

For Orange Biscuits, add grated rind of half an orange to dry ingredients. Roll, cut, and press into center of each biscuit a cube of sugar dipped into orange juice. Or roll dough thin, cut with large cutter, spread with softened butter, place section of orange dipped into sugar on each, fold over to cover orange and press edges together.

For Cheese Biscuits, add $\frac{1}{4}$ cup grated cheese and $\frac{1}{4}$ teaspoon paprika to sifted dry ingredients before moistening.

For Drop or Emergency Biscuits, add enough additional liquid (about 2 tablespoons) to make dough soft and sticky; then, instead of rolling and cutting, drop onto greased pan from tip of spoon.

For Sandwich Biscuits, divide dough into two portions and roll each into thin rectangle. Spread one portion with filling, cover with remaining dough. Cut into squares, brush with milk or softened butter.

Suggested fillings are: deviled or potted meat; minced ham with mustard; thin spreading of uncooked sausage meat (bake this slowly); chopped candied fruit peel mixed with half its bulk chopped dates (spread dough with sof-

tened butter before adding); equal parts butter and brown
sugar creamed together then blended with chopped pecans
or other nuts; a layer of cream cheese, then one of orange
marmalade.

The reason for suggesting cutting these filled or Sandwich Biscuits square rather than round is to avoid any
fragments or left-over scraps.

For Molasses Nut Biscuits, mix thoroughly together
1½ tablespoons melted butter, ¼ cup molasses, and ⅛
teaspoon ground cinnamon. Put a half tablespoon of the
mixture into each of four well-greased muffin pans. Roll
biscuit dough into an oblong sheet, spread with remaining
molasses mixture, and sprinkle with chopped nuts. Roll
up, cut into four portions and place cut side down in
prepared pans. Remove from pans as soon as baked to
avoid sticking.

BISCUIT SHORTCAKE

1 cup sifted flour	2 tablespoons sugar
1 teaspoon baking powder	4 tablespoons shortening
¼ teaspoon salt	Scant ½ cup milk

Sift together all dry ingredients, work in shortening, and
mix to smooth dough with milk. Divide into two portions,
turn one onto slightly floured board and roll out about
one-half inch thick. Spread lightly with softened butter,
top with the second portion similarly rolled out, brush
top surface also with softened butter and bake in hot oven,
450° F., about twenty minutes. Separate the layers, fill with
crushed sweetened fruit, putting more fruit over the top.
Serve plain or with cream.

For Individual Biscuit Shortcakes, roll out and cut with
large-sized biscuit cutter, placing one portion on top of
the other as directed.

QUICK COFFEE CAKE

1 cup sifted flour
1 teaspoon baking powder
⅓ teaspoon salt
3 tablespoons sugar

3 tablespoons shortening
1 small egg, well beaten
About 3 tablespoons milk

FOR THE TOPPING:

1 tablespoon melted butter
2 tablespoons sugar
1½ teaspoons flour

¼ teaspoon ground cinnamon

Sift together twice, flour, baking powder, and salt; add sugar, and work in shortening. Combine egg and milk and use to moisten dry ingredients. When thoroughly blended, spread evenly in shallow greased baking pan or divide into greased muffin pans. Brush surface with melted butter and sprinkle with sugar, flour, and cinnamon stirred together. Bake in hot oven, 400° F., twenty-five to thirty minutes.

MUFFINS

1 cup sifted flour
2 teaspoons baking powder
⅓ teaspoon salt
1 tablespoon sugar, optional

1 small egg
About ½ cup milk
1 tablespoon melted shortening

Sift together flour, baking powder, and salt. Add sugar, if used, and moisten with beaten egg, milk, and melted shortening. Beat well, transfer to greased muffin pans and bake in hot oven, 400° F., from twenty to twenty-five minutes.

For Cereal Muffins, add to sifted dry ingredients ½ cup cooked or flaked cereal. With cooked cereal, slightly reduce the quantity of milk used; with flaked cereal, slightly increase it.

For Corn Muffins, use ½ cup flour and ½ cup corn meal in place of all flour.

For Graham or Whole Wheat Muffins, use ½ cup Graham or whole wheat flour in place of white flour, and add a tablespoon additional liquid.

For Cheese Muffins, stir ⅓ cup grated cheese into muffin batter.

For Ham or Bacon Muffins, stir ⅓ cup diced cooked ham or bacon into muffin batter.

For Fruit or Nut Muffins, stir ½ cup diced pitted dates, seedless or halved seeded raisins, or coarsely chopped nut meats into muffin batter.

BRAN MUFFINS

½ cup bran
Scant ½ cup milk
½ cup sifted flour
1¾ teaspoons baking
   powder

¼ teaspoon salt
1½ tablespoons sugar
1 small egg
1½ tablespoons melted
   shortening

Pour milk over bran and let stand ten minutes. Sift together flour, baking powder, salt, and sugar. Then combine the two mixtures, add egg and shortening and mix, beating as little as possible. Turn into well-greased muffin pans and bake in hot oven, 400°-425° F., twenty to twenty-five minutes.

POPOVERS

⅔ cup sifted flour
⅓ teaspoon salt

2 small eggs
⅔ cup milk

Sift flour and salt. Make a hollow in the center, and pour in beaten eggs with half the milk. Mix until smooth, gradually adding remaining milk, then beat hard for two minutes. Pour into sizzling-hot well-greased heavy gem pans and bake in moderately hot oven, 375°-400° F., about thirty-five minutes.

HONEY NUT BREAD

1 cup sifted white flour
1 cup whole wheat flour
4 teaspoons baking powder
½ teaspoon salt
½ cup bran

½ cup chopped nut meats
1 beaten egg
⅓ cup honey
1 cup milk

Sift together the two flours, baking powder, and salt, add the bran and nut meats, then moisten with beaten egg, honey, and milk lightly beaten together. Turn into well-greased bread pan and bake in moderate oven, 350°-375° F., about one hour.

Makes delicious sandwiches with filling of cream cheese, cottage cheese, or orange marmalade.

DATE BRAN BREAD

1 cup sifted flour
1½ teaspoons baking
   powder
⅛ teaspoon baking soda
⅓ teaspoon salt
⅔ cup bran
1 small egg

⅓ cup molasses
½ cup milk
½ cup chopped pitted
   dates
2 tablespoons melted shortening

Sift flour, baking powder, soda, and salt. Add bran, and blend with beaten egg, molasses, and milk. Stir in dates and shortening. Bake in shallow greased pan in moderate oven, 350° F., about forty minutes.

SPOON BREAD

½ cup corn meal	1 tablespoon shortening
1 cup boiling water	½ teaspoon salt
½ cup milk	1 egg

Stir corn meal gently into rapidly boiling water and cook, stirring constantly, for five minutes. Remove from fire, add milk, shortening, and salt, and finally the well-beaten egg. Beat and mix very thoroughly. Turn into a well-buttered pan, and bake in hot oven, 400° F., about twenty-five minutes. Serve with a spoon from the dish in which it is baked.

CORN BREAD

½ cup corn meal	1 small egg
½ cup sifted flour	½ cup milk
2 teaspoons baking powder	1 tablespoon melted short-
¼ teaspoon salt	ening
1 tablespoon sugar	

Sift together the dry ingredients, and mix to a rather soft consistency with the beaten egg, milk, and melted shortening. Turn into a greased shallow pan, and bake in moderately hot oven, 375°-400° F., about twenty-five minutes.

GRIDDLE CAKES

1¼ cups sifted flour	¾ cup milk
1¼ teaspoons baking powder	2 eggs, slightly beaten
½ teaspoon salt	2 tablespoons melted butter or other shortening

Sift dry ingredients thoroughly. Combine eggs and milk and add gradually, working to a smooth creamy batter.

Add shortening last, and bake on hot griddle. (One tea-spoon sugar may be added with the flour if desired.)

Some cooks contend that beating the egg whites stiffly, and adding just before baking, makes lighter cakes. With this method, mix the batter with egg yolks and milk only, then finally fold in the stiffly beaten egg whites.

Do not forget that there are many prepared griddle and pancake mixes (and they make excellent cakes) which need only the addition of milk or water to moisten to the desired consistency. Many of these flours are of blended grains, thus giving good variety. There is no law against enriching them, if one wishes, by the addition of egg and melted shortening, but they are good used just as they come from the package.

Rules for Baking Griddle Cakes

Some griddles are designed for baking without any greasing whatever. If, however, yours needs greasing, let it be done very lightly and with an unsalted fat. Wiping over with an oiled cloth before and between bakings is usually sufficient.

Heat the griddle slowly and evenly. Test for heat by pouring onto it a few drops of cold water which should immediately form sputtering, quickly disappearing bubbles.

If a spoon or spouted ladle large enough to hold batter for one griddle cake is available, use it for pouring, otherwise the simplest plan is to turn the batter, after mixing, into a narrow-mouthed pitcher.

With a properly heated griddle the cakes will begin to sizzle, set, and bake immediately. Turn once only as soon as thoroughly puffed, the under side browned, and the top evenly covered with bubbles.

SOUR MILK GRIDDLE CAKES

1¼ cups sifted flour	1 teaspoon sugar, optional
½ teaspoon salt	1 egg, beaten
⅔ teaspoon baking soda	1 tablespoon melted butter
1 cup sour milk	or shortening

Sift together flour, salt, and soda, add sugar if used, and mix to light batter with beaten egg and milk. Stir in shortening, and bake on hot griddle.

CORN MEAL GRIDDLE CAKES

¼ cup sifted flour	¾ cup milk
2 teaspoons baking powder	1 scant tablespoon molasses
⅓ teaspoon salt	1 beaten egg
¾ cup corn meal	2 teaspoons melted butter

Sift flour, baking powder, and salt, add corn meal, then moisten with remaining combined ingredients. Beat thoroughly, and bake on hot greased griddle. Very good with broiled ham.

CRÊPES SUZETTE

2 small eggs	1½ teaspoons powdered
½ cup milk	sugar
¼ cup sifted cake flour	⅛ teaspoon salt
	Grated rind ½ orange

Beat eggs slightly and combine with milk. Sift flour, sugar, and salt, add orange rind, and mix to light batter with eggs and milk. Beat until perfectly smooth. Bake preferably in a heavy, small frying pan that the cakes may be exactly even in size, having pan well greased with butter. Turn to brown both sides. As soon as done, roll and

keep hot while doing remainder of baking. If desired, a
teaspoon of sugar may be sprinkled over each crêpe before
rolling.

When ready to serve melt a tablespoon of Suzette Sauce,
lift a pancake carefully, unroll and turn about in sauce
until this is completely absorbed by the cake. Re-roll for
service.

WAFFLES

2 cups sifted flour   3 eggs
2 teaspoons baking powder 1 cup milk
½ teaspoon salt   ¼ cup melted butter

Sift together flour, baking powder, and salt. Beat egg
yolks until light, combine with milk and melted butter.
Add to sifted dry ingredients and beat until perfectly
smooth. Fold in stiffly beaten egg whites, and bake in hot
waffle iron.

For variety add ⅓ cup crumbled cooked bacon, ½ cup
grated cheese, or ½ teaspoon ground cinnamon, stirring
any of these into the dry ingredients before mixing.

CHOCOLATE OR DEVIL'S FOOD WAFFLES

½ cup butter   ½ teaspoon salt
¾ cup sugar   ½ cup milk
2 eggs   1 teaspoon vanilla
1½ cups sifted flour   2 squares (ounces) unsweet-
1½ teaspoons baking   ened chocolate, melted
   powder

Cream butter and sugar, add well-beaten eggs, then
sifted dry ingredients alternately with milk and vanilla.
Stir in chocolate last, and bake in waffle iron not quite as

hot as usual (chocolate burns readily). Serve with whipped cream or ice cream, or make into ice cream sandwiches.

MELBA TOAST

Cut day-old bread into very thin slices. Place on oven rack and bake in cool oven, not over 325° F., until crisp and golden brown throughout. The bread will curl slightly during the drying process.

MILK TOAST

Place freshly made toast in deep plates; pour slightly salted, scalded milk over and serve immediately.

CREAM TOAST

Place freshly made toast in deep plates, and pour over it a thin White Sauce to which, for added richness, a spoonful or two of light cream may be added.

FRENCH TOAST

4 slices day-old bread	½ cup milk
1 egg	Butter or other shortening

Crusts may be removed or left as preferred. Beat egg until light, combine with milk, lay slices of bread in the mixture, and turn in it two or three times until all liquid is absorbed. Fry golden brown on both sides in a little butter or other shortening. Serve with butter, sirup, or honey.

CINNAMON TOAST

Butter freshly made toast generously, then spread with a sugar and cinnamon mixture, using one part cinnamon to three parts sugar. If convenient, place in the oven for a moment or two before serving, to allow sugar to partially melt into the toast.

HONEY TOAST

Spread hot buttered toast with honey, and if desired squeeze a few drops of lemon juice over this.

CRANBERRY BANANA TOAST

Toast bread on one side, turn; butter untoasted side, then spread generously with cranberry sauce; top with sliced bananas, sprinkle with brown sugar, and dust with cinnamon. Place under broiler until banana slices brown slightly and cranberry sauce bubbles.

ROLLS AND BREAD

RAISED REFRIGERATOR ROLLS

⅓ cup shortening, scant	1 yeast cake or 1 package
¼ cup sugar	dry granular yeast
1 teaspoon salt	2 tablespoons lukewarm
1 cup boiling water	water
1 egg, beaten	4 cups sifted flour, about

Combine shortening, sugar and salt in large bowl. Pour boiling water over and cool to lukewarm. Soften yeast in lukewarm water. Add to first mixture with egg and half of flour. Beat well, gradually adding remaining flour to make a smooth elastic dough. Knead lightly. Grease surface of dough, cover and keep in refrigerator until needed. Cut off portions, shape into small round balls, place close together in greased shallow pan, cover and let rise until doubled in bulk, about 1½ hours. Brush with melted shortening and bake in hot oven, 425 degrees F., twelve to fifteen minutes.

For immediate use shape dough as soon as mixed, let rise and bake as directed.

PULLED BREAD

Decrust freshly baked bread. Then, using two forks, pull apart in rough irregular pieces. Place on flat pan and bake in slow oven, 325 degrees F., until delicately browned.

GARLIC BREAD

Cut inch-thick diagonal slices almost through a loaf of French or Italian bread. Spread generously with garlic butter (butter creamed in a bowl well rubbed with a cut clove of garlic), press slices back into place, and heat thoroughly in moderately hot oven, 400 degrees F., eight to ten minutes.

Soft Bread Crumbs

Crumble day-old decrusted bread with fingers or pass through sieve. For stuffings, crumbling is sufficient; for covering croquettes, sifting is preferable.

Dry Bread Crumbs

Thoroughly dry stale bread (placed in paper bag) in very cool oven. Crumble, roll with rolling pin and pass through sieve.

Buttered Crumbs

Melt 2 tablespoons butter for each ½ cup soft crumbs. Blend thoroughly. For browned crumbs sauté crumbs and butter in shallow pan or brown gently in oven, stirring frequently.

CHAPTER FIVE

CEREALS

(Including Macaroni, Noodles and Rice)

The majority of cereals require just as much cooking as they ever did, but today much of that cooking is done in the plant in which they are made, rather than in the home kitchen. We can now cook our breakfast cereal practically while the coffee is being made. The quantity of water required varies with the type of cereal, but explicit directions for preparation can be found on each package. Remember that for greater nutritive value cereals may be cooked with part or all milk, in place of part or all water.

Left-over cereal can always be used to advantage. It may be reheated or molded in small cups, chilled and served with cream or top milk and stewed or fresh fruit; it may be sliced after chilling, sautéed, and served with bacon or eggs, or as fried mush with sugar or sirup.

When it comes to ready-to-eat cereals there are literally scores from which to select. Thanks to modern scientific packaging these retain their natural crispness usually throughout the life of the package. If that crispness is lost, however, it may be restored by toasting a few minutes in the oven; indeed many prefer their cereals served warm.

Do not forget that cereals, both cooked and ready-to-eat, may form an important ingredient in meat loaves, steamed puddings, muffins, and cookies, while the ready-to-eat variety in particular make excellent toppings for casserole dishes in place of crumbs.

MACARONI, SPAGHETTI, AND NOODLES

Macaroni, spaghetti, and noodles are essentially alike in composition, being made from hard (durum) wheat mois-tened and pressed into shape, the perforations in the plate of the cylinder through which they pass in their manufacture determining their character and appearance.

Generally speaking, we think of macaroni and spaghetti merely in terms of long, more or less slender, strands; but actually there is a vast assortment of these pastes, ranging from broad ribbons to fine threads, with tubes, elbows, alphabets, shells, stars, and other fancy forms.

Noodles differ slightly from macaroni, eggs and some-times vegetable coloring being used in their manufacture. They are rolled thin, then cut into strips of varying width.

All three are low-cost foods with high energy value. They keep well and are quickly cooked. But remember to cook rapidly in an abundance of boiling salted water, stirring occasionally to prevent sticking. Just as soon as tender, drain, season, and add such other ingredients as are to be incorporated. All members of the macaroni fam-ily are best when served hot and freshly cooked.

All three products are usually purchased in package form. Weights may vary, but the 8-ounce package is a good standard.

BOILED (BUTTERED) MACARONI OR SPAGHETTI OR NOODLES

For two servings allow one-half package, 1 quart boiling water, 1 teaspoon salt, and cook as directed on package, from nine to twelve minutes, or until soft. Drain. then add butter and pepper.

MACARONI AND CHEESE

½ package macaroni   ¾ cup grated cheese
Boiling salted water   2 tablespoons grated cheese,
2 cups well-seasoned Me-   additional
  dium White Sauce

Cook macaroni in boiling salted water until tender.
Drain, then blend with white sauce, add cheese, turn into
buttered baking dish or casserole, sprinkle with remaining
cheese, and bake in moderately hot oven, 375°-400° F.,
until thoroughly hot and delicately browned. If desired
use 1 tablespoon grated cheese and 1 tablespoon buttered
crumbs for the topping.

For Baked Macaroni with Meat, substitute minced
cooked ham, tongue, or left-over cold meat, with appropriate seasoning, for the cheese.

For Baked Macaroni with Fish, substitute canned fish,
salmon, tuna fish, shrimps, or left-over boiled or baked
fresh fish, with appropriate seasoning, for the cheese.

SPAGHETTI AND TOMATO CASSEROLE

2 slices diced raw bacon   1½ cups canned tomatoes
1 tablespoon minced onion   ½ package spaghetti
1 chicken liver   Salt and pepper
2 tablespoons diced mush-   2 tablespoons buttered
  rooms, fresh or canned   crumbs
½ teaspoon paprika   1 tablespoon grated cheese

Cook bacon until fat flows freely, then add onion and
chicken liver, and cook five minutes. Drain off any excess
bacon fat, add mushrooms, paprika, and tomatoes, and let
all simmer together gently for twenty minutes. Meanwhile
cook spaghetti until tender in boiling salted water, then
drain. Combine with first mixture, season, turn into cas-

serole or baking dish, and top with crumbs into which cheese has been stirred. Bake in moderately hot oven, 375°-400° F., about ten minutes.

BAKED NOODLES WITH TOMATOES AND GREEN PEPPERS

½ package broad noodles
2 tablespoons butter
1 medium-sized onion, minced
1 green pepper, minced

4 tomatoes, peeled and thickly sliced
Salt and pepper
Buttered crumbs

Cook noodles in boiling salted water until tender, then drain. Melt butter, cook onion in it until just beginning to color, add green pepper, and cook a moment longer. Put half the noodles in greased casserole, top with half the sliced tomatoes, then half the onion-pepper mixture. Sprinkle with salt and pepper and repeat layers. Top with crumbs and bake in moderate oven, 375° F., twenty minutes. If desired, other cooked vegetables, such as diced carrots, cauliflower flowerets, green peas, or beans, about ⅔ cup, may be substituted for, or added with, the tomatoes.

NOODLE RING

1 package noodles
Boiling salted water
3 eggs, beaten

1¼ cups milk
½ teaspoon salt
¼ teaspoon pepper

Cook noodles in boiling salted water until just barely tender, drain and blend with remaining ingredients. Turn into a well-greased ring mold; set it in a pan of hot water, and bake in moderate oven, 375° F., about three-quarters of an hour. Let stand for a moment, unmold onto platter, and fill center as desired.

Suggested fillings: Creamed tuna fish with mushrooms, creamed fresh fish, or canned red salmon, cooked mixed vegetables, with or without sauce, creamed chicken and peas, creamed dried beef. Serves four.

RICE

Rice is perhaps the oldest edible cereal, and still one of the most important. It is high in starch content and obviously contains less protein than wheat. White rice may be either of the polished or unpolished type; brown rice is the same grain, from which only the hull has been removed. Because it retains some of the bran coats it has greater mineral and vitamin content. It also takes a little longer to cook than white rice, but is of infinitely richer flavor.

Wild rice, or water rice, is the seed of a tall water grass and is much more expensive than ordinary rice. It is usually reserved for service with game and other strong-flavored meats.

There are two methods of boiling rice each entirely different, each thoroughly satisfactory.

BOILED RICE, INDIAN METHOD

Use 1 quart rapidly boiling water and 1 teaspoon salt to ½ cup well-washed rice. Shake rice gently into water. (If water is kept at a violent boil, no stirring is necessary, the water keeping the rice in motion, but. if boiling ceases, the rice may stick to the bottom of pan.) Cook until thoroughly tender fifteen to twenty-five minutes, then turn into sieve or colander, and pour over it an abundance of hot water to wash off loose starch. Cover lightly with cloth and set over pan containing a little hot water to fluff and separate the grains. Serve as a cereal with milk and sugar, or as a vegetable with butter.

BOILED RICE, CHINESE METHOD

Use ¾ cup boiling water and ½ teaspoon salt to ½ cup well-washed rice. Place in upper part of double boiler over direct heat, and again bring to a rapid boil, then cook very gently for ten minutes by which time the water should all be absorbed. Now set over hot water and continue cooking for a further ten to fifteen minutes. Remove cover and allow steam to escape.

STEAMED RICE

Place well-washed rice in a perforated steamer or sieve, over pan containing furiously boiling water. Cover closely and steam about half an hour. Salt lightly before serving.

OVEN STEAMED RICE

Cook rice by Chinese method over open fire for first ten minutes, being careful to use a heavy pan, then cover and complete cooking in oven. This method is suggested for use when the oven is being used for other cooking.

BOILED WILD RICE

Pick over rice, wash, then cook in boiling salted water, allowing 3 cups water, 1 teaspoon salt, and ¾ cup rice, until rice is tender and water absorbed, thirty to forty-five minutes. Add butter and serve with beef or game.

RICE RING

Pack cooked rice into well-buttered ring mold, steam over hot water, or set in pan containing a little hot water in the oven, and reheat. Unmold and fill with creamed meat, fish, or vegetables.

RICE TIMBALES

Prepare exactly as rice ring, packing into individual buttered cups or molds.

BAKED RICE AND CHEESE

Arrange in baking dish alternate layers of cooked rice and cheese sauce. Top with buttered crumbs, and bake in moderately hot oven, 375°-400° F., fifteen to twenty minutes.

CREOLE OR SPANISH RICE

1 very small onion, minced
1 slice bacon, diced
1½ cups cooked rice
1 cup canned tomatoes
Salt and pepper
1 tablespoon minced green pepper

Cook onion and bacon together until onion begins to color. Add all remaining ingredients, blend thoroughly, and continue cooking over gentle heat, twenty minutes or longer. Or if the oven is in use, turn mixture into baking dish, top with buttered crumbs or not as preferred, and complete cooking in moderate oven, 350° F., about twenty minutes.

CHAPTER SIX

EGGS AND CHEESE

The most important fact to remember about egg cookery is that eggs are toughened and made indigestible by fast cooking at a high temperature. Cooked slowly and at low temperature, eggs are tender and readily assimilated.

SOFT-COOKED AND HARD-COOKED EGGS

We commonly speak of "boiled eggs" but actually eggs should never be boiled. They may be soft cooked by starting in cold water and bringing slowly just to the boiling point, or by placing them in boiling water, covering, reducing the heat, and keeping just below boiling point, for from five to eight minutes.

For hard-cooked eggs, follow the second method just described, but leave eggs in the water (just below boiling point) from fifteen to twenty minutes. Be sure to use enough water, the ideal amount has been found to be 1½ cups to each egg, a rule which may be followed both in poaching and cooking in the shell.

POACHED EGGS

Have boiling salted water ready in a shallow pan. Break eggs separately into a saucer, then slip them gently into the water, cover and cook until set, never allowing water to boil after eggs have been put into it. Lift out carefully with perforated spoon and serve on plain buttered toast or anchovy toast (buttered toast lightly spread with commercial anchovy paste).

Poached eggs may also be served on boiled rice, topping with Shrimp Sauce and dusting with paprika, or they may be masked with Cheese or Tomato Sauce, Hollandaise or Mock Hollandaise. Then too, milk may be used in place of water for poaching, this being thickened and seasoned as an accompanying sauce.

SCRAMBLED EGGS

3 eggs
1/3 cup milk
1/3 teaspoon salt

1/8 teaspoon pepper
2 tablespoons butter

Beat eggs slightly, then combine with milk and seasonings. Melt butter in upper part of double boiler, add egg mixture, and cook over hot water just until set, stirring constantly to lift thickened part of mixture from bottom of pan. Be careful not to overcook. Serve plain, or on toast, or with bacon garnish.

Canned or stewed tomatoes may be substituted for the milk; or any of the following may be added to the eggs when almost cooked: 1/2 cup grated cheese, 1/2-cup minced cooked chicken, tongue, dried beef, ham, or chicken liver, or 1 teaspoon minced parsley and a few drops onion juice.

SHIRRED OR BAKED EGGS

3 eggs
2 tablespoons butter

Salt and paprika

Melt butter in a shallow baking dish, break eggs in gently, sprinkle with salt and paprika, and bake in moderately hot oven, 375° F., just until set. Serve in dish in which they were cooked, garnishing with mushrooms, peeled, halved, and cooked in a little butter; with sausages, broiled, fried, or baked, or with chicken or calf's liver diced and sautéed in a little butter. Or arrange left-over spinach in baking dish, break eggs onto this, top with White Sauce, and sprinkle generously with grated cheese before baking.

PLAIN (FRENCH) OMELET

3 eggs	1½ tablespoons butter
3 tablespoons milk or cream	Salt and paprika

Beat eggs slightly with milk or cream and seasonings. Melt butter in pan, allowing it to become thoroughly hot, but not brown. Pour in egg mixture and cook gently until eggs begin to set at outer edge of pan. Tilt pan slightly and draw omelet together at one side of pan, shaking pan gently meanwhile so that omelet may not stick. When golden brown on under side, fold together, turn onto hot platter and serve at once.

Any of the following may be either blended with the eggs before cooking or spread over the surface of the omelet just before folding together: cooked minced heated kidneys, chicken liver, ham, tongue, or mushrooms; cooked vegetables heated in a little sauce or butter; minced parsley, chives, or grated onion.

PUFFY OMELET

3 eggs	¼ teaspoon salt
3 tablespoons milk or water	1 tablespoon butter

Separate whites from yolks of eggs, beat whites with salt until very light and puffy. Beat yolks until light, add milk or water, combine, and turn into pan containing butter, heated but not browned. Cook until mixture begins to set on bottom and sides of pan, then place in moderately hot oven, 375° F., and cook until firm. Fold together, turn onto hot platter and serve at once.

DESSERT OMELET

3 eggs	Apricot or peach preserves
3 tablespoons water	Whipped cream
⅙ teaspoon salt	Finely chopped toasted al-
¼ cup sugar	monds
1½ tablespoons butter	

Beat egg whites until stiff, yolks until light. Add water, salt, and sugar to yolks, combine with whites, and turn into large omelet pan in which butter has been melted and heated, but not browned. Cook very gently until omelet begins to set on bottom and edges, then transfer pan to a hot oven, 400° F., and bake about five minutes. Spread with preserves, fold omelet, turn onto hot platter, spread more preserves on top, garnish with cream, and sprinkle with nuts.

EGGS BAKED IN ROLLS

Cut a slice from the top of each roll, scoop out the soft crumb, brush inside of roll with softened butter, break an egg into each, replace top and bake in moderately hot oven, 375° F., about ten minutes. Or prepare and bake the rolls, then fill with creamed diced hard-cooked eggs and reheat in oven before serving.

STUFFED OR DEVILED EGGS

3 hard-cooked eggs	⅙ teaspoon mustard
1 tablespoon butter	2 teaspoons mayonnaise
1 tablespoon grated cheese	Salt and paprika

Divide eggs lengthwise, remove yolks, press these through sieve, season, and blend with any of the following: minced sardines, shrimps, pimiento, deviled ham or tongue, chicken liver, a little anchovy paste, a few finely chopped capers or indeed almost any available savory ingredient. Pile in halved egg whites and chill. Serve in a nest of lettuce. If for picnic service, press two halves of stuffed egg together and wrap immediately in waxed paper.

EGGS BENEDICT

1 English Muffin, split, or 2 slices bread	2 eggs
2 thin slices ham	⅓ cup Hollandaise or Mock Hollandaise

Toast and butter the muffin or bread; broil or pan broil the ham; poach the eggs. Arrange for individual service a portion of ham on each half muffin or slice of bread, an egg over this, topping all with Hollandaise or Mock Hollandaise. Dust with paprika and garnish with parsley. Slices of broiled well-seasoned tomato may be substituted for the ham, the eggs then being topped with sautéed mushrooms.

Good Uses for Left-over Egg Whites

All kinds of meringues.
Cake frostings.
Angel cake, white cake or macaroons.
Fruit sherbets, parfaits, snow puddings.

Good Uses for Left-over Egg Yolks

Baked or boiled custards.
Mayonnaise and boiled salad dressing.
Eggnogs.
As a binder for meat and vegetable loaves and to color and reinforce sauces.

WELSH RAREBIT

1 tablespoon butter	1½ cups diced American
1 teaspoon cornstarch or	cheese
flour	½ teaspoon mustard
½ cup milk	Salt and pepper
	Cayenne

Blend butter and cornstarch or flour smoothly in saucepan; then add milk, bring to boiling point, stirring constantly, and cook three minutes. Add cheese and stir over gentle heat until melted. Season and serve on rusk or toast. If preferred, beer may be substituted for the milk in this rarebit.

SAVORY RAREBIT

⅓ cup condensed tomato soup or seasoned prepared tomato sauce	½ package Liederkranz cheese
3 tablespoons top milk or light cream	Toast or crackers

Heat soup and milk or cream in upper part of double boiler or chafing dish. Cut cheese into pieces, blend in thoroughly, and serve piping hot on toast or crisp crackers.

CHEESE SOUFFLÉ

1½ tablespoons butter	Pepper
1½ tablespoons flour	Salt
½ cup milk	2 eggs
½ cup grated cheese	

Combine butter and flour in saucepan, and blend thoroughly without browning. Add milk gradually, bring mixture to boiling point stirring constantly, then add cheese

and seasonings. (Remember cheese is salty.) When cool,
beat in egg yolks. Blend thoroughly, and finally fold in
gently the stiffly beaten egg whites. Turn into deep well-
greased dish and bake in moderate oven, 350°-375° F.,
about twenty-five minutes. Serve immediately. If desired,
prepare in individual ramekins or baking dishes, in which
case bake fifteen to eighteen minutes.

CHEESE FONDUE

⅔ cup milk
⅔ cup soft bread crumbs
⅔ cup mild cheese, cut
   small

2 teaspoons butter
⅓ teaspoon salt
2 eggs

Scald milk, pour over crumbs, and let stand until milk is
absorbed. Add cheese, butter, salt, and beaten egg yolks.
When these are thoroughly blended, fold in gently the
stiffly beaten egg whites. Turn into buttered baking dish
and bake in moderate oven, 350° F., twenty minutes. Serve
at once.

SWISS FONDUE

½ pound thinly sliced
   cheese
⅓ cup white wine

2 tablespoons brandy
French bread or garlic
   bread

Pour wine over cheese in shallow pan. A French casserole
which can be sent to table is perfect. Let stand two hours,
then place over gentle heat and stir and toss until cheese
melts.

Add brandy, reheat, and serve with French bread cut
into small chunks and dunked in the melted cheese mixture; or serve with hot crisp Garlic Bread.

CHEESE TRAY

More and more we are coming to appreciate the occasional service of cheese at the close of a meal in place of rich sweet desserts. One or two or a greater variety of cheese may be offered on a cheese board or tray, with knife for serving, plus crisp crackers, plain or toasted. Sometimes jelly accompanies the cheese. In France this would probably be replaced by fresh fruit, especially crisp apples and juicy pears.

BACON AND EGGS

The secret of crisp bacon is to cook it very, very slowly, and to pour off the melted fat as it collects in the pan. Start by placing slices of bacon in *cold* frying pan over low heat and cook until bacon is crisp, turning once if desired. Drain on paper towel placed on a heated plate to keep bacon hot.

For the eggs, pour 2 tablespoons fat back into frying pan and allow this to heat. Then carefully drop eggs into the fat. Cook gently until set, dipping fat over eggs with spoon while cooking, or you can cover the pan and cook three to five minutes until eggs set. Season lightly with salt and pepper, or paprika. With a spatula arrange eggs on the hot plate with the bacon.

CHEESE AND BACON TOAST

Arrange thin slices of American cheese on slices of bread. Brush lightly with mustard and top with uncooked bacon cut to fit (use scissors). Place in broiling oven under moderate flame and cook until bacon is crisp and cheese melted. Allow two slices of bread for each serving. For hors d'oeuvres cut each slice into three sections before broiling. Serve very hot.

CHAPTER SEVEN

SOUPS

The twosome family is unlikely to make much soup stock, depending rather on the cream soups and chowders made without stock or upon the convenient and excellent canned soups. Even so, it may not be amiss to know how to make this good base for soups and sauces.

STOCK FOR SOUPS AND SAUCES

The coarser lean cuts of meat are suitable for stock— neck, shank or shin of beef, breast or neck pieces of lamb, or knuckle of veal. Trimmings, bones, fragments of vegetables, together with fresh uncooked vegetables, all help the stock. Wipe meat, cut into small pieces, chop bones small, and cover with cold water, using one pint to each pound of meat. Cook very slowly to draw meat juices into liquid. After meat and bones have cooked two hours, add vegetables—a stalk of celery, a carrot, leek or onion, parsley, a half bay leaf, and two or three peppercorns for added flavor. Season with salt and pepper when adding vegetables, and cook half an hour longer, adding more water if needed. Skim off all fat before using. If stock is allowed to become cold, the fat can be lifted off in a solid cake.

BOUILLON

Bouillon is clarified, well-seasoned, fat-free beef stock made without vegetables. Serve hot or jellied.

TO CLARIFY STOCK

Beat one egg white slightly, and add it with the crushed washed shell to each quart of stock. Bring to boiling point, beating or stirring constantly, then cook five minutes without further stirring. Add ½ cup cold water, and after five minutes strain through flannel or doubled cheesecloth previously wrung out of very hot water.

JELLIED BOUILLON

Allow one-half envelope gelatin to each pint of bouillon. Soften in cold water to cover, add to boiling liquid, and when cold break up or cut into cubes. Serve in bouillon cups. To darken, add a few drops Kitchen Bouquet.

TOMATO BOUILLON

Simmer together for twenty minutes equal parts canned or fresh tomatoes and clarified stock with 2 slices onion. Strain through fine cheesecloth, season, and serve. Use celery salt instead of plain salt if desired.

CONSOMMÉ

Consommé is a first cousin to bouillon but the stock is usually made of at least two kinds of meat. Clarify, flavor, and season as directed for bouillon. Serve hot or jellied.

For Consommé Royale, garnish with Royale Custard.

For Consommé Julienne, add ¼ cup very finely shredded cooked vegetables, carrot, turnip, celery, beans, or peas (whole), to each 2 cups of consommé.

CLAM BROTH

4 large chowder clams   Pepper
Water

Scrub clams thoroughly, using several waters. Place in kettle, add cold water almost to cover, bring to boiling point and simmer, closely covered, fifteen minutes. Strain through doubled cheesecloth, reheat, and season with pepper.

OYSTER STEW

2 tablespoons butter	Pepper
1½ dozen shucked oysters	2 cups scalded milk
½ teaspoon salt	Paprika

Melt two-thirds of the butter in deep saucepan. Add oysters with their liquor (pick them over first in case there are any bits of shell attached) and seasonings, and bring just to boiling point. As soon as the oysters look plump and edges begin to curl, add milk and cook a minute longer without actually boiling. Turn into cups or bowls, add remaining butter, and dust with paprika.

ONION SOUP

2 large onions	Salt and pepper
¼ cup butter	2 small slices toast
3 cups stock	Grated cheese

Peel and slice onions very thinly, cook slowly in butter until clear, but not browned. Add stock, bring to boiling point, and season.

Onion soup is generally served in earthen pots (marmites) in which case the cheese-sprinkled toast is set on top of each portion and the whole placed in a hot oven, 400°-425° F., until cheese is melted. Failing earthen pots, sprinkle toast with cheese, place in oven until cheese is melted, and transfer to soup plates or cups at moment of serving.

Canned bouillon, or bouillon cubes and water, may be

substituted for stock, cooking the onion as directed, then adding liquid.

LAMB BROTH

1 pound neck of lamb	1 small onion, sliced
1 quart cold water	1 stalk celery, diced
½ teaspoon salt	1 tablespoon barley
⅓ cup diced carrot	1 teaspoon minced parsley
⅓ cup diced turnip	Additional salt and pepper

Wipe meat, cut into small pieces, and place in saucepan with water, bring slowly to boiling point, add salt and sim-mer one hour, skimming occasionally. Add vegetables and barley and cook until vegetables are tender. Season to taste, and add parsley just before serving.

VICHYSSOISE

2 leeks	2 cups chicken stock
2 tablespoons butter	Salt and pepper
½ cup thinly sliced raw	⅓ cup light cream
potato	Minced parsley or chives

Remove roots, also green tops of leeks, leaving about two inches above the white portion, and slice. Melt butter in saucepan, add leeks, and sauté five minutes. Add pota-toes and stock, and cook over medium heat until potatoes are tender. Press through sieve, reheat, add seasonings and cream. Garnish with parsley or chives. Vichyssoise may also be served cold, in which case be sure it is very thoroughly chilled.

CREAM OF VEGETABLE SOUP

To 1½ cups Thin White Sauce (page 168) add 1½ cups sieved cooked vegetable, fresh or canned, as celery, peas, spinach, asparagus, carrots or corn. Use as part of the measure the liquor in the can or that in which vegetable was cooked. Before serving, dust lightly with nutmeg, paprika or parsley.

CREAM OF TOMATO SOUP (TOMATO BISQUE)

1½ cups tomatoes, stewed fresh or canned
1 slice onion
Small piece bay leaf

1½ cups thin White Sauce (page 168)
Salt and pepper

Cook tomatoes, onion, and bay leaf for ten minutes. Press through sieve forcing through as much pulp as possible. Reheat and combine with Foundation White Sauce and seasonings. This blending should not be done until the moment of serving. If the sauce and tomato stand together for any length of time they are apt to curdle. If this occurs while mixing, beat vigorously for a moment with rotary beater.

VEGETABLE SOUP

1 large soup bone (about 2 pounds)
2 quarts cold water
2 tablespoons barley
2 carrots
2 stalks celery
1 small turnip

1 large onion
1 potato
1 green pepper
2 cups tomatoes, fresh or canned
1 teaspoon salt
⅛ teaspoon pepper

Have butcher crack bone (any attached meat may be cut from it and lightly browned to add flavor). Cover with cold water, add barley and simmer two hours, replenishing water as it boils away. Peel or scrape vegetables, dice and add to soup stock with tomatoes and seasonings. Simmer one hour longer; remove bone and serve.

MANHATTAN CLAM CHOWDER

¼ cup diced fat salt pork	2 cups boiling water
1 small onion, diced	6 large chowder clams in
1 cup diced potato	shells
½ cup diced celery	½ teaspoon salt
1 cup canned tomatoes	⅛ teaspoon pepper

Cook pork until fat flows freely, then remove and cook onion in fat until it just turns color. Add potato, celery, tomatoes, and 1 cup of water. Cover and simmer twenty minutes. Meanwhile, scrub clams and steam with remaining water until shells open. Discard shells, set aside soft portions of clams, chop hard portions finely, and cook fifteen minutes with water in which they were steamed. Strain through doubled cheesecloth, and add liquor and soft parts of clams to first mixture. Continue cooking until potatoes are quite tender. Season with salt and pepper, and serve with pilot crackers.

If a more spicy chowder is desired a pinch of marjoram, thyme, or summer savory may be added to the chowder when nearly cooked.

NEW ENGLAND CLAM CHOWDER

1 cup clams	Dash of pepper
¼ cup diced fat salt pork	1 cup boiling water
1 small onion, sliced	1 cup scalded milk
1 cup diced potato	2 tablespoons butter
1 teaspoon salt	2 teaspoons flour

Clean and pick over clams (shucked), rinse in ½ cup cold water. Drain, reserve liquor, heat to boiling point and strain. Cook pork until fat flows freely, add onion, cook five minutes, and strain into saucepan. Add potato and hard part of clams finely chopped, with salt, pepper, and boiling water, and cook ten minutes. Then add milk with soft portions of clams and half the butter, and cook three minutes longer. Blend remaining butter with flour, add clam water which was strained and set aside. Bring slowly to boiling point, cook two minutes, and combine with chowder just before serving. Do not add this clam water until the last moment, as it has a tendency to cause milk to curdle. Serve with pilot crackers.

FISH CHOWDER

2 slices fat salt pork, diced	Boiling water
1 onion, chopped	1 pint milk
½ pound raw fish, diced	Pepper and salt, if needed
3 small potatoes, sliced	

Fry pork in deep saucepan; when crisp remove pieces of pork, and fry onion until just beginning to color. Add fish and potato, and just cover with boiling water. Simmer until potatoes are tender (about half an hour), add milk, and return pieces of pork to chowder. Cook five minutes longer, season with pepper and additional salt, if needed. Serve with pilot crackers.

For Canned Salmon Chowder, substitute 1 cup flaked canned red salmon.

CANNED SOUPS

Now a word about canned soups. While these are delicious and appetizing, and save time and labor when served just as they come from the can (extended when necessary), there are any number of ways of adding a distinctive touch, either by combining two varieties, or by adding individual flavorings and garnishes. A group of such good combinations with appropriate garnishes follows:

Combine For	Garnish With
Soup Provençale	
Equal parts condensed chicken soup, condensed celery soup, and water.	Minced pimiento or minced parsley.
French Pea Soup	
Equal parts ready-to-serve chicken soup and ready-to-serve cream of pea soup.	Finely shredded lettuce and a dash of onion juice.
Purée Mongole	
Equal parts condensed tomato soup, condensed pea soup, and water.	Croutons.
Tomato Clam	
Condensed tomato soup extended with clam broth in place of water.	Croutons fried in bacon fat.
Chicken Clam	
Equal parts ready-to-serve chicken noodle soup and clam broth.	Salted whipped cream.
Suprême	
Equal parts condensed mushroom soup, condensed chicken soup, and water.	Whipped cream flavored with lemon juice or grated horseradish. Paprika.

SOUP GARNISHES AND ACCOMPANIMENTS
CROUTONS

Toast day-old bread, then cut into half-inch squares; or cut day-old bread into half-inch squares, sauté lightly in butter, then drain on soft paper.

For company service, bread for croutons should be de-crusted.

CHEESED FINGERS

Spread day-old bread lightly with softened butter, sprin-kle generously with grated cheese, cut into finger strips, then place in hot oven, 425° F., just until cheese is browned. Pile log cabin fashion.

ROYALE CUSTARD

Use half quantity baked custard, omitting sugar and va-nilla. Turn into shallow buttered pan, having mixture not more than one-third inch thick. Bake as directed, then cut into cubes or diamonds. Decorative cutters may also be used but they must be *very* small.

Use as garnish for clear soups only—consommé and bouillon. (Do not attempt to shape custard until it has been well chilled in refrigerator.)

For additional soup accompaniments see also Melba Toast, page 90; Pulled Bread and Garlic Bread, page 92.

CHAPTER EIGHT

MEATS AND POULTRY

For the characteristics of good meat, the cuts best adapted to various cooking processes, and for meat marketing tips, see under Marketing for Meats. All meats should be wiped with a damp cloth before cooking.

ROASTING

There are two methods of roasting meat:

Searing Method

Meat is first seared at a high temperature, 450°-500° F., from twenty to thirty minutes, after which temperature is reduced to 300°-325° F. for remainder of cooking period. This results in a crisp outer surface with juicy interior, but the meat shrinks, especially if cooked to the well-done stage.

Constant Temperature Method

Here an even, constant temperature of approximately 300°-350° F. is maintained throughout the entire cooking period. This means that the outer surface of the meat will be somewhat less crisp, the interior juicy and tender, and shrinkage reduced to a minimum.

Meat Roasting Thermometer

The only absolutely correct way to determine the doneness of meat is by the use of a roasting thermometer which registers the internal temperature of the meat. Prepare roast for oven, then press skewer into thickest part of meat and carefully insert thermometer. The pointed end should be in center of meat and must not contact bone, gristle, or fat. Place meat in oven with thermometer inserted, and leave thermometer there during entire cooking process. Remove meat from oven when the black liquid in the tube registers the desired stage.

Always place meat in roasting pan, fat side up. Also remember that boned cuts, because they are solid meat, require about ten minutes per pound longer cooking time than when the bone is retained.

Certain meats now on the market have received preliminary preparation which cuts down the cooking time. For these follow packers' directions.

BROILING

As with roasting, there are two methods of broiling:

Searing Method

With gas or electric range, when using the searing method, set regulator to "Broil" (about 550° F.) and preheat. Place meat on heated greased broiler rack having top surface of meat one and one-half to two inches below source of heat (slashing fat aids in minimizing curling). Brown both surfaces at this temperature, then reduce heat with a gas broiler by turning down flame, with an electric broiler by moving to a point farther from it. Turn meat occasionally so that cooking may be uniform. A thermom-

ROASTING TIME AND TEMPERATURE CHART

Meat	Method One			Method Two		
	Searing Temperature	Searing Time (minutes)	Reduce to	Constant Temperature	Internal Temperature Registered on Meat Thermometer	Approximate Cooking Time (Minutes per Pound)
Beef						
Standing Ribs						
Rare	500° F.	20–25	300°–325° F.	300°–350° F.	140° F.	18–20
Medium					160° F.	22–25
Well done					180° F.	27–30
Rolled Roast						Add 10 min. per pound to above directions because meat is solid
Rare	500° F.	20–25	300°–325° F.	300°–350° F.	140° F.	
Medium					160° F.	
Well done					180° F.	
Veal	500° F.	15–20	275°–325° F.	300°–350° F.	170° F.	25–30
Lamb						
Medium	450°–500° F.	30	325° F.	300°–350° F.	170° F.	25–30
Well done					180° F.	30–35
Pork (Fresh)						
Small and rolled roasts	500° F.	15–20	300°–325° F.	300°–350° F.	185° F.	40–45
Ham						
Half (without preboiling)				300°–350° F.	170° F.	30
Poultry						
Chicken and Capon	450°–475° F.	20–25	325° F.	325°–350° F.	Well done	25–30
Turkey	450°–475° F.	20–25	325° F.	325°–350° F.	Well done	18–25
Duck and Goose	450°–475° F.	15–20	325° F.	325°–350° F.	Well done	20–25

Remember that small roasts, under five pounds, will take the longer number of minutes per pound indicated. Searing time is included in minutes per pound.

eter may be used with this method, but must be very carefully handled because of the several turnings necessary.

Constant Temperature Method

Preheat broiler to 350° F. Set meat in position on rack, having top surface of meat about three inches from source of heat. (If the depth of the broiler does not permit this much space between heat and meat, reduce temperature a few degrees.) When half done and surface is browned, season with salt and pepper, turn and cook under side in same manner. When turning always be sure to insert fork in fat only, not in lean of meat.

If using a thermometer, insert it from side of steak through fat to center of meat, do not let it touch the bone. At turning time, thermometer should read approximately 100° F. for rare to medium steak; or approximately 135° F. for medium to well-done lamb chops.

When cooking is completed, rare steak should have an internal temperature of 130° F.; medium 160° F.; lamb chops 170° F. Be careful not to injure thermometer while turning meat.

Combination Broiling-Roasting

A combination broiling-roasting method which has definite advantages is sometimes used. Preheat broiler, place meat on it as directed, sear five minutes on each side, then when sufficiently browned, transfer meat to oven, and complete cooking at 250° F. Because of the lower temperature, this obviously means a little longer cooking, but on the other hand after the searing is done it requires less attention. Especially good for very thick steaks, chops or young chicken.

BROILING CHART FOR BEEF, LAMB CHOPS, PORK, AND POULTRY

Meat	Method One			Method Two	
	Thickness	Searing Temperature	Reduce to	Constant Temperature	Approximate Cooking Time (minutes)
Beef					
Steaks:					
Club, Porterhouse or T-bone, Small Sirloin, Filet Mignon	1″	500° F.	350° F.	350° F.	Rare 10–15 / Medium 15–20 / Well done 20–30
Hamburg	1″	500° F.	350° F.	350° F.	Rare 15 / Medium 20 / Well done 25
Minute or Cubed Steak	¼–½″	500° F.	350° F.		Rare 3 / Medium 4 / Well done 5
Lamb Chops					
Loin	¾–1″	500° F.	350° F.	350° F.	Medium 10–15 / Well done 15–25
Rib	¾–1″	500° F.	350° F.	350° F.	12
English Kidney Chops	2″	500° F.	350° F.	350° F.	20–35 Lamb chops are never served rare
Pork					
Ham Slice	½″			350° F.	15–20
Tendered Slice	¾–1″			350° F.	10–12
Bacon				350° F.	4–5
Sausage Meat Patties	¾–1″	Pan broil			15
All of the above meats may be pan broiled, that is, cooked over open flame in a heated pan rubbed over with fat or oil to prevent sticking. Be sure to pour off fat as it collects.					
Poultry					
Broilers and Duckling	Split	450° F.	325° F.	350° F.	20–30
Squab	Split	450° F.	325° F.	350° F.	25–35 / 20 All well done

BROILING CHART FOR FISH, SWEETBREADS, BRAINS, AND GAME

Food		Broiling Temperature	Time (minutes)
Fish			
Fillets of Sole and Flounder		400°–450° F.	8–12
Bluefish and Mackerel	Split	400°–450° F.	12–20
Halibut	Slice	350°–375° F.	15–25
Shad Roe	Parboiled	375°–400° F.	8–10
			All well done
Sweetbreads	Parboiled and split	450° F.	10
Brains	Parboiled and split	450° F.	10
			Both well done
Game			
Wild birds—			
Duck	Split	350° F.	Medium 15–20
Partridge	Split	350° F.	Well done 25–30
Quail	Split	350° F.	Well done 10–15

BEEF

ROAST OF BEEF

For *Standing Rib Roast,* that is with bones in, wipe meat with damp cloth. Place fat side up in open roaster. Season lightly with salt and pepper. (If meat thermometer is used insert as directed on page 118.) Do not add water and do not cover. Roast by Searing or Constant Temperature method (pages 119 to 120). Serve with Brown Gravy and Yorkshire Pudding (page 176).

For *Rolled Roast,* follow directions for Standing Rib Roast, remembering that boned cuts, because they are solid meat, will require ten minutes per pound longer cooking time by either roasting method.

BROWN GRAVY

Pour from roaster all but 2 tablespoons of fat, but leave any brown meat juices in pan. Place pan on top of stove. Sprinkle 2 tablespoons flour over fat in pan. Brown very gently, stirring constantly. Gradually add 1½ cups water, still stirring. Bring slowly to boiling point, simmer three minutes, season with salt and pepper, and, if desired, add 1 teaspoon Worcestershire or other sauce.·

BROILED STEAK

Wipe steak with damp cloth. Trim off excess fat and slash remainder in four places to prevent curling. Broil according to desired method (pages 119 to 120). When done, transfer to hot platter and spread with butter or Maître d'Hôtel Butter (page 173).

HASH FROM STEAK OR ROAST BEEF

Add to 1 cup leftover meat passed through food chopper (coarse knife), 1 small minced onion and 1 cup diced cooked potato. Season, toss lightly together and moisten with 3 or 4 tablespoons gravy, stock, milk or water. Turn into well-greased frying pan and cook gently until crust is formed on under side. Fold together and serve plain or with Poached Eggs (page 100).

PLANKED STEAK

Broil tender thick steak on one side, season, place on heated plank, broiled side down, and almost complete cooking under broiler. Arrange border of well-seasoned mashed potato around edge of plank and return to oven to brown lightly. Garnish with colorful cooked vegetables, dot steak with butter or Maître d'Hôtel Butter (page 173) and reheat before serving. This is a company dish because the steak used *must* be of generous size.

STUFFED ROUND STEAK

¾ pound round steak
Savory bread or oyster stuffing
2 tablespoons seasoned flour

Bacon fat or drippings
1½ cups water or stock
1 teaspoon Worcestershire or other table sauce

Have meat cut very thin (in one piece) or pound with rolling pin between pieces of waxed paper. Spread with stuffing (half recipe), roll up and tie with thread into compact shape. Roll in seasoned flour, and brown in hot bacon fat or drippings. Arrange in baking dish, add flour to hot fat, cook gently until browned, then add water or stock, bring to boiling point, add additional seasoning if needed, also table sauce. Pour over and around meat and bake in moderate oven, 350° F., about one and a half hours. If preferred, and the oven is not in use for another purpose, after the gravy is made the meat may be put back into it and cooked over the fire. Remove threads before serving.

BAKED ROUND STEAK CREOLE

¾ pound round steak, cut thick
2 medium-sized onions, sliced

1 green pepper, shredded
½ bay leaf
2 cups canned tomatoes
Salt and pepper

Brown meat in frying pan on all sides in a very little hot fat. Transfer to baking dish, add onion, pepper, bay leaf, and tomatoes. Cover and bake in slow oven, 325°-350° F., one and a half to two hours. Season with salt and pepper at end of first hour, at which time, if necessary, add a little more canned tomato.

For Round Steak in Casserole with Potato Balls, add 1 cup potato balls or large dice, at end of first hour of cooking.

STEAK AND KIDNEY PIE

¾ pound round steak	Dash of ground cloves
1 lamb's kidney	1 small onion, minced
1 tablespoon flour	Water
½ teaspoon salt	Pastry or baking powder
Dash of pepper	biscuit crust

Cut meat into thin strips and kidney into slices, discarding white core. Dip each piece of meat into flour to which seasonings have been added, then form into a roll, with a piece of kidney in the center of each strip of steak. Place in baking dish, add onion and fill dish two-thirds with cold water. Cover and bake in slow oven, 325°-350° F., one hour. Meanwhile, prepare and roll crust out thinly, cover meat in baking dish with it, wetting edge of dish that crust may adhere. Return to moderately hot oven, 375°-400° F., and bake about twenty minutes longer. If gravy in dish has boiled down too much, add a little more liquid before putting crust on pie.

For Meat and Potato Pie, add diced potato or potato balls. If using raw potato cook with meat; with cooked potato add before covering with crust.

POT ROAST OF BEEF

3 pounds bottom round of beef	2 cloves
3 tablespoons fat	1½ teaspoons salt
1 cup boiling water	⅓ teaspoon pepper
2 cups canned tomato	4 small onions
1 bay leaf	4 carrots, halved

Brown meat on all sides in the heated fat, add water, tomato, bay leaf, and cloves, cover closely, and simmer two to three hours, adding seasonings and vegetables at end of first hour.

To thicken gravy blend smoothly two tablespoons flour and four tablespoons cold water. Add to the hot gravy after removing meat and vegetables from pan and simmer five minutes, keeping meat and vegetables hot meanwhile.

This is a large roast for two but is good enough to serve twice, with some left over for Shepherd's Pie or other cold meat cookery.

BEEF STEW WITH DUMPLINGS

1 pound round, shin, or rump of beef
1 tablespoon flour
1 onion, sliced
1½ tablespoons fat
1 pint water or stock

Small piece bay leaf
¾ teaspoon salt
⅙ teaspoon pepper
½ cup sliced carrots
½ cup diced celery
Dumplings

Cut meat into medium-sized pieces, roll each in flour, and brown with onion in fat. Add water or stock, bring to boiling point, then simmer about two hours, adding seasonings and vegetables at end of first hour with a little more liquid if needed. Then add dumplings and cook, closely covered, for fifteen minutes.

SHEPHERD'S PIE

1 to 1½ cups cold cooked beef
½ cup left-over gravy or canned tomato

1½ to 2 cups well-seasoned mashed potatoes

Arrange meat and gravy or tomato in small casserole or individual baking dishes. Top with mashed potatoes,

roughening surface with fork and bake in hot oven, 400°
F., until meat is hot and potatoes lightly browned.
Other cold meats may be substituted for the beef if de-
sired.

CHOPPED BEEF

When the budget simply refuses to budge, it is chopped
beef or hamburg to the rescue! That need not mean same-
ness of service, for appearance, flavorings, and seasonings
can be infinitely varied. Here are just a few suggestions to
lead you off the beaten track.

Encircle the patties with strips of bacon and bake in deep
muffin pans as individual meat loaves.

Shape into cutlets with a simulated bone of macaroni
and serve with fried onion rings.

Add a savory sauce of vinegar, Worcestershire, catsup,
and minced onion heated in the fat in which the ham-
burgers were cooked and serve as barbecued patties with
boiled potatoes.

For a very special occasion, plank the hamburg and serve
with a generous garnish of vegetables—baked potatoes on
the half shell, peas in potato nests, potato croquettes, glazed
sweet potatoes, broiled halved tomatoes, glazed onions, corn
fritters, broiled bananas, pineapple wedges, apricot or
peach halves, spiced pears—not all at once, of course, but
just two or three items used in combination, and all served
on one handsome plank.

BEEF PATTIES WITH FRUIT

½ pound chopped beef   ⅙ teaspoon pepper
3 tablespoons soft crumbs   ¼ teaspoon mustard, op-
3 tablespoons milk   tional
⅔ teaspoon salt

Combine meat, crumbs, milk, and seasonings; when thoroughly blended, form into small balls or flattened cakes. Broil or pan fry in a little hot fat and serve either on rounds of sautéed pineapple or with a garnish of glazed peaches or apricot halves. For these, drain canned fruit, sprinkle with sugar, dot with butter, and broil under hot flame or bake in very hot oven, 450° F., ten minutes.

SWEDISH MEAT BALLS

1 very small onion, minced	⅓ cup water
2 tablespoons hot fat	1 small egg
½ pound chopped beef	⅔ teaspoon salt
3 tablespoons bread crumbs	⅛ teaspoon pepper

Brown onion lightly in hot fat then strain onion from fat and blend with all other ingredients, mixing very thoroughly until smooth. Form into small balls, and brown evenly in the hot fat, then transfer to saucepan. Cover with gravy made by browning 1 tablespoon flour in fat remaining in pan, then adding 1 cup water or stock, and stirring until mixture boils. Season and add a few drops of Kitchen Bouquet. Simmer half an hour and serve with plain boiled potatoes, boiled rice, macaroni, noodles, or mashed potatoes.

Swedish cooks often add a little heavy cream to the gravy just before serving and frequently use a blend of pork and beef in making the meat balls.

INDIVIDUAL MEAT ROLLS WITH MUSHROOM SAUCE

Prepare Swedish Meat Ball mixture. Shape into four rolls like croquettes, and brown in hot fat, but do not overcook. While meat is cooking, prepare and thinly roll out Baking Powder Biscuit dough, cutting it into squares. Lay a meat roll on each piece of dough, brush edges with milk or

water, press firmly together over meat, brush surface with
milk, and bake in moderately hot oven, 375°-400° F., about
fifteen minutes. Serve with Mushroom Sauce.

SAVORY MEAT LOAF

1 thin 2-inch slice salt pork, diced	1 very small onion, minced
1 pound chopped beef	1 cup canned tomatoes
¼ cup quick-cooking tapioca	1 teaspoon salt
	⅛ teaspoon pepper

Fry pork until golden brown, then combine (with drippings), with all other ingredients. Mix very thoroughly,
turn into greased loaf pan, and bake in hot oven, 450° F.,
about fifteen minutes. Then decrease heat to moderate,
350° F., and bake thirty minutes longer. Serve hot with
gravy or tomato sauce, or cold sliced with a salad. Planned
for two meals, hot on the first day, cold on the second.

CORNED BEEF WITH VEGETABLES

3 pounds corned beef, plate, brisket or round, as preferred	3 potatoes
	1 small yellow turnip
3 carrots	Water

Place meat in large pan, cover with cold water, and
bring slowly to boiling point. With very salt meat, discard
this water, add fresh cold water, and bring again to boiling
point. Reduce heat and simmer for two hours. At end of
first hour add turnip, thickly peeled and cut into chunky
pieces, and fifteen minutes later the carrots, scraped and
halved, also the thinly peeled potatoes. Serve all on same
platter. This will serve more than one meal, but it is not
profitable to cook less than three pounds.

CORNED BEEF HASH WITH POACHED EGGS

Follow recipe for Hash from Steak or Roast Beef (page 123) substituting chopped cooked (or canned) corned beef and omitting salt.

PORK

ROAST PORK

Wipe meat with damp cloth. Season with salt and pepper. Place fat side up in open roaster. If meat thermometer is used, insert as directed on page 118. Do not add water and do not cover. Roast by Searing or Constant Temperature method, pages 119 to 120. Serve with baked apples (page 231) or apple sauce (page 177).

SAUTÉED PORK CHOPS

Select lean rib or loin chops, sauté in a little tried-out pork fat obtained from excess fat cut from edge of chops. Cook gently, turning to brown both sides, and seasoning when half done. When brown add one-half cup water, cover pan, and cook very gently fifteen to twenty minutes. Serve with sautéed apple, pineapple, or orange slices, or with cranberry sauce.

STUFFED PORK CHOPS

Follow recipe for Stuffed Lamb Chops using apple, apple and raisin, sage and onion, or savory bread stuffing (one-fourth recipe).

FRENCHED PORK TENDERLOIN

1 fresh pork tenderloin,   Butter or other fat
  about ¾ pound   Salt and pepper

Cut tenderloin crosswise into four portions. Place these, cut sides up and down, between waxed paper and pound to flatten (the butcher will do this upon request). Sauté in a little butter or other fat about fifteen minutes, turning to brown both sides, and seasoning when half done.

STUFFED PORK TENDERLOIN

1 fresh pork tenderloin,   raisin, or other desired
  about ¾ pound   stuffing
Bread, apple, apple and   Salt and pepper

Wipe tenderloin and split lengthwise almost through. Put a layer of stuffing (one-fourth recipe) between the two pieces of meat, sandwich fashion; fasten together with tooth-picks and cord, dot with butter and place in baking pan with one-half cup water. Cover and bake in moderate oven, 375° F., three-quarters of an hour, basting two or three times with liquid in pan, seasoning when half done, and uncovering for the last fifteen minutes of cooking. Serve with baked or plain boiled potatoes.

BAKED HAM SLICE

There are a number of savory media in which a ham slice may be baked. In every instance have the ham wiped and excess fat removed. Place in shallow baking dish and pour around it the liquid ingredient which may be cider, pineapple juice, grapejuice, cranberry juice, gingerale, or milk. A small slice of ham, suited to service for two, will need one to one and one-half cups liquid. Bake in moderate oven, 350°-375° F., about forty minutes, having ham covered during first half of the baking period.

BOILED HAM

Scrub ham (whole or half) with stiff brush, place in large pan, cover with boiling water, reduce heat and simmer (covered) allowing twenty-five to thirty minutes per pound. If to be served cold sliced, that is, not cut at all while hot, let the ham cool in the water in which it was cooked, then remove rind and slice thinly as needed.

BAKED (PREBOILED) HAM

Cook ham (whole or half) as directed for boiled ham al lowing twenty minutes to the pound. Lift from water into baking pan, carefully cut and tear away rind (unless it is a rindless ham), stud with cloves, sprinkle with blended brown sugar and bread crumbs (two tablespoons of each to a whole ham), place in hot oven, 400°-425° F., and bake twenty to thirty minutes.

BAKED TENDERIZED HAM
(WHOLE OR HALF)

Since tenderized ham is already fully cooked all that is necessary is to heat it; but it must be thoroughly heated right to the bone. Place in roasting pan, fat side uppermost, and heat in slow oven, 300° F., allowing ten minutes per pound. Stud with cloves, sprinkle with brown sugar and crumbs and return to hot oven, 400° F., for a further fifteen to twenty minutes.

BAKED FRESH SPARERIBS

1½ pounds fresh spareribs   Salt and pepper

Choose meaty spareribs. Cut into pieces convenient for serving, lay in baking pan, cover and bake in hot oven, 400°-425° F., half to three-quarters of an hour, turning once or twice during the baking, and seasoning when half done. Remove cover during last fifteen minutes in order to brown. Parboiled white or sweet potatoes are good, placed in the pan with the spareribs and allowed to browr.

BROILED SPARERIBS

Prepare as for baking then broil under hot flame turning two or three times during the cooking and allowing about twenty minutes. Season with salt and pepper.

BARBECUED SPARERIBS

Follow recipe for broiled or baked spareribs, basting three or four times while cooking with Barbecue Sauce.

STUFFED FRANKFURTERS

Parboil frankfurters, split lengthwise. Lay thin cheese strips between halves, fasten with toothpicks and bake in hot oven, 425° F., until slightly browned.

LAMB

ROAST LAMB

Wipe meat with damp cloth. Season with salt and pepper. Place fat side up in open roaster. If meat thermometer is used insert as directed on page 118. Do not add water and do not cover. Roast by either Searing or Constant Temperature method, page 119 to 120. Serve with Brown Gravy (page 123) or Mint Sauce (page 172).

STUFFED LAMB CHOPS

2 thick lamb chops   Salt and pepper
Mushroom or oyster stuff-   Maître d'Hôtel Butter
   ing

Split chops lengthwise right down to the bone. Trim
off any excess fat. Prepare one-fourth of either stuffing;
press this between halves of chops, and tie or fasten together with wooden toothpicks. Brown on both sides under
broiler, then reduce heat and complete cooking, or after
browning transfer to hot oven, 400° F., and bake about
twenty minutes, seasoning with salt and pepper when
about half done. Serve with Maître d'Hôtel Butter.

PLANKED LAMB CHOPS WITH PINEAPPLE

Trim excess fat from loin lamb chops, cut off tails, then
broil on one side only; after which arrange on heated
plank, broiled side down, and season with salt and pepper.
Dip slices of drained canned pineapple into melted butter,
then sprinkle with brown sugar, and arrange on plank
with chops. Complete broiling under moderately hot flame.
Garnish with potatoes on the half shell and mounds of
green peas. Pass Mint Sauce or jelly separately.

PLANKED LAMB CHOPS JARDINIÈRE

Follow recipe for Planked Lamb Chops with Pineapple,
garnishing with nests of mashed potato filled with well
seasoned diced carrots and (or) small whole beets hollowed
and filled with seasoned green peas. Return to oven for a
moment after arranging vegetables so that everything may
be piping hot. Put a pat of mint butter on each chop or
pass separately.

BREADED SHOULDER LAMB CHOPS

2 shoulder chops   ½ teaspoon mixed herbs
Milk   2 tablespoons grated cheese,
Dry bread crumbs   optional
Salt and pepper

Trim chops, removing any excess fat. Dip first into milk then into crumbs with which salt, pepper, herbs, and cheese, if used, have been blended. Repeat this dipping, then place in a baking dish and bake in moderately hot oven, 375° F., about half an hour. Or, if preferred, sauté golden brown in a little hot fat, then cover and cook gently for twenty minutes longer. Serve with peas and Tomato Sauce or with brown gravy and mint jelly. Cooked in this way, shoulder chops are tender and delicious.

BRAISED SHOULDER LAMB CHOPS

3 shoulder chops   1 tablespoon melted fat
1½ tablespoons flour   4 small onions
½ teaspoon salt   2 carrots
Dash of pepper   1½ cups stock

Trim chops, removing any excess fat. Roll in blended flour, salt, and pepper, then brown on both sides in the hot fat. Place in casserole with peeled onions, and carrots, scraped and quartered lengthwise. Two peeled, quartered potatoes may be added also if desired. Add remaining seasoned flour to fat in pan, brown, then add stock (or water in which a bouillon cube has been dissolved). Bring to boiling point, stirring constantly, pour over meat and vegetables, cover and bake in a slow oven, 325° F., one and a half hours, adding a little more liquid if necessary during the cooking.

Peas, lima beans, celery, etc., may be substituted for the onions and carrots.

TOMATO-BAKED SHOULDER CHOPS

Trim chops, removing any excess fat, arrange in baking dish, season with salt and pepper; then cover with thinly sliced onion, green pepper, and lemon, allowing one slice of each to each chop. Pour canned tomato sauce, canned seasoned tomato or extended tomato soup around, cover and bake in moderate oven, 350°-375° F., one and a half to two hours. Serve hot with baked potatoes.

Equally good for both pork and lamb chops.

MIXED GRILL

Allow one rib chop, one sausage, one lamb kidney, one slice bacon, and one slice pineapple for each service. Wipe chop, split and fasten kidney open with toothpick, prick sausage with fork. Broil all meats gently and season with salt, pepper, and plain or Maître d'Hôtel Butter. Pat pineapple dry, brush with butter, and broil with meats.

Serve as individual "blue plates" with French fried, shoestring, or hashed browned potatoes, and a green salad.

Broiled banana halves, broiled peach halves, or orange or apple slices may be substituted for the pineapple.

LAMB SIZZLE PLATTER

This consists of broiled lamb patties, grilled onion rings, broiled bananas or peaches, Duchesse potatoes, and spinach timbales, all attractively arranged on a piping-hot metal sizzle platter. The cooking of chops, onion, and fruit may be commenced under the broiler; the foods then transferred to the sizzle platter, potato border added, and broiling completed; the spinach timbales being put in place at the last moment.

Other vegetables may be used in place of spinach as broiled tomatoes, cauliflower sections topped with grated cheese, or carrots and peas.

LAMB STEW WITH VEGETABLES

1 pound shoulder or breast and neck of lamb	3 carrots, scraped and halved
2 tablespoons fat	2 stalks celery, diced
1 tablespoon flour	1 small green pepper, minced
1½ cups canned tomatoes	
2 potatoes, quartered	⅔ cup peas
4 small onions, peeled	⅔ teaspoon salt
	⅙ teaspoon pepper

Trim off any excess fat, cut meat into convenient pieces for serving, and brown in hot fat; then place in saucepan with vegetables and seasonings. Discard all but one tablespoon of fat, brown flour in this, add tomatoes, bring to boiling point then pour over meat. Cover closely and simmer about one and a half hours.

IRISH STEW

1 pound shoulder or neck of lamb	4 small onions, peeled
2 cups water	¾ teaspoon salt
3 halved potatoes	⅙ teaspoon pepper

Cut meat into convenient pieces for serving, place in saucepan, add water, cover and simmer three-quarters of an hour. Put in vegetables and seasonings, and continue cooking very gently until these are tender, about one hour longer.

VEAL

ROAST VEAL

Wipe meat, season and place skin side up in open roaster without water. If thermometer is used, insert as directed on page 118. Roast by either method, pages 119 to 120. Serve with Brown Gravy (page 123).

BREADED VEAL CHOPS

Have chops cut about three-fourths inch thick. Trim, egg and bread crumb, and sauté in a little hot fat, turning to brown both sides. Cover and continue cooking very gently for fifteen minutes, or transfer to moderate oven, 350°-375° F., still covered, and complete cooking. Season when half-cooked with salt and pepper. Being a dry, close-fibered meat, veal needs long, slow cooking.

VEAL CUTLET

½ pound veal cutlet, cut very thin
Beaten egg
1 cup soft bread crumbs
Salt and pepper
1 teaspoon poultry seasoning
¼ teaspoon thyme
1 teaspoon minced parsley
Heated fat

Cut veal into convenient pieces for serving, and pound between sheets of waxed paper that it may be very thin (the butcher will do this upon request). Dip first into beaten egg, then into crumbs with which seasonings and flavorings have been blended. Cook gently, about ten minutes, in a little hot fat, turning to brown both sides. Any left-over seasoned crumbs may be browned in fat remaining in pan, and served with the cutlets. Serve plain or with Tomato or Mushroom Sauce.

VEAL STEW

1 pound veal	¼ teaspoon pepper
1 medium-sized onion	1 teaspoon minced parsley
2 tablespoons melted fat	Slight grating lemon rind,
1 tablespoon flour	optional
1 teaspoon salt	2 cups stock or water

Slice onion, and cook golden brown in hot fat. Cut veal into convenient-sized pieces and roll in blended flour, seasonings, parsley and lemon rind, if used. Remove onion from fat, cook meat in same fat until slightly browned, add any remaining seasoned flour, replace onion, add water or stock. Cover and simmer gently until tender, about one hour. If to be served with dumplings, lay these in the pan twenty minutes before serving time, cover, and do not remove cover from pan until dumplings are done. If necessary, add a little more stock or water before putting in the dumplings.

VEAL POT PIE

Prepare and cook veal as for Veal Stew. Then, instead of adding dumplings, cover with baking powder biscuit crust cut to fit top of pan, which should be a rather shallow one so that the crust may not be too thick. Cover and cook as for dumplings, allowing half an hour. To serve, cut crust carefully into wedge-shaped pieces, turn meat onto platter, and top with the crust. Or bake and serve in covered casserole.

LIVER, SWEETBREADS, KIDNEYS, AND TONGUE

SAUTÉED LIVER AND BACON

4 slices bacon	½ teaspoon salt
1 cup sliced onions	⅛ teaspoon pepper
½ pound beef liver, cut moderately thick	1 tablespoon flour
	¾ cup water

Fry bacon until crisp and keep hot. Fry onions in bacon fat, drain, and keep hot. Dip liver into boiling water, drain, pat dry, and cook gently about ten minutes in remaining fat in pan, turning to cook both sides by slipping spatula under liver (do not pierce with fork), and seasoning when half done. Arrange on platter with onions and bacon and keep hot. Brown flour in frying pan in which other ingredients were cooked, then add water, bring to boiling point, stirring constantly, and cook five minutes, adding additional seasoning if necessary. Pour gravy around liver on serving dish.

CASSEROLE OF LIVER AND BACON

3 slices bacon	1 cup mushrooms, fresh or canned
½ pound beef liver	
1½ cups diced potatoes	1 cup brown gravy

Cut bacon into small pieces, and cook gently until fat flows freely. Take out bacon and sear liver on each side in the fat. Place both liver and bacon in casserole with mushrooms and potatoes. Cover with gravy made by browning 1½ tablespoons flour in the bacon fat (after removing liver); then add 1½ cups water or stock, stir until boiling, and cook five minutes. Season with pepper, salt may not be needed because of the bacon. Cover and bake in moderate oven, 350° F., one hour.

SPANISH LIVER

½ pound liver	Juice ½ lemon
Thin slices bacon	1 cup prepared tomato
⅓ teaspoon salt	sauce (Commercial)
⅙ teaspoon pepper	Toast

Cut liver into pieces the size of a large oyster, wrap each in a thin slice of bacon, and arrange in shallow baking dish. Sprinkle with seasonings and lemon juice, pour tomato over and around, and bake in moderate oven, 350°-375° F., twenty to twenty-five minutes. Serve on toast, pouring the sauce over all and garnish, if desired, with fried parsnips or fried bananas.

SWEETBREADS—TO BLANCH

Sweetbreads are the thymus glands of the calf, somewhat expensive but very delicate in flavor. They must be used promptly and, no matter what the method of cooking, are always first blanched, that is covered with cold water for half an hour, then drained, and simmered fifteen minutes in slightly salted boiling water to which two tablespoons lemon juice or vinegar has been added. After cooking, plunge into cold water, and when cool enough to handle, skin, trim and split.

BROILED SWEETBREADS

1 pair sweetbreads	Melted butter or Maître
⅔ teaspoon salt	d'Hôtel Butter
¼ teaspoon pepper	

Blanch sweetbreads as directed; then broil about six minutes, turning to cook both sides. Season when half done with salt and pepper, and serve with a little melted

butter poured over, or pass Maître d'Hôtel Butter separately.

CREAMED SWEETBREADS

Blanch sweetbreads as directed; then cut into large dice
and reheat in Medium White Sauce to which a little extra
butter, or one or two tablespoons of cream, has been added.
Serve on toast.

For Sweetbread Patties fill puff-paste patty shells with
creamed sweetbreads.

STEWED KIDNEYS

4 lamb or 2 veal kidneys	½ teaspoon mustard
2 slices fat bacon, diced	½ teaspoon salt
1 medium-sized onion, diced	Dash of pepper
	1 tablespoon flour

Split lamb kidneys, or cut veal kidneys into convenient-
sized pieces. Cover with water, bring to boiling point, discard first water and cover with fresh. Add bacon, onion,
and mustard, cover closely and simmer until tender, one
to one and a half hours. Season, then thicken with the
flour rubbed smoothly with two tablespoons cold water.
Simmer five minutes after flour is added so that it may be
thoroughly cooked. Serve on toast or garnish with toast
points.

BOILED TONGUE

Place tongue in saucepan, cover with cold water, bring
slowly to boiling point and cook gently until tender, about
two hours for a two to three pound tongue. Skin and serve
hot with Raisin Sauce. If not to be served until cold, leave
the tongue in the water in which it was cooked until cold,
as it will then be more juicy.

The choice cuts are in the center of the tongue, the tip and root are best passed through the food chopper, then added to scrambled eggs, omelets, or used for sandwiches.

It is sometimes possible to buy a small smoked calf's tongue which is of more convenient size for the small family. Obviously being smaller, less cooking time will be necessary, one to one and a quarter hours.

POULTRY

The term poultry includes such domesticated food birds as chicken, turkey, duck, goose, pigeon, and squab. For proper selection, see section on Marketing.

PREPARATION AND ROASTING OF POULTRY

Most of us need have little concern regarding the cleaning and drawing of poultry, as the butcher is likely to attend to it for us. But be sure to have him draw the tendons, for this will make the drumsticks infinitely more tender. If not asked to draw them, he is apt merely to chop off the feet, leaving the tendons themselves imbedded in the flesh.

Remove any pin feathers either with thumb and finger, with tweezers, or with the tip of a knife pressed against the thumb to provide leverage. Next, singe to remove any hairs by holding and turning the bird over a low flame. With duck or goose a teaspoon of alcohol, rubbed over the skin before singeing, helps materially in removing all fuzzy down.

Cut off neck close to body, also wing tips. Do not forget the oil sac—that very small protuberance just above the tail tip—which is easily removed by making a sharp cut at either side, then pressing the sac out. Finally, wash and dry, or wipe both inside and out with a damp cloth. Then the bird will be ready for stuffing.

Lightly fill body cavity with any desired stuffing, a little of which pressed into the crop cavity helps round it out and improve the appearance of the bird after roasting. Draw neck skin down under back of bird and sew or fasten with small skewer. Then close opening through which stuffing was inserted by sewing or, better still, lacing with white cord passed around toothpicks or small skewers made for the purpose.

Truss with skewers and cord, or cord alone, pressing legs close to body, pulling wings back, and, as low as possible, tying the legs and tail tip together compactly. Be sure that the cord is carried under the back, never over the breast, of the bird. Naturally all cords and skewers are removed before serving.

With dry-fleshed birds, lay thin strips of fat salt pork or bacon over the breast and, as in the case of all meats, unless a covered roaster is used, baste frequently during the roasting with the fat in the pan or with seasoned water or stock. See Roasting Chart, page 119, for time and temperatures.

GIBLET GRAVY

Wash giblets—heart, gizzard, liver, neck. Place in saucepan with water to cover, together with a small onion, one or two outside stalks of celery, and a bay leaf. Simmer gently for one hour (the liver may be removed after the first half hour), then season with salt and pepper. Pick meat from bones of neck, and chop all giblets finely. Strain the liquor.

Pour off all but 2 tablespoons of fat from the roasting pan, add 2 tablespoons flour, and allow this to brown in the pan. Add 1½ cups strained broth, bring to boil, stirring constantly, and cook five minutes. Add the chopped giblets and additional seasoning, if needed, and heat through.

FRIED CHICKEN

1 small chicken
1½ tablespoons flour
⅔ teaspoon salt

¼ teaspoon pepper
Hot fat

Clean chicken, cut into convenient pieces for serving and roll in the blended flour, salt, and pepper. Sauté gently in hot fat about twenty-five minutes, covering as soon as browned and reducing heat that it may cook through thoroughly. If desired the cooking may be completed in the oven.

CHICKEN MARYLAND

Cook chicken as directed for fried chicken. Arrange in center of platter, pour around it a thin white sauce made with half chicken stock and half top milk, and garnish with corn fritters. The neck, wing tips, and feet will make the chicken stock.

BROILED CHICKEN

Select a plump young chicken, allowing one-half chicken for each service. Split, place flesh side up on broiler, brush over with melted butter and broil about three minutes. Turn, brush skin side with melted butter, and broil until golden brown, turning two or three times during cooking. After browning, reduce heat or place farther away from it, to finish cooking without burning. Season when half done. Dot with butter, and garnish with parsley and cut lemon. See Broiling Chart for time and temperatures.

CHICKEN CASSEROLE WITH HERBS

Half a 3½-4 lb. chicken
2 tablespoons flour
⅔ teaspoon salt
⅙ teaspoon pepper
1 teaspoon minced parsley

½ teaspoon thyme
2 tablespoons butter or shortening
¾ cup water or stock

Cut up chicken as for fricassee, and roll each piece in the blended flour, salt, pepper, parsley, and thyme. Arrange in casserole, sprinkle over the chicken any remaining seasonings, dot with butter or shortening, and pour water or stock around. Cover and bake in moderately hot oven, 375° F., about one and a half hours.

CHICKEN FRICASSEE (WHITE)

1 small fricassee chicken
1 onion
2 cloves
Boiling water
Small piece salt pork, optional

½ teaspoon celery salt
½ teaspoon plain salt
¼ teaspoon pepper
1 tablespoon butter
1 tablespoon flour

Cut up chicken as for frying, wipe, and place in saucepan with onion into which cloves have been pressed. Add water to half cover and simmer gently, closely covered, until chicken is tender, about one and a half hours. If pork is used, dice and cook with chicken. Season when half done. Dish chicken, thicken gravy with butter and flour smoothly blended, simmer five minutes, and pour over chicken.

If dumplings are to be served with the chicken add them

twenty minutes before serving time. Be sure not to remove cover from pan while they are cooking. Serves four.

CHICKEN FRICASSEE (BROWN)

Follow recipe for Chicken Fricassee (White), but roll pieces of chicken in flour, and brown in a little hot fat before adding water. To enrich color of gravy, add a few drops Kitchen Bouquet.

CHICKEN PIE

Cook chicken as for white fricassee, arrange in baking dish with gravy and one cup cooked peas or diced potatoes, optional. Cover with flaky pastry or baking powder biscuit dough rolled thin, and bake in hot oven, 400° F., twenty-five to thirty minutes.

CHICKEN À LA KING

6 peeled sliced mushrooms or ½ cup canned mushrooms	½ teaspoon salt
	Dash of paprika
	1 egg yolk
1½ tablespoons butter	3 tablespoons cream
¾ cup thin white sauce	1 teaspoon lemon juice
1 cup diced cooked chicken	

Cook mushrooms in butter for five minutes, then add to white sauce (in double boiler). Add also chicken and seasonings, and heat thoroughly. Just before serving, put in egg yolk beaten with cream, and make very hot; but do not allow the mixture to boil after egg is added. Finally stir in lemon juice, and serve on toast, garnishing with parsley and cut lemon.

TURKEY OR CHICKEN CROQUETTES

½ cup well-seasoned me-
dium White Sauce, hot
Scant teaspoon gelatin
1 tablespoon cold water

¾ cup minced cooked tur-
key or chicken
Slight grating lemon rind
Beaten egg
Bread crumbs

Add gelatin, first softened in cold water, to white sauce
and stir until dissolved. Then blend with turkey or chicken
and lemon rind, and spread on a plate to cool. Divide into
four portions, shape into croquettes, egg and bread crumb,
and fry in deep hot fat, 375°-390° F. Drain on soft paper.
The croquettes may, if preferred, be baked in a hot oven,
400°-425° F., until brown.

CHICKEN NORMANDY

1 young chicken
2 tablespoons flour
1 teaspoon salt
⅙ teaspoon pepper
¼ cup oil

2 tomatoes, quartered
1 clove garlic
6 stoned ripe olives
6 sliced mushrooms
1 cup white wine

Cut chicken into pieces convenient for serving. Roll in
blended flour, salt and pepper. Then place in heated oil.
When chicken is browned, cover closely, reduce heat and
continue cooking until tender, about thirty minutes. Pour
off any excess oil, add tomatoes, garlic, olives and mushrooms, with wine. Cover again and simmer twenty minutes. Remove garlic before serving.

CHAPTER NINE

FISH AND SHELLFISH

Directions for the selection of fish will be found under Marketing for Fish.

To Clean Fish

Although fish is usually cleaned and dressed at market, it should be wiped with a cloth wrung out of cold water to remove any clotted blood from the inside and any loose scales from the surface.

With whole fish it may sometimes be necessary to scrape the skin a little with a dull knife to remove any attached scales. For this, work from the tail toward the head, slanting the knife a little so that it may catch and detach such scales.

The entrails are removed through an incision made on the under side of the fish. Heads and tails may be discarded or retained as preferred; with small fish they are frequently left, with larger ones they are usually removed.

To Skin Fish

If a fish must be skinned at home, first remove the fins with a sharp pointed knife or kitchen shears, then insert the knife (sharp side up) at one side of the back fin, and make an incision the entire length of the fish. Do the same on the other side of the back fin. This bony strip can then easily be pulled out intact.

Then beginning at the head, close to the gills, insert knife between skin and flesh and, guiding knife to keep it close to skin, pull it off gently. If flesh is soft, work very carefully as it tears easily. Remove skin from second side of fish in same manner.

To Bone or Fillet a Fish

Clean and skin as directed, then beginning at the tail slip a sharp knife under the flesh right down to the backbone. With long even strokes separate flesh from bone, making as clean a cut as possible. Turn and repeat. This is usually done at market, though occasionally (after a fishing trip for example) one may have to do it at home.

To Boil Fish

Use either small whole fish or thick chunky cuts of larger ones. Wipe as directed, then wrap in cheesecloth and place in hot water, being sure to use enough to cover the fish. Bring quickly to boiling point, then reduce heat, as hard boiling is apt to break the tender flesh. One teaspoon of salt and 1 tablespoon of vinegar or lemon juice may be added to each 2 quarts of water in order to season, whiten, and firm the flesh. Allow six to ten minutes to the pound, depending on thickness. For additional flavor, a slice or two of onion, celery, and carrot, with a clove or half a bay leaf, may be added to the water in which the fish is cooked.

To Steam Fish

Prepare as directed for boiling, wrap in cheesecloth, and place in steamer with boiling water in lower compartment. A little longer cooking time must be allowed when steaming, because in this case the fish is not actually immersed in water—ten to fifteen minutes per pound.

If desired, fish to be boiled or steamed may be placed on a plate, both fish and plate being wrapped in cheesecloth. In this way the fish is easily lifted from the pan after cooking.

Fish suited to boiling or steaming are cod, halibut, hake, cusk, mackerel, salmon, etc. Boiled fish usually needs a rich flavorful sauce such as egg, oyster, anchovy, shrimp, Hollandaise, or Béchamel.

To Bake Fish

The richer fish, bluefish and mackerel for example, need no basting, their own juices preventing the flesh from drying out. Dry fish such as weakfish and haddock, however, must be basted frequently with a little fat to keep the flesh and skin moist. These dry fish are improved by being stuffed; to insure greater richness and moisture, thin strips of bacon or fat salt pork, or even a little bacon fat, may be spread over the surface before baking.

Thin steaks or fillets of fish should be dipped into slightly salted milk, then drained and coated with bread crumbs before baking. The fish is then placed in a greased baking pan, dotted with fat (optional) and baked. Fillets bake very quickly, ten minutes in a very hot oven, 500° F., being sufficient. For larger fish allow about forty minutes, having the oven very hot, 500° F., for the first ten minutes, after which reduce to 400° F.

In placing a whole fish on the pan for baking, it may lie flat in the pan (and also subsequently on the platter), but is more attractive if skewered and tied into a curve or "s" shape, then placed upright (as it swims) in the pan.

Fillets may be spread with stuffing, then rolled and skewered for baking, or two fillets (or steaks) may have stuffing placed between them, like a sandwich.

Whole fish suited to baking are bluefish, haddock, mackerel, flounder, whitefish, weakfish, etc. Steaks or fillets include flounder, halibut, haddock, salmon, cusk, etc. Sauces for service with baked fish are egg, oyster, drawn butter, tomato, Hollandaise, Sauce Tartare. Good fish stuffings are savory bread, pickle, oyster, shrimp, and potato.

To Broil Fish

If fish is quite small, smelts or panfish, broil without splitting, and with heads and tails left on. Split larger fish down the back, and remove head and tail. Cut cod, salmon, and halibut into slices or steaks about one inch thick. Fillets may also be broiled, being brushed or rubbed over with melted fat before cooking.

If cooking over an open fire, place close to the fire to sear the outer surface as quickly as possible, thus retaining the juices, after which turn and sear the other side quickly; then complete cooking a little distance from the fire. With oven broiling, place fish quite near the heat at first, afterwards reducing the heat or lowering the broiling pan. In either case season when partly done with salt and pepper.

Thick slices of fish may be partly cooked under the broiler, the cooking then completed by baking in a hot oven, 400°-425° F., to insure thorough cooking without burning or over-browning.

Fish suited to broiling are shad, salmon, mackerel, smelts, bluefish, swordfish, pompano, small whole fish, or fish fillets. Accompanying sauces are Maître d'Hôtel, Hollandaise, melted butter. See Broiling Chart, page 122.

To Sauté or Pan Fry Fish

Small panfish, fish steaks, or fillets may be cooked by this method.

Dip the fish first into milk or beaten egg, then into

seasoned flour or crumbs, shake off any which do not adhere firmly, lay gently in frying pan containing two or three tablespoons of heated fat (oil, butter, or any other preferred fat). When brown on one side, turn carefully, using broad spatula, and brown other side.

To Deep Fat or French Fry Fish

Steaks and fillets are best suited to this method. Pat dry, egg, and bread crumb, shaking off any loose crumbs, then fry in deep hot fat, 375°-390° F., three to six minutes, depending on the thickness of the fish. Drain on soft paper.

For either type of fried fish, Hollandaise, Maître d'Hôtel, or Sauce Tartare is suitable.

Garnishes for the Fish Platter

Parsley: plain or minced.

Lemon: sliced; quartered; in fancy shapes; as a container for various fish sauces.

Cucumber: thinly sliced, plain or marinated in French dressing; in long wedges; as cups for mayonnaise.

Watercress; hard-cooked egg; radish roses; small pickles, mustard pickles.

Beets: sliced, or as cups for peas.

Pimiento: in narrow strips, or small fancy shapes.

Hard-cooked egg: sliced, or whites cut into rings with yolks pressed through sieve.

SEA FOOD CASSEROLE

1 cup flaked cooked fish	1 tablespoon minced pimiento or green pepper
1 teaspoon lemon juice	
1/3 teaspoon salt	1 teaspoon Worcestershire sauce
Dash of pepper	
1 cup medium white sauce	1 diced hard-cooked egg
1/2 cup diced celery	1 cup buttered crumbs

Add lemon juice, salt, and pepper to fish, then put a layer of fish in each of two individual casseroles. Cover with sauce to which celery, pimiento or green pepper, Worcestershire sauce, and hard-cooked egg have been added. Next a layer of crumbs, then repeat, having crumbs for top layer. Bake in moderately hot oven, 375°-400° F., about twenty minutes.

Fresh, smoked, or salt fish may be used.

SALT AND SMOKED FISH

To prepare salt fish for cooking, place in cold water to draw out salt. The length of time needed for this freshening depends on the saltiness and the size of the fish; salt cod slices for example, are likely to be sufficiently freshened in an hour or so; salt mackerel, on the other hand, may need from twelve to twenty-four hours. In the last instance, or indeed when soaking any whole salt fish be sure to lay it flesh side down in the water. It is well to change the water once or twice during the freshening period.

Smoked fish, which is preserved by both salting and smoking, is less salty than when brine or dry salt alone is used. Such fish, kippered herring and finnan haddie, rarely need freshening. Salt herring, however, usually requires as much soaking as mackerel,

CREAMED SALT CODFISH

½ pound salt codfish   Toast
1 cup thin white sauce   Paprika

Freshen fish as directed, separate into flakes, cover with cold water, bring slowly to boiling point, then simmer ten minutes. Add to sauce (made without salt) cook five min-utes, and serve on toast, dusting with paprika.

CODFISH CAKES

1 cup shredded codfish	¼ teaspoon pepper
1 cup hot mashed potato	1 tablespoon butter
1 egg	

Freshen codfish by placing in sieve and running cold water from the faucet through it for a moment. Then place in cold water, bring to boiling point, cook five minutes and drain. Combine with remaining ingredients, beating all well together. Shape into cakes and sauté in a little hot fat (tried-out salt pork or bacon fat are both good) turning to brown both sides.

For Codfish Puffs, drop mixture from tip of tablespoon into deep hot fat, 375°-390° F., and cook golden brown. Drain on soft paper, and serve plain or with tomato sauce.

NEW ENGLAND SALT FISH DINNER

¾ pound salt codfish	2 slices salt pork
4 small beets	1 cup egg sauce
4 small potatoes	Parsley
2 white onions	

Freshen fish as directed, place in cold water, bring slowly to boiling point; if still too salt, pour off water and replace with fresh, then cook until tender, half to three-quarters of an hour. Cook vegetables separately. Dice pork and cook until crisp and brown in frying pan. Place fish on large platter, pour sauce over and garnish with pork, vegetables, and parsley.

STEAMED FINNAN HADDIE

Wipe small fillet, place in cold water and bring to simmering point. If very salt, pour off water and replace with fresh; with lightly smoked fish the one water will suffice. Cook about fifteen minutes, drain and spread with softened butter.

BAKED FINNAN HADDIE

Bring fish to boiling point in water as directed for Steamed Finnan Haddie. Transfer to baking dish, pour ⅔ cup milk over, dot with butter, and bake in moderately hot oven, 375° F., about twenty-five minutes, basting with milk in pan.

Any left-over fish may be flaked and reheated in a medium white sauce, then served on toast.

KIPPERED HERRING

This savory salt smoked fish needs but a few minutes broiling under hot flame (oven broiling), or over a hot flame (open fire). Pour a teaspoon of melted butter over each fish when serving, no other seasoning is needed.

BROILED SALT MACKEREL

Freshen fish as directed. Pat dry, and broil, placing flesh side first toward the fire, then turning to broil other side. Or, partly broil, then complete cooking in moderately hot oven, 400° F. Serve with cut lemon and plenty of butter.

SALMON LOAF

1 small can red salmon	1 tablespoon butter
⅓ cup finely diced celery	½ cup scalded milk
¼ teaspoon salt	1 egg
⅛ teaspoon pepper	Dry bread crumbs
½ cup soft bread crumbs	

Flake salmon, removing all skin, oil, and bone. Combine with celery, seasonings, crumbs, butter, and milk.

Cover and let stand for five minutes, then add beaten egg, and turn into a small deep pan which has been well greased and sprinkled with dry bread crumbs. Place in a pan of hot water, and bake in moderately hot oven, 375°-400° F., about half an hour.

SALMON CROQUETTES OR CUTLETS

Follow recipe for Lobster Croquettes or Cutlets under Shellfish, substituting flaked canned red salmon for the lobster.

SALMON IN RICE NESTS

1 cup medium white sauce
1 egg yolk
1 teaspoon lemon juice
1 tablespoon sherry, optional
1 small can red salmon
1 small can mushrooms, sliced
1½ cups cooked rice
1 hard-cooked egg
Parsley

Add beaten egg yolk, lemon juice, and sherry if used, to white sauce; failing sherry, use an additional teaspoon lemon juice. Flake, and add salmon, also mushrooms, and heat thoroughly. Arrange rice on plates for individual service, making a depression or nest in each. Fill with salmon and garnish with the quartered hard-cooked egg and parsley.

FISH SOUFFLÉ

2 tablespoons quick-cooking tapioca
½ teaspoon salt
¼ teaspoon pepper
½ cup shredded celery
1 cup milk
½ cup flaked canned salmon or tuna fish
2 eggs
1 teaspoon lemon juice
1 teaspoon minced parsley or green pepper, optional

Combine tapioca, seasonings, celery, and milk in upper part of double boiler; place over boiling water, bring to boiling point and cook five minutes, stirring frequently. Add fish, beaten egg yolks, lemon juice, and parsley or green pepper if used. Finally fold in stiffly beaten egg whites and turn into well-greased deep baking dish. Set in pan of hot water and bake in moderate oven, 350° F., about forty minutes.

Left-over boiled, steamed, or baked fresh fish may be substituted for the canned.

SHELLFISH

FRIED OYSTERS

Pat oysters separately in cheesecloth until dry. Dip in beaten egg, then into crumbs seasoned with celery salt and paprika. Fry golden brown in deep hot fat, 375°-390° F., drain on soft paper and serve with Sauce Tartare.

Frequently oysters are set aside for half an hour after egging and bread crumbing, the process then being repeated. This gives a heavier crust.

SCALLOPED OYSTERS

¼ cup melted butter	1 teaspoon lemon juice
¼ teaspoon salt	1 cup soft bread crumbs
Dash of pepper	1 dozen oysters

Add butter, seasonings, and lemon juice to crumbs, and arrange in fireproof baking dish in alternate layers, first half the oysters, then half the crumbs. Repeat layers, pour into dish any oyster liquor, and bake in hot oven, 425° F., about twenty minutes. Never have more than two layers of oysters in this dish, otherwise those at the top and bot-

tom would be over-cooked before those in the center are
done.

OYSTERS CASINO

12 oysters in shells	2 slices bacon, finely
1 tablespoon finely minced	minced
green pepper	Squeeze of lemon juice
	Dash of salt and pepper

Have oysters on deep shells. Blend pepper, bacon (raw),
and lemon juice, and use to top oysters. Bake in hot oven,
425° F., ten minutes. Season with a very little pepper and
salt and serve immediately.

STEAMED CLAMS

Allow 12 to 20 clams per portion. Scrub with brush and
wash very thoroughly. Fresh clams have tightly closed
shells or they close when touched. Never use clams if
shells are gaping open. After scrubbing, place in saucepan
with ½ cup boiling water to each 2 portions. Cover closely
and steam about twenty minutes, or until shells open.
Serve very hot, accompanied by strained clam broth
(liquid in which clams were cooked), in cups, with small
dishes of melted butter to which a squeeze of lemon juice
has been added. The clams are dipped into this before
eating.

FRIED CLAMS

Use soft clams discarding tough necks, then follow recipe
for Fried Oysters.

CLAM FRITTERS

1½ dozen clams	¼ teaspoon salt
½ cup flour	1 egg
½ teaspoon baking powder	

Chop clams very fine or pass through food chopper. Drain, measure liquor, and if necessary add milk to make ¼ cup. Sift dry ingredients, add chopped clams, and moisten with beaten egg and liquid. The mixture should be the consistency of a heavy drop batter. Cook golden brown on both sides in frying pan, or on griddle well greased with bacon fat or salt pork, dropping mixture into pan from spoon.

If preferred the mixture may be dropped by scant table-spoonfuls into deep hot fat, 360°-375° F., cooked golden brown, then drained on soft paper.

SCALLOPS

There are two types of scallops, the small delicate bay scallop and the larger sea scallop. Both are prepared in the same manner except that the larger variety needs a little longer cooking.

To sauté: Pat scallops dry in a cloth, dust with flour, dip each separately into beaten egg, and roll in bread crumbs. Cook golden brown in a little hot butter or oil, turning to brown all sides. Serve with melted butter and lemon juice, or Sauce Tartare.

To broil: Roll scallops in flour, dip into melted butter, then broil until golden brown, about six minutes, turning to brown all sides. Season lightly with salt and pepper when half done.

CREAMED SCALLOPS

Parboil scallops five minutes in salted water. Drain and reheat in Medium White Sauce using part of liquor in which scallops were cooked in making the sauce.

TO BOIL LOBSTER

A live lobster is dark green in color and should be active. If purchased already boiled, test by straightening the tail which should spring back quickly, this indicating that the lobster was alive—as it should be—when boiled.

To boil at home, have ready a large kettle two-thirds filled with boiling well-salted water (1 tablespoon salt to each quart water). Pick up lobster behind head or, better still, take it up with tongs. Plunge head first into the boiling water, cover, and keep water actively boiling. A one to one and one-half pound lobster will take about twenty minutes to cook. Plunge at once into cold water; and when cool enough to handle take meat from shell.

First break off claws, then split body lengthwise (heavy kitchen shears easily cut through both shells). Discard black intestinal vein which runs the full length of the solid meat, keep any red coral and greenish fat. Discard all spongy tissue and the sac near the head, commonly called the lady. Split or break claws and pick meat from them.

Be sure to use a silver or stainless steel knife when cutting lobster meat, as a steel one somewhat discolors it. Use for salad, Newburg, cocktail, etc.

TO BROIL LOBSTER

Place lobster on its back on a board and kill by inserting a sharp knife at the joint where tail and body shells come together, thus cutting through the spinal cord. Be sure that the claws are plugged before attempting this. Split lengthwise from head to tail with large sharp knife. The fish dealer will usually take care of all of this if requested, delivering the lobster at the time it is to be cooked.

Discard soft spongy tissue, small sac near head (the lady), also the black intestinal vein which runs the length of the meat. Crack claws with hammer or nut cracker, place flesh side uppermost on greased broiler, brush generously with melted butter, and broil about twenty minutes. Additional butter may be brushed over the lobster during the cooking. If desired, partly broil then finish cooking in a hot oven, 425° F.

Some prefer to boil lobster first, then split, clean, brush over with butter, and broil, basting while cooking with more butter, but the first method is preferable.

Serve with melted butter, cut lemon, and chili sauce.

LOBSTER NEWBURG

2 tablespoons butter
1½ cups diced lobster meat, fresh cooked or canned
Salt and paprika

Slight grating nutmeg
1 tablespoon sherry
1 egg yolk
¼ cup cream

Melt butter and cook lobster in it for three minutes. Add seasonings and sherry, then beaten egg yolk with cream. Heat thoroughly without boiling and serve immediately.

LOBSTER CROQUETTES OR CUTLETS

1 teaspoon gelatin
1 tablespoon cold water
½ cup thick white sauce
¾ cup finely diced lobster, fresh cooked or canned
Slight grating nutmeg

¼ teaspoon salt
Dash of pepper
1 teaspoon lemon juice
Egg and bread crumbs
Frying fat

Add gelatin, first softened in cold water, to white sauce while sauce is still scalding hot. Stir until dissolved, then add lobster, seasonings, and flavorings, and turn onto plate, spreading smoothly about three-quarters inch thick. Set aside to chill, divide into four or six portions and shape either as croquettes or cutlets. Egg, and bread crumb, then fry golden brown in deep hot fat, 375°-390° F., and drain on soft paper.

If preferred bake in a very hot oven, 450° F., about fifteen minutes.

The cutlets are very attractive if a stick of macaroni about one and one-half inches long is pressed into the narrow end of each to simulate a bone.

CRABS

Both hard and soft shell crabs are the same species, the shells being hard except during the shedding season. Soft crabs are those which have just cast off or shed their old shell, the new one not yet having become hard. Hard crabs are boiled like lobster, the meat then being removed from the shells and used in salads, cocktails, and a variety of other dishes.

FRIED SOFT SHELL CRABS

Wash crabs, remove pointed apron on under side and discard all spongy material beneath it, also the points at each end of the shell. Season with salt and pepper, roll in flour, then in beaten egg, and finally in bread crumbs. Fry in deep hot fat, 360°-375° F., three to five minutes. Drain on soft paper. The crabs will rise to the surface of the fat and must be turned to brown both sides. Sometimes soft shell crabs are dipped in light batter instead of flour, egg, and crumbs, before frying.

BROILED SOFT SHELL CRABS

Clean crabs exactly as for frying but, instead of rolling in egg and crumbs, brush over with melted butter to which a little lemon juice, salt, and pepper have been added. Broil seven to eight minutes, turning two or three times during the cooking.

CRABMEAT À LA KING

Follow recipe for Chicken à la King, substituting crabmeat, fresh cooked or canned, for the chicken. Season with slight grating of nutmeg.

CRABMEAT RAVIGOTE

½ cup crabmeat, fresh or canned
⅓ teaspoon salt
⅙ teaspoon pepper
Dash of paprika
¼ teaspoon mixed mustard

2 teaspoons salad oil
½ teaspoon minced parsley
½ hard-cooked egg, finely chopped
Ravigote mayonnaise

Combine crabmeat with all ingredients except mayonnaise, blend thoroughly, arrange in two scallop shells, spread with mayonnaise and garnish with latticed narrow strips of green pepper or strips of anchovy, the remaining hard-cooked egg, and parsley. Chill thoroughly before serving.

CRABMEAT NEWBURG

Follow recipe for Lobster Newburg, substituting crabmeat, fresh or canned.

CRABMEAT MOUSSE

1 envelope gelatin
1/4 cup cold water
3/4 cup boiling water
1/2 cup mayonnaise
1 cup crabmeat, fresh or canned
1/2 cup heavy cream, whipped

1/4 teaspoon salt
1/6 teaspoon paprika
1 teaspoon lemon juice
Stuffed olives
Pimiento
Parsley, watercress, or lettuce

Soften gelatin in cold water, then add boiling water, and stir until dissolved. Chill, and when mixture begins to thicken fold in mayonnaise, crabmeat, cream, and seasonings. Turn mixture carefully into a mold previously dipped into cold water, and chill. Unmold for service and garnish with stuffed olives, strips of pimiento and parsley, cress, or lettuce. Serves four. This is especially good for company service.

TO BOIL SHRIMPS

Plunge shrimps into boiling salted water (1 tablespoon salt to 1 quart water) and cook until they turn pink, about fifteen minutes. Remove shells and discard black intestinal veins as with lobster.

CURRIED SHRIMPS

2 tablespoons butter
1 teaspoon finely minced onion
1/2 clove garlic, optional
1 cup halved shrimps, fresh cooked or canned

1 tablespoon flour
1 teaspoon curry powder
1 cup milk
Salt and paprika
1 teaspoon lemon juice
2 cups cooked rice

Heat butter, cook in it gently for five minutes the onion and garlic, if used. Take out garlic, add shrimps, flour, and curry powder. Blend smoothly, add milk, and stir until boiling. Season, cover, and let stand just below boiling point for twenty minutes. Finally add lemon juice, and serve wtih boiled rice.

SHRIMP SCRAMBLE

1 cup shrimp, fresh cooked   ⅔ teaspoon anchovy paste
  or canned   2 eggs
⅓ cup light cream

Combine all ingredients and cook over hot water (double boiler) until mixture thickens. Serve at once on buttered toast, dusting with paprika or minced parsley.

SHRIMP CREOLE

1 tablespoon butter   Dash of pepper and
1 small onion, minced   paprika
2 tablespoons minced   1 cup solid canned
  green pepper   tomatoes
½ clove garlic, minced   1 pound raw shrimp
¼ teaspoon salt   1 teaspoon minced parsley

Melt butter and cook in it for three minutes the onion, green pepper, garlic and seasonings, stirring constantly. Add tomatoes, cover and simmer fifteen minutes. Add raw shrimp (shelled and with black intestinal vein removed). Cover and simmer ten minutes. Serve on hot buttered toast, sprinkling with minced parsley.

If preferred, the shrimp may be served in a border of steamed rice.

CHAPTER TEN

SAVORY SAUCES, STUFFINGS, AND MEAT ACCOMPANIMENTS

Sauces are valuable primarily because they contribute to the food value and appearance of foods, as well as adding flavor where it may be lacking. They also help to make dry dishes more palatable by the moisture they provide.

Sauces should not be hurriedly made, for flavor is developed almost as much by cooking as by the actual ingredients used in making the sauce. Good sauces are perfectly blended, smooth, and free from lumps; neither too heavy nor too thin. Seasonings and flavorings are highly important also, though both must be used with discretion.

If you can make a good white sauce and a good brown sauce, you have the foundation for all sauces, as others depend chiefly for their variety on individual seasonings and flavorings. For example, egg, parsley, shrimp, anchovy, and oyster sauces are all developments of white sauce; while olive, mushroom, piquant, and many more, have brown sauce as their base.

Actually, there are three white sauces, thin, medium, and thick, the difference consisting only in the proportions of butter and flour used in their making. Thin White Sauce forms an excellent base for cream soups; Medium White Sauce is the one commonly served with fish, vegetables, and meats; Thick White Sauce is chiefly used as a foundation for croquettes and cutlets.

WHITE SAUCE

THIN

1 tablespoon butter	¼ teaspoon salt
1 tablespoon flour	⅛ teaspoon pepper or
1 cup milk	paprika

MEDIUM

2 tablespoons butter	¼ teaspoon salt
2 tablespoons flour	⅛ teaspoon pepper or
1 cup milk	paprika

THICK

3-4 tablespoons butter	¼ teaspoon salt
3-4 tablespoons flour	⅛ teaspoon pepper or
1 cup milk	paprika

Melt butter, add flour, and blend the two until perfectly smooth. Until you become thoroughly accustomed to the making of sauces, it is better to do this away from the fire. Then add the milk, a little at a time, and cook over gentle heat, stirring constantly, continuing the cooking several minutes after the sauce boils. It is advisable to use a double boiler so that the cooking may proceed slowly with no fear of burning. Season.

The expert cook often scalds the milk before adding to the butter and flour; but the novice had better add it cold, as then there is less likelihood of burning.

For Egg Sauce, add to Medium White Sauce 1 hardcooked egg, diced, finely minced, or crushed with a fork.

For Parsley Sauce, add to Medium White Sauce 2 teaspoons finely minced parsley. To prepare parsley, wash and dry, then mince it. Gather together in a piece of fine cheesecloth or corner of a towel, hold under water faucet and press out the liberated green coloring, which otherwise would make the sauce a dull grayish green. The sauce should be creamy white with parsley specks floating in it.

For Shrimp Sauce, add to Medium White Sauce ⅓ cup diced shrimps, fresh cooked or canned, with a very slight grating of nutmeg.

For Cheese Sauce, add to scalding hot Medium White Sauce 4 tablespoons grated cheese and beat in thoroughly.

For Scandinavian Sauce, add to Medium White Sauce ½ cup mayonnaise, juice of ½ lemon and 1 egg yolk beaten until light. Reheat in double boiler, but do not actively boil.

For Oyster Sauce, add to ½ cup Thick White Sauce 6 oysters scalded in their own liquor then coarsely chopped. Add also the strained oyster liquor, and season with a few drops lemon juice.

For Egg and Olive Sauce, add to ½ cup Thick White Sauce ¼ cup fish stock, 1 hard-cooked egg, diced, finely minced, or crushed with a fork, and ½ dozen sliced stuffed olives.

BÉCHAMEL SAUCE

2 tablespoons butter
2 tablespoons flour
½ cup veal or chicken stock
½ cup light cream
¼ teaspoon celery salt
⅛ teaspoon pepper or paprika

Prepare exactly as White Sauce.

TOMATO SAUCE

1 cup canned tomatoes
1 sliced small onion
½ bay leaf
2 cloves
¼ teaspoon salt
⅛ teaspoon pepper
1 teaspoon sugar, optional
2 tablespoons butter
1½ tablespoons flour

Cook together for ten minutes tomatoes, onion, bay leaf, cloves, salt, pepper, and sugar if used. Then press through sieve. Combine butter and flour smoothly in saucepan, add tomato mixture and cook, stirring constantly, until boiling, then simmer five minutes.

Remember that excellent commercial tomato sauce, richly flavored and spicy, comes in cans requiring only heating.

BROWN SAUCE

2 tablespoons butter	1 cup brown stock
1 sliced small onion	¼ teaspoon salt
3 tablespoons flour	⅛ teaspoon pepper

Cook onion in butter until it turns yellow. Stir in flour, and when golden brown add stock slowly. Bring to boiling point, stirring constantly, season, and strain to remove onion. Half a small bay leaf may be cooked with the sauce if desired; but because bay leaf has a very strong flavor be careful not to use too much.

The reason for the larger amount of flour in this sauce is because flour loses some of its thickening properties when browning.

For Brown Mushroom Sauce, add to Brown Sauce, after straining, 1 cup fresh mushrooms, sliced and sautéed in a little butter. Canned mushrooms may be used instead.

For Piquant Sauce, add to Brown Sauce, after straining, 1 tablespoon each vinegar, minced pickles, capers, and olives.

SPANISH OR CREOLE SAUCE

1 tablespoon minced onion   ½ cup solid tomatoes,
2 tablespoons minced green   canned or fresh
    pepper   ⅛ teaspoon salt
1 tablespoon butter   Dash of pepper
6 minced olives   1 cup Brown Sauce

Cook onion and green pepper in butter for three minutes. Add tomatoes, olives, and seasonings, simmer gently for ten minutes, then combine with brown sauce.

HOLLANDAISE

½ cup butter   ⅓ cup boiling water
2 egg yolks   ¼ teaspoon salt
1 tablespoon lemon juice   Dash of cayenne

Divide butter into three portions. Place one in upper part of double boiler with egg yolks and lemon juice. Cook over hot water, stirring constantly, until butter is melted, then add second portion of butter and continue cooking, still stirring. As mixture thickens, add remaining butter and cook until sauce coats the spoon. Add boiling water gradually with salt and cayenne, and cook one minute. Keep water under sauce hot; *never let boil.*

Hollandaise must be watched very carefully while cooking lest it curdle. Should it do so, add gradually 1 to 2 tablespoons heavy cream.

MOCK HOLLANDAISE

3 tablespoons butter   ⅙ teaspoon paprika
2 tablespoons flour   Juice ½ lemon
1 cup water   1 whole egg or 2 egg yolks
½ teaspoon salt

Combine half of the butter with flour in saucepan, blend smoothly, add water, and bring to boiling point, stirring constantly. Season, add lemon juice, and pour while boiling hot over beaten egg. Finally add remaining butter, a little at a time, beating well into sauce.

BARBECUE SAUCE

¼ cup butter
2 tablespoons minced onion
2 slices lemon
1 green pepper, finely chopped
2 tablespoons chili sauce

1 tablespoon Worcestershire sauce
¼ cup brown sugar
½ teaspoon dry mustard
½ teaspoon chili powder
1 cup vinegar

Combine all ingredients in saucepan, and cook over gentle heat until butter is melted and ingredients thoroughly blended. Use with barbecued meats, or as a sauce for sandwiches, or as a basting for steaks and similar cuts of meat.

RAISIN SAUCE

1 tablespoon butter
1 tablespoon flour
1 cup cider

¼ teaspoon salt
⅛ teaspoon paprika
¼ cup seedless raisins

Blend butter and flour until smooth, then gradually add cider, bring to boiling point, stirring constantly; add salt, paprika, and raisins, and simmer ten minutes.

MINT SAUCE

½ cup mild vinegar
2 tablespoons sugar

2 tablespoons finely minced mint leaves

Combine vinegar and sugar, stirring until sugar is dissolved; then add mint, washed, dried, and very finely minced.

SAUCE TARTARE

½ cup mayonnaise
1 tablespoon minced sour pickles
1 teaspoon minced capers
1 teaspoon minced chives

2 teaspoons minced parsley
Few drops onion juice
2 teaspoons plain or tarragon vinegar

Combine all ingredients and chill thoroughly.

MAÎTRE D'HÔTEL BUTTER OR SAUCE

2 tablespoons butter
1 teaspoon lemon juice
1 teaspoon minced parsley

Few drops onion juice
Salt and pepper

Cream butter until quite light, add lemon juice slowly, stir in parsley, onion and seasonings. Form into balls or pats, and chill.

STUFFINGS

SAVORY BREAD STUFFING

2 cups crumbled bread
½ cup minced celery
1 tablespoon minced parsley
1 slice onion, minced
½ teaspoon grated lemon rind

1 teaspoon salt
½ teaspoon poultry seasoning
¼ teaspoon pepper
Dash of paprika
3 tablespoons butter, melted

Combine and blend all ingredients thoroughly. Use for chicken, lamb, or veal; for turkey, double or treble the recipe according to quantity needed. There are also excellent commercial packaged stuffings which need only moistening before using. Either the homemade Savory Bread Stuffing or the prepared stuffing may be varied as follows:

For Giblet Stuffing, add giblets which have been simmered in water until tender, then finely chopped.

For Oyster Stuffing, add 6 oysters, diced, moistening with a little oyster liquor.

For Sausage Stuffing, omit butter and substitute ¼ pound sausage meat, cooked ten minutes, then broken or cut small.

For Chestnut Stuffing, add ½ pound chestnuts which have been boiled until tender, shells and brown skins removed, and nuts chopped.

For Cooked Stuffing, use double the amount of butter called for, melt and heat it in frying pan, then sauté dry ingredients in it.

For Corn Bread Stuffing, substitute crumbled left-over corn bread for white bread in Savory Bread, Oyster, or Sausage Stuffings.

SAGE AND ONION STUFFING

6 onions	1 teaspoon salt
1 tablespoon powdered sage	¼ teaspoon pepper
½ teaspoon poultry season- ing	2 cups crumbled bread

Peel onions, boil until tender, drain, then chop finely. Add remaining ingredients and mix thoroughly. If bread is very dry, soak in cold water before crumbling, then squeeze as dry as possible. Use with duck, goose, or pork.

For Apple Stuffing, substitute diced uncooked apples for onions, omit sage, and add grated rind ½ lemon.

For Apple and Raisin Stuffing, add 1 cup halved seeded raisins to Apple Stuffing.

POTATO STUFFING

1 cup mashed potato	½ teaspoon powdered sage
½ teaspoon salt	2 tablespoons cream
Dash of paprika	1 tablespoon butter
Slight grating of onion	1 beaten egg yolk

Have potato thoroughly mashed and free from lumps. Combine with all other ingredients and beat well.

OYSTER STUFFING

1 cup oysters	⅔ teaspoon salt
1½ cups soft bread crumbs	¼ teaspoon pepper
¼ cup melted butter	

Pick over oysters, scald in their own liquor, drain, and chop coarsely. Add to bread crumbs with melted butter and seasonings, and moisten with a little of the oyster liquor, using enough to soften the crumbs but not to make the mixture too moist. Use as stuffing for baked fish.

PICKLE STUFFING

2 cups crumbled bread	1 tablespoon finely chopped
¼ cup melted butter	parsley
1 teaspoon onion juice	¼ cup chopped sweet
Celery salt and pepper	pickles

Blend ingredients in order given, pack loosely in body of fish. Either sew up or fasten with toothpicks, or spread between fillets of fish, and bake.

SHRIMP STUFFING

2 tablespoons butter	Lemon juice
2 tablespoons flour	½ cup chopped cooked or
¾ cup milk or fish stock	canned shrimps
Salt and pepper	

Blend butter and flour in saucepan, add milk or stock slowly, stir until boiling, season, and add shrimps. Spread between fish fillets.

MEAT ACCOMPANIMENTS

DUMPLINGS

½ cup sifted flour	⅛ teaspoon salt
¾ teaspoon baking powder	Milk

Sift flour, baking powder, and salt, and mix to a light dough with milk, as for biscuit. Drop by small spoonfuls into hot gravy, stew, or fricassee; cover and cook twenty minutes without removing saucepan lid.

YORKSHIRE PUDDING

½ cup sifted flour	1 egg
¼ teaspoon salt	½ cup milk

Sift flour and salt, add egg slightly beaten with just enough milk to moisten. Beat until perfectly smooth, then add remaining milk. Turn into shallow pan in which 2 tablespoons fat from roasting beef have been poured and allowed to become thoroughly hot. Bake in moderately hot oven, 350°-375° F., twenty to thirty minutes. Cut into squares for serving. If preferred, bake in muffin pans in which the fat has been heated.

APPLE SAUCE

Wipe, pare, core, and cut apples into eighths. To 2 cups of apples add ¼ cup water, cover, and cook gently until apples are tender. If a smooth sauce is desired, press through sieve, in which case the apples need be neither pared nor cored. Add ¼ to ⅓ cup sugar depending on tartness of apples, and cook three minutes longer. Serve plain or flavored with a grating of nutmeg, a dash of cinnamon, or a very little grated lemon rind. The flavor of insipid apples is improved by the addition of a squeeze of lemon juice.

For Raisin Apple Sauce, add ¼ cup seedless or halved seeded raisins with the sugar.

For Cranberry Apple Sauce, use three-fourths apples and one-fourth cranberries, slightly increasing the amount of sugar.

TEN MINUTE CRANBERRY SAUCE

1 cup sugar	2 cups cranberries
1 cup water	

Boil sugar and water together for five minutes. Add cranberries and boil, without stirring, until all the berries burst; five minutes is usually sufficient. Remove from fire and cool.

MOLDED STRAINED CRANBERRY SAUCE

2 cups cranberries	1 cup sugar
1 cup water	

Cook cranberries in water until all the berries burst. Strain, add sugar, and stir until dissolved. Then boil rapidly until a drop tested on a cold plate jellies, about ten to fifteen minutes. (If using a sugar thermometer, it should register 220° F.) Turn into mold previously dipped in cold water and chill.

CRANBERRY ORANGE RELISH

2 cups cranberries   1 cup sugar
1 orange

Put cranberries through food chopper. Quarter orange, remove seeds, and pass orange also through food chopper. Add sugar and mix well. Chill before serving. This will keep well in refrigerator for several weeks.

BEET HORSERADISH RELISH

1 cup finely chopped well-   Juice ½ lemon
  drained canned beets   1 tablespoon sugar
2 tablespoons horseradish,   ½ teaspoon salt
  bottled or fresh grated

Blend all ingredients thoroughly. Will keep several days in refrigerator.

CHAPTER ELEVEN

VEGETABLES

All vegetables require thorough washing in cold water before cooking. A small stiff-bristled brush is a wonderful help in cleaning root vegetables and celery, while for spinach a spray attached to the faucet dislodges sand quickly and effectively.

Never use soda when boiling green vegetables. It may help to retain bright color but it destroys essential vitamins and influences flavor.

For marketing tips on fresh vegetables see Marketing, page 49. There also will be found suggestions for the home care of vegetables.

Boiled Vegetables

Use fresh boiling salted water. With small amounts of water (up to one quart) use one-half teaspoon salt; with large amounts of water one teaspoon salt to each quart.

Cook vegetables rapidly and just until tender. Overcooking, or slow cooking, impairs color and flavor. The time required depends on the age, tenderness, and freshness of the vegetable. Obviously, diced turnips or sliced carrots will cook more quickly than the whole or even halved vegetable.

Generally speaking, all green vegetables are cooked uncovered. Spinach, being cooked with practically no water, is covered during the first few minutes of cooking.

TIMETABLE FOR BOILING VEGETABLES

Vegetable	Regular Saucepan		Pressure Saucepan	
	Amount of Boiling Salted Water	Cooking Time (Minutes, except as indicated)	Amount of Water	Cooking Time (Minutes) 15 lbs. 250°F.
Artichokes, French,	To cover	20–40	½ cup	10–12
Jerusalem	To cover	20–30	½ cup	4–10
Asparagus	To cover	15–25	½ cup	1–2
Beans, Green or Wax	To cover	20–40	½ cup	3–4
Lima, fresh	To cover	25–40	½ cup	2–3
Lima, dried	Abundant	1½–2 hrs.	3 cups	25
Beets, young	To cover	30–60	½ cup	8–10
old	Abundant	1–2 hrs.	½ cup	10–18
Beet greens	Abundant	20–30	½ cup	2–3
Broccoli	Abundant	15–30	½ cup	2–3
Brussels Sprouts	Abundant	15–20	½ cup	3
Cabbage	Abundant	8–15	½ cup	3–4
Carrots, new	To cover	10–20	½ cup	3–5
old	To cover	20–30	½ cup	8–10
Cauliflower, flowerets	Abundant	8–10	⅔ cup	2–3
whole	Abundant	15–25	1 cup	5
Celeriac	To cover	15–25	½ cup	2
Celery	To cover	20–30	½ cup	2–3
Chard, Swiss	Very little	15–30	½ cup	2–3
Corn, green	To cover	8–12	⅔ cup	3–5
Cucumber	Very little	6–15	½ cup	1
Dandelion Greens	Abundant	20–30	½ cup	3
Eggplant	Very little	15–20	½ cup	1
Kale	Abundant	25–30	½ cup	2
Kohlrabi	Abundant	25–40	½ cup	6
Leeks	Abundant	15–25	½ cup	2–3
Okra	To cover	20–30	½ cup	3
Onions	Abundant	20–40	½ cup	5–7
Oyster Plant (Salsify)	To cover	25–45	½ cup	7–10
Parsnips	To cover	25–45	½ cup	7–10
Peas	Very little	15–30	½ cup	1–2
Potatoes, White	To cover	20–40	½ cup	8
Sweet	To cover	20–30	½ cup	10
Spinach	Very little	8–10	½ cup	2
Squash, Summer	Very little	15–20	½ cup	6–8
Winter	Very little	20–30	½ cup	10–12
Tomatoes	Very little	15–25	½ cup	1
Turnips	Abundant	20–35	½ cup	5–12
Turnip Greens	Abundant	20–30	½ cup	3–5

The minimum time indicated is for young, tender, fresh vegetables, the maximum applies when they are maturer or less tender.

After cooking, drain and reserve any drained-off liquid for soups, sauces, or gravies; it contains valuable, soluble minerals and vitamins which must not be wasted. Season with butter, pepper, and additional salt if needed.

The cooking time for quick-frozen vegetables is shorter than for those which have not been quick-frozen. Follow directions on container.

When cooking vegetables by the pressure cooker method, the cooking period is minimized. Follow directions which come with your individual cooker.

The so-called waterless method of cooking, that is, cooking in a very heavy utensil with practically no water, is to be recommended highly as it retains the maximum amount of flavor, color, and vitamins.

Steamed Vegetables

Prepare vegetables as for boiling, sprinkle lightly with salt, and cook in perforated steamer placed over rapidly boiling water. The steamer must have a tightly fitting cover. Season after cooking with butter, pepper, and additional salt if needed. Allow from one-fourth to one-third longer cooking time for steaming than for boiling.

Buttered Vegetables

This means boiled or steamed seasoned vegetables with the addition of 1 to 1½ teaspoons butter per serving, added after cooking and draining.

Creamed Vegetables

Use ½ cup Thin White Sauce to 1½ to 2 cups cooked vegetables.

For Creamed Parsley Vegetables, add 1 teaspoon minced parsley to the White Sauce.

For Creamed Pimiento Vegetables, add 1 tablespoon minced pimiento to the White Sauce.

Scalloped Vegetables

Scalloped means alternate layers of vegetables and Medium White Sauce, the vegetables being boiled or steamed, seasoned, and usually sliced or diced. Top with buttered crumbs and bake in moderately hot oven, 375° F., until browned and piping hot.

Vegetables au Gratin

Prepare as for Scalloped Vegetables, but use equal parts buttered crumbs and grated cheese for the topping. If desired, a little cheese may also be sprinkled over each layer of White Sauce.

ARTICHOKES

There are two kinds of artichoke and they are entirely different: the globe or French artichoke, and the Jerusalem artichoke. The first is a green vegetable of the thistle family; the second a tuber, having some of the characteristics of chestnuts and sweet potatoes as regards flavor.

BOILED GLOBE OR FRENCH ARTICHOKES

Discard mature or withered outer leaves, and cut stems so that each artichoke will stand firmly when served. Then cut off prickly tips and tie with cord to prevent leaves spreading. If artichokes must be kept waiting before cooking, let them stand in cold water to which a little vinegar, 2 tablespoons to the quart, has been added. Cook in boiling salted water (see Time Table for Boiling Vegetables). Test by pulling out a leaf; when it parts easily from the stem the artichokes are done; the length of time of cooking depends on size. Drain upside down to allow any water to run off, and serve on individual plates accompanied by melted butter or Hollandaise.

In eating, each leaf is pulled separately from the stem, dipped into butter or sauce, and the fleshy portion drawn from the fiber with the teeth. The choke is inedible and must be removed either before or after cooking; but the heart at the base of the leaves is most delicate. These hearts are often sold commercially in bottles or cans to be heated with butter, and served as a vegetable; they are also packed in oil or brine for hors d'ocuvrc or salads.

BOILED JERUSALEM ARTICHOKES

Wash and scrape artichokes; then immediately drop them into cold water in which a little vinegar, 2 tablespoons to the quart, has been added to prevent discoloration. Rinse, before cooking, in fresh water. Cook in slightly salted boiling water until tender (see Time Table for Boiling Vegetables); or steam, following recipe for Steamed Vegetables. Drain, season, and serve with melted butter, White Sauce, or Hollandaise.

BOILED ASPARAGUS

Cut off tough ends of stems. (Use them for cream of asparagus soup.) Wash, scrape, and tie asparagus in bundles, then cook until tender in boiling salted water (see Time Table for Boiling Vegetables). Drain thoroughly, and serve plain or on toast with melted butter, Medium White Sauce, Hollandaise, or Mock Hollandaise.

As the tender tips cook more quickly than the lower part of the stalk, asparagus can also be prepared by plunging the lower ends into the saucepan of boiling water, and covering the pan with another inverted pan, thus permitting the tender tips to be cooked by steaming.

ASPARAGUS WITH BROWN CRUMBS

Boil or steam asparagus; drain, sprinkle with sautéed buttered crumbs seasoned with onion juice, grated lemon rind, and paprika. If desired, a tablespoon of grated cheese may also be added.

ASPARAGUS WITH BROWN BUTTER

Boil or steam asparagus, drain and pour over it 2 tablespoons butter which has been heated, slightly browned, and seasoned with salt, pepper, and lemon juice.

BOILED GREEN OR WAX BEANS

Break off stem and tip ends of beans, then either cut crosswise into inch lengths or, better still, French by cutting into slender one and a half inch slanting slices. Wash, then cook just until tender in boiling salted water (see Time Table for Boiling Vegetables). Drain and season. A little minced parsley may be added to the beans with the seasonings.

BOILED LIMA BEANS

Shell beans, and cook just until tender in boiling salted water (see Time Table for Boiling Vegetables). Drain and season.

BOILED DRIED LIMA AND OTHER BEANS

This group includes lima, black, soy, pea, navy, yellow eye, and other members of the bean family. Pick over care-

fully, rejecting any imperfect ones. Wash, then soak overnight in cold water. Cook, covered, in boiling salted water
until tender, usually two to three hours. (Soy beans will
take almost double this time.) A slice of salt pork, a ham
bone, or a strip of bacon adds flavor to dried beans. Drain
and season with salt and pepper. One cup uncooked dried
beans will yield two to three cups after cooking.

LIMA BEAN CASSEROLE

1 cup cooked dried lima beans	¾ cup Medium White Sauce
2 tablespoons minced pimiento	½ cup grated cheese
	¼ cup soft bread crumbs
¼ teaspoon salt	1 tablespoon butter, melted
1 tablespoon tomato catsup	

Combine beans, pimiento, seasonings, white sauce, and
two-thirds of the cheese and turn into buttered casserole
or baking dish. Blend crumbs, butter, and remaining
cheese, spread over top and bake in moderate oven, 350°-
375° F., about thirty minutes. If preferred substitute well-
seasoned Tomato Sauce for the White Sauce and omit
catsup.

NEW ENGLAND BAKED BEANS

2 cups pea or navy beans	2 tablespoons dark molasses
¼ pound salt pork	½ teaspoon mustard, optional
1 teaspoon salt	
1 tablespoon brown sugar	Boiling water

Wash, then soak beans overnight in cold water. Drain,
add fresh water, and simmer until skins break. (Test by
taking two or three beans on spoon and blowing gently on
them; if skins break readily the beans are sufficiently

cooked.) Turn into bean pot; add pork, scoring rind with sharp knife that it may more easily divide after cooking; add all other seasonings and flavorings with water just to come to top of beans. Cover and bake in slow oven, 250°-300° F., five to six hours, adding additional water as needed to keep beans just covered. During last half hour, remove cover to brown surface.

SPICY BAKED BEANS

1 medium-sized can baked beans	½ teaspoon salt
	¼ teaspoon pepper
1 cup canned tomatoes	½ teaspoon mustard
1 minced pimiento	½ teaspoon curry powder, optional
1 small minced onion	
1 tablespoon salad oil	2 tablespoons molasses

Combine all ingredients thoroughly. Turn into a bean pot or casserole, and bake in a slow oven, 300°-325° F., about one and a half hours.

BOILED BEETS

Wash, but do not peel beets. Leave tapering root and at least two inches of stem on beets. If skin is cut, or stems cut too short, beets will bleed and lose their rich color. Cook in boiling salted water (see Time Table for Boiling Vegetables), drain and season.

FIVE-MINUTE BEETS

Wash and peel beets thinly, then grate on coarsest grater. Place in saucepan with a very little water, about two tablespoons to each medium-sized beet. Cover and cook until tender, about five minutes. Practically all the water will be absorbed during the cooking. The beets may be seasoned with salt, butter, and pepper.

PICKLED BEETS

Slice cold boiled beets and cover with vinegar. If desired add 1 tablespoon grated horseradish to each 2 cups beets.

HARVARD BEETS

¼ cup sugar	1 tablespoon salad oil
⅓ tablespoon cornstarch	6 small beets, cooked or
2 tablespoons water	canned
2 tablespoons vinegar	Salt and pepper

Combine sugar and cornstarch, add water and mix smoothly. Then add vinegar and oil, and boil five minutes, stirring constantly. Add diced beets and seasonings, and let all stand together over gentle heat for half an hour.

BROCCOLI

Discard all mature leaves. Peel stems if at all tough, and split if unduly large. Cook, uncovered, in boiling salted water (see Time Table for Boiling Vegetables). Drain and season with salt, pepper, and melted butter; or serve with Hollandaise, Mock Hollandaise, or Cheese Sauce; or with melted butter and lemon juice; or with buttered crumbs.

BOILED BRUSSELS SPROUTS

Remove any wilted leaves and tough stem. Wash thoroughly, then soak in well-salted water half an hour. Drain, cover with boiling salted water and cook, uncovered, until tender (see Time Table for Boiling Vegetables). Drain and season.

BOILED CABBAGE

Discard any wilted leaves, cut into sections, let soak in slightly salted water until ready to cook. Then boil, uncovered, until just tender (see Time Table for Boiling Vegetables). Drain and season.

CHINESE CABBAGE

Boil like ordinary cabbage, or prepare and serve like Hot or Cole Slaw.

HOT SLAW

2 cups shredded cabbage   2 tablespoons hot vinegar
1 egg yolk   ¼ teaspoon salt
2 tablespoons cold water   Dash of pepper
2 teaspoons butter

Crisp cabbage in ice water; then drain and dry thoroughly. Meanwhile combine all remaining ingredients and cook over hot water (double boiler), stirring constantly until thickened. Add cabbage and serve as soon as hot.

BOILED CARROTS

Scrub, then scrape carrots, leave whole, or cut into rounds, or lengthwise halves. Cook in boiling salted water until just tender (see Time Table for Boiling Vegetables). Drain and season.

CARAMELED CARROTS

Use left-over boiled or steamed carrots. Slice lengthwise or crosswise as preferred. For 3 carrots heat 2 tablespoons butter or other fat in heavy frying pan; add carrots, sprinkle lightly with salt, pepper, and granulated sugar, and cook very slowly until golden brown. Garnish with minced parsley.

For Lyonnaise Carrots, add 2 tablespoons minced onion and a squeeze of lemon juice.

For Minted Carrots, substitute 1 teaspoon minced mint for the onion in Lyonnaise Carrots.

BOILED CAULIFLOWER

Discard coarse stems and outer leaves. Place flower side down in a pan of cold salted water for half an hour. If preferred, the cauliflower may be broken into small flowerets, in which case it will cook more quickly than if left whole. Cook in boiling salted water (see Time Table for Boiling Vegetables), drain and season. Serve with White Sauce, thin or medium, Hollandaise, Mock Hollandaise, Cheese, or Mustard Sauce.

The leaf stalks of cauliflower may be cut into finger strips or large dice, boiled or steamed until tender, then drained and served with White or Cheese Sauce.

CAULIFLOWER WITH BROWN CRUMBS

Boil or steam cauliflower (see Time Table for Boiling Vegetables), drain, dust with salt and paprika, and sprinkle with sautéed buttered crumbs. If desired, a tablespoon of grated cheese may be added to the crumbs after browning.

STEWED CELERY

Use outer stalks allowing three or four stalks per portion. Scrub, scrape, and cut into three to four inch lengths. Tie together, and cook in boiling salted water just until tender (see Time Table for Boiling Vegetables). Drain and serve with melted butter, Cheese Sauce, or Mock Hollandaise.

BRAISED CELERY

Prepare celery as for stewing, then sauté in 2 tablespoons butter in heavy frying pan until delicately browned. Add ¾ cup stock (or bouillon cube and water) and continue cooking until celery is tender, about twenty minutes. Serve plain or on toast.

CORN ON THE COB

Do not husk until ready to cook; remove all silk using stiff vegetable brush. See Time Table for Boiling Vegetables.

SUCCOTASH

1 cup young lima beans	½ cup milk
1 cup corn cut from cob	1 tablespoon butter
Dash of pepper	1 teaspoon sugar, optional
⅓ teaspoon salt	

Cook beans until tender in boiling water (see Time Table for Boiling Vegetables). Add corn, cook twelve minutes longer, season, add milk and butter, and heat, adding sugar if corn is not young and sweet.

Kidney beans, also canned corn, may be used if desired.

CORN CUSTARD

1 cup uncooked corn cut from cob	2 teaspoons melted butter
2 small eggs	¼ teaspoon salt
1 cup milk	Dash of pepper

Beat eggs and combine with milk, butter, and seasonings. Stir in corn and turn mixture into buttered custard cups. Place these in a pan of hot water, and bake in moderate oven, 350° F., until just set, twenty to thirty minutes. Test by inserting blade of knife in center of custard; if it comes out clean custard is done, if milky cook a little longer.

CORN FRITTERS

⅓ cup flour
½ teaspoon baking powder
⅙ teaspoon salt

⅛ teaspoon pepper
1 small egg
½ cup corn, cooked

Sift together flour, baking powder, and seasonings, add beaten egg and corn (cut from cob or canned vacuum packed), and a little milk, if necessary. The batter should be soft enough to drop easily from spoon. Drop by spoonfuls onto hot well-greased griddle or frying pan and cook golden brown, turning to brown both sides. If cream-style canned corn is used, add an additional tablespoon of flour.

STUFFED EGGPLANT

½ eggplant
Boiling salted water
1 teaspoon minced onion
1 tablespoon minced green
  pepper
1 tomato, diced

⅙ teaspoon pepper
1 tablespoon melted butter
1 cup minced cooked meat
  —beef, tongue, ham, etc.
Buttered crumbs

Split eggplant lengthwise. Cook one half in boiling salted water for twenty minutes. Cool, then scoop out most of the flesh, chop, and combine with onion, pepper, tomato, seasonings, and meat. Replace in shell, sprinkle with buttered crumbs, and bake in moderate oven, 350° F., about forty-five minutes. Wrap the remainder of the eggplant in waxed paper and keep in the refrigerator for subsequent use sautéed or scalloped.

SAUTÉED EGGPLANT

Cut half an eggplant (peeled) into slices about one-third inch thick. Dip first into beaten egg, then into seasoned bread crumbs, and sauté golden brown on both sides in a little hot fat, draining afterwards on soft paper.

FRENCH FRIED EGGPLANT

Slice peeled eggplant about three-fourths inch thick then cut into finger strips. Dip first into beaten egg then into seasoned bread crumbs, shaking off any loose crumbs. Fry golden brown in deep hot fat, 375°-390° F. Drain on soft paper.

BOILED ONIONS

Select onions of the same size so that they may cook evenly. Peel, then cook in boiling salted water (see Time Table for Boiling Vegetables). Drain very thoroughly, and season with butter and pepper. If boiling water is poured over the onions and they are allowed to stand a moment, the skins will slip off more easily.

FRIED ONIONS

Peel and slice mild onions, then sauté in a little butter or other fat until tender and brown, stirring occasionally so that they may cook evenly. Drain off any excess fat before serving.

FRENCH FRIED ONIONS

Peel mild onions, cut into quarter-inch slices and separate into rings. Dip in milk, drain, toss in flour, and fry in deep hot fat, 380° F., until golden brown. Drain on soft paper, sprinkle with salt, and serve immediately.

GLAZED ONIONS

1 dozen small white onions	Salt and paprika
1 tablespoon butter	2 teaspoons sugar
2 tablespoons stock or water	

Peel onions, cook five minutes in boiling salted water, drain thoroughly, and turn into small baking dish with butter, stock or water, salt, and paprika. Cover and bake in moderately hot oven, 375° F., half an hour; then remove cover, sprinkle with sugar, and allow onions to brown.

BAKED STUFFED ONIONS

Peel onions of even size, and parboil fifteen minutes in slightly salted water. Take out centers, chop them, and blend with seasoned bread crumbs, plain or flavored with grated cheese, or a little bit of cold cooked minced ham, chicken, or sausage meat. Refill cavities, place in baking dish, put a small piece of butter on top of each onion, and bake in moderate oven, 375° F., half an hour, having dish covered for first fifteen minutes.

BOILED OYSTER PLANT (SALSIFY)

Cut off tops and scrape roots. Then immediately plunge into water containing two teaspoons vinegar to the quart; unless this is done oyster plant will quickly turn brown.

Rinse, then cook in boiling salted water (see Time Table for Boiling Vegetables), drain, cut into inch lengths, and season. Reheat before serving.

VEGETABLE OYSTERS

Prepare oyster plant as directed, mash after boiling. When cool enough to handle, season, form into small flat cakes, and roll in flour. Sauté in a little hot fat, turning to brown both sides.

BOILED PARSNIPS

Wash, scrape, cut in pieces, and cook in boiling salted water until tender (see Time Table for Boiling Vegetables). Drain, season, and serve with hot melted butter or White Sauce. Or after draining, mash very thoroughly and season with butter, pepper, and salt.

For Parsnip Cakes, form mashed parsnips into small flat cakes, roll in flour and sauté in hot butter or other fat, turning to brown both sides.

For Fried Parsnips, boil as directed, drain, roll in flour, and fry golden brown in a little butter or drippings.

BOILED PEAS

Do not shell peas until just before cooking time in order to avoid loss of flavor. Cook in boiling salted water just until tender (see Time Table for Boiling Vegetables). Drain reserving liquor for soups or sauces, and season with butter and pepper.

Small quantities of peas may be served as a garnish in combination with other vegetables, such as hollowed-out cooked beets, small onions, small white turnips, or mashed potato nests filled with hot buttered peas.

PEAS WITH ROSEMARY

1 tablespoon butter	1 cup water
1 tablespoon flour	Salt and pepper
1½ cups shelled peas	1 teaspoon sugar
2 or 3 sprays parsley	1 egg yolk
4 shallots or tiny onions, peeled	1 tablespoon butter, additional
1 small spray or ¼ teaspoon dried rosemary (or basil)	

Combine the first tablespoon of butter, flour, peas, parsley, shallots or onions, rosemary or basil, and water, and simmer until peas are tender. Discard parsley and herb (tying these together assures easy removal). Season with salt, pepper, and sugar. Just before serving, add egg yolk and additional butter, and toss and stir together to blend. Serve very hot.

FRIED PEPPERS

Wipe peppers, then pierce with fork and hold over flame until thin outer skin blisters, and can easily be rubbed off. Cut out stem end, discard seeds and connecting fiber, and cut peppers into slices, narrow or wide as preferred. Sauté in a little butter or other preferred fat, five to seven minutes, turning to cook both sides. Usually served as a steak accompaniment.

STUFFED PEPPERS

Wipe, skin, discard seeds and fiber as directed for fried peppers. Stuff with any of the fillings suggested for stuffed tomatoes. Place close together in deep baking dish, pour a little water, stock, or canned tomato around and bake in moderately hot oven, 375° F., about half an hour. Very large peppers may be halved instead of stuffed whole.

BOILED POTATOES

Choose potatoes of even size so that they will all cook in the same time. Whenever possible, cook potatoes in their jackets as this conserves the mineral salts. If they are to be pared, peel off only the thinnest possible layer of skin, and do it as short a time before cooking as possible. For boiling directions, see Time Table for Boiling Vegetables. As soon as tender, drain; if a floury surface is desired shake lightly. If they must be kept a short time, sogginess and discoloration may be prevented by covering with a cloth, never with the pan lid.

PARSLEY POTATOES

Dice peeled potatoes or cut into small balls with a vegetable cutter; or use very small whole new potatoes. Boil, drain, and season with melted butter, finely minced parsley, and a dash of paprika.

For Minted Potatoes, add with the parsley three or four minced fresh mint leaves.

MASHED POTATOES

Drain boiled potatoes thoroughly, then mash until perfectly smooth. Add for each 4 potatoes, 1½ tablespoons butter, about 3 tablespoons scalded milk, and a dash of paprika; then beat with fork until light and fluffy.

For Fried Potato Cakes, form leftover mashed potatoes into three-quarter inch round cakes, dust with flour and brown on both sides in hot bacon or other meat drippings.

For Duchesse Potatoes, place mounds of mashed potato

on baking sheet, roughen surface with fork and bake in hot oven, 400°-425° F., until lightly browned.

For Potato Puff, add one beaten egg yolk to mashed potato, and pile roughly on shallow baking dish. Place in moderate oven, 350°-375° F., to reheat and slightly brown.

BAKED POTATOES

Use large potatoes, scrub thoroughly, and bake in moderately hot oven, 350°-375° F., until tender, about fifty minutes. Serve at once. If they must be kept a short time, burst skins to permit escape of steam. A pat of butter may be pressed into this opening and a sprinkling of salt and dash of paprika added. The baking time may be shortened if potatoes are parboiled for ten to fifteen minutes before placing in the oven.

(A top-of-the-range oven for small quantity baking is a wonderful fuel-saver.)

POTATOES ON THE HALF SHELL

Bake large potatoes, split lengthwise, scoop out potato, and mash, adding a generous seasoning of salt, pepper, butter, and a little hot milk or cream. Replace in halved skins, and return to oven to color surface delicately.

For Surprise Potatoes, replace half the mashed, seasoned potato in the skin, put a small ball of cooked sausage meat or hamburg in center, top with more potato, and reheat.

STUFFED POTATOES

Bake potatoes, cut open without actually dividing, scoop out potato, mash, season with butter, salt, paprika, minced parsley, a few drops onion juice, optional, and add any one of the following: 2 tablespoons grated cheese, diced crisp cooked bacon, cooked frizzled dried beef, or minced ham or tongue. Return to shells, reheat and brown.

For Creamed, and Creamed Pimiento Potatoes, see recipes for Creamed, and Creamed Pimiento Vegetables.

FRENCH FRIED POTATOES

Cut medium-sized peeled potatoes into thick finger strips. Let stand in cold water one hour, drain, and pat dry in cloth. Fry, a few at a time, in deep hot fat, 375°-390° F. Drain thoroughly on soft paper, sprinkle with salt, and serve immediately.

JULIENNE POTATOES

Cut peeled potatoes into thin slices, then into strips not over one-fourth inch thick. Let stand in cold water one hour, drain, pat dry in cloth, and cook as directed for French Fried Potatoes.

For Shoestring Potatoes, cut into the thinnest possible strips.

FRANCONIA (BROWNED) POTATOES

Use potatoes of even size. Parboil ten minutes (potatoes may be peeled either before or after parboiling); then ar range in roasting pan around meat, and bake about forty minutes, basting three or four times with fat in pan.

HASHED BROWN POTATOES

2 tablespoons fat   Dash of pepper and salt
2 cups finely diced cooked
   potatoes

Any preferred fat may be used, butter, bacon fat, drippings, etc. Heat, then add seasoned potato, mix with fat, and cook gently for five minutes, stirring occasionally, after which allow potato to brown on under side. Fold together like an omelet and turn onto hot platter.

For Cottage Fried Potatoes, slice instead of dicing potatoes, and cook in the fat, turning to brown both sides. Stirring is not necessary as each slice of potato browns separately.

LYONNAISE POTATOES

2 teaspoons minced onion
2 tablespoons hot fat
2 cups cooked potatoes, sliced or diced

Salt and pepper
1 teaspoon minced parsley

Cook onion in hot fat until it begins to color. Add potatoes, seasonings, and parsley, and heat thoroughly; then cook gently until under surface is brown. Fold omelet fashion onto hot platter.

POTATO PANCAKES

¼ cup sifted flour
1 teaspoon baking powder
½ teaspoon salt

⅙ teaspoon pepper
2 large raw potatoes, grated
1 egg

Sift flour, baking powder, salt, and pepper; add to potatoes with well-beaten egg. A little more, or less, flour may be needed according to proportion of water in potato. (The mixture should be the consistency of drop batter.) Drop by tablespoons into shallow pan containing a little hot fat. Cook golden brown on both sides. Serve with gravy as a meat accompaniment or with apple sauce.

BOILED SWEET POTATOES

Sweet potatoes should be boiled in their skins, then peeled after cooking. Select potatoes of the same size so that they may cook evenly. Cook in boiling salted water until tender (see Time Table for Boiling Vegetables).

For Baked Sweet Potatoes, see recipe for Baked Potatoes, remembering that sweet potatoes cook in about one-third less time than white ones.

For Mashed Sweet Potatoes, boil or bake sweet potatoes in their skins until tender. Discard skins, mash potato, and season with butter, pepper, and salt.

SOUTHERN (CANDIED) SWEET POTATOES

2 large sweet potatoes   3 tablespoons butter
⅓ cup brown sugar

Boil sweet potatoes until just tender, peel, slice, and arrange in layers in buttered baking dish, sprinkling each layer with sugar and dotting with butter. Cover and bake in moderately hot oven, 375°-400° F., about half an hour.

Maple sirup, crushed maple sugar, or honey may be substituted for brown sugar; a little grated orange rind may be added, or alternate layers of sweet potato and sliced or crushed canned pineapple, or pared, cored, sliced tart apple may be used.

BOILED SPINACH

When boiling spinach use no water except that which clings to the leaves after washing. The washing must be very thoroughly done (see introduction to vegetable recipes). Cut stems in small pieces and cook with leaves. Spinach is the one exception to the rule of cooking green vegetables uncovered, because of the very small amount of water used. By covering the pan for the first five minutes steam is generated, which quickly wilts the spinach and liberates its juices, in which the cooking is completed.

Cook only until tender (see Time Table for Boiling Vegetables), drain very thoroughly, and reserve any remaining liquid for soup. Chop fine, reheat, and season with butter, pepper, and salt. Garnish with sliced, chopped, or quartered hard-cooked egg, if desired.

SPINACH RING

Press cooked, seasoned, chopped spinach into a buttered ring mold and allow it to stand a moment; then unmold onto serving platter and fill center with any desired creamed mixture, meat, fish, or another vegetable.

For Molded Spinach for plate service, press spinach into individual buttered cups or molds.

BUTTERED SUMMER SQUASH

Wash, cut into chunky pieces, and cook until just tender, with as little boiling salted water as possible (see Time Table for Boiling Vegetables). Drain very thoroughly, mash, and season with pepper, salt, and butter. Very tender summer squash need not be peeled, if at all mature peel thinly and discard large seeds.

STEAMED OR BOILED WINTER SQUASH

Wash squash, then cut into small pieces, peel, and remove spongy portion and seeds. Steam or boil until tender (See Time Table for Boiling Vegetables, or recipe for Steamed Vegetables). Drain thoroughly then mash and season with pepper, salt, butter, and a little top milk or cream.

BAKED WINTER SQUASH

Wash and cut squash into sections, discarding spongy portion and seeds. Place in roasting pan, flesh side down, and bake in moderate oven, 350°-375° F., twenty minutes. Then turn flesh side up and put a dot of butter into each portion with a generous sprinkle of salt and pepper. Complete baking until tender, about twenty-five minutes longer. Serve with additional butter.

BAKED ACORN SQUASH

Wash, cut squash into halves crosswise, and bake as winter squash, serving in the shells. This will take about half an hour to bake, and will cook more quickly if first parboiled for ten to fifteen minutes.

Baked acorn squash may be served as the main course at a luncheon, if, when partly cooked, a pat of sausage meat or hamburg is placed in it; this in turn being covered by a slice of apple or a layer of cranberry sauce; the whole being then baked together until the squash is tender and the meat cooked.

FRIED CROOKNECK SQUASH

Wash squash, cut into crosswise slices one to one and a half inches thick. Discard spongy portion and seeds. Cook gently in frying pan in a very little hot butter, bacon fat, or sausage fat.

BROILED TOMATOES

Wipe and halve medium-sized firm tomatoes. Arrange on broiler, season with salt and pepper, and dot with butter or drippings. Place under broiler flame, and cook five to seven minutes, or until lightly browned; then transfer to hot oven, 425° F., for ten minutes to complete cooking. Serve piping hot.

STEWED TOMATOES

Use either fresh or canned tomatoes. With fresh, wipe and cut up adding a tablespoon of water to start the cooking; canned tomatoes will not need this. Cook ten to twenty minutes until texture is thoroughly broken down. Season with salt, pepper, and butter. If desired, shortly before serving, add for each cup of tomatoes half a slice of diced day-old bread, or fried bread croutons.

SCALLOPED TOMATOES

Use fresh, stewed fresh, or canned tomatoes. Season with salt, pepper, and butter or drippings. Arrange in baking dish alternate layers of seasoned tomato and bread crumbs. Top with buttered crumbs and bake in moderate oven, 375°-400° F., twenty to thirty minutes. If desired, use plain crumbs for topping, and when partly baked arrange strips of bacon, lattice fashion, over top of dish.

STUFFED TOMATOES (HOT)

2 firm tomatoes	⅙ teaspoon pepper
½ cup soft bread crumbs	1 teaspoon minced parsley
¼ cup chopped celery	2 tablespoons buttered
1 teaspoon grated onion	crumbs
½ teaspoon salt	

Cut a thin slice from the stem end of each tomato, and scoop out pulp with a teaspoon. Combine crumbs, celery, and seasonings, and moisten with tomato pulp, using as much as is needed to thoroughly soften the crumbs. Fill hollowed-out tomatoes with mixture, top with buttered crumbs, and bake in moderately hot oven, 375° F., half an hour. If desired, celery salt may be used in place of chopped celery and part of the plain salt.

Tomatoes may also be stuffed with well-seasoned left-over chicken or other meat extended with bread crumbs (corn bread is especially good); with cooked rice or potatoes, using gravy or tomato pulp to moisten; with macaroni and cheese; or with cooked fresh or canned corn moistened with tomato pulp and seasoned with minced green pepper, onion juice, salt, pepper, and a little butter.

MASHED YELLOW TURNIPS

Peel turnip thickly, then cut into chunky pieces, or slice and dice. Cook in boiling salted water just until tender (see Time Table for Boiling Vegetables). Drain very thoroughly, season, and mash. For a more delicate flavor turnips are often mashed, and combined with an equal quantity of mashed potato.

SCANDINAVIAN VEGETABLE PLATE OR DINNER

Arrange in concentric circles for individual service any desired combination of cooked vegetables, spinach molds or timbales, cauliflower flowerets, green peas, boiled onions, carrots, broccoli, whole steamed tomatoes, etc., then pour Scandinavian Sauce over all and serve very hot.

Vegetable Plate Combinations

Spinach ring filled with creamed onions, alternate mounds parsley potatoes, carrots and peas.

Stuffed Idaho potato halves, cauliflower au gratin, Harvard beets, buttered green beans.

Stuffed green pepper, creamed potatoes, minted carrots, buttered lima beans.

Rice or noodle ring with creamed mushrooms, buttered broccoli or Brussels sprouts, buttered beets.

Corn-stuffed tomato, buttered string beans with onion, steamed winter squash.

Asparagus bundles with Hollandaise or Mock Hollandaise, buttered peas and carrots, parsley potatoes.

VEGETABLES FOR PARTIES

SCALLOPED POTATOES
(8 servings)

8 medium-sized potatoes	3 tablespoons butter
Salt and pepper	4 cups scalded milk
Flour	

Peel potatoes and slice thinly. Arrange one-third in buttered casserole, sprinkle with seasonings and dredge with flour. Repeat twice. Melt butter in milk and pour over potatoes. Cover and bake in moderate oven, 375° F., half an hour, then uncover and bake 15 minutes longer to delicately brown. Watch during earlier part of cooking lest milk boil over. If it does, uncover and continue baking at 350° F.

One teaspoon grated onion or two tablespoons grated cheese may, if desired, be sprinkled over each layer of potatoes.

SAVORY BAKED TOMATOES

Wipe, then cut ripe tomatoes in halves crosswise. Arrange in greased shallow casserole, cut sides up, dot with butter, sprinkle with salt, pepper, minced parsley and chives. Bake in moderate oven, 350-375° F., until tender, about 25 minutes. Allow one large half for a serving.

CHAPTER TWELVE

SALADS AND SALAD DRESSINGS

Salads have so steadily increased in popularity that they are now conceded an important place in at least one meal every day, usually in two. Originally, salads were introduced into a meal to stimulate or refresh the appetite after the hearty meat course; nowadays, we often serve them as the main part of the meal, as the dessert, or even as an appetite teaser at the beginning of the meal. Salads are highly important as tonic foods, being replete with vitamins and mineral salts; and they deserve much greater consideration than most of us give them.

A salad of whatever variety should always have as its base some form of green, not always lettuce, but sometimes cress or watercress, endive, chicory, escarole, romaine, or perhaps shredded cabbage, white or red. Nor should we overlook the spring possibilities of so many of the "green things growing," dandelion, lamb's lettuce, sorrel, and purslane—to mention only a few.

There are certain important points in the preparation of all salads which must be emphasized:

Have ingredients cold and crisp.

Be sure that lettuce, celery, etc., are thoroughly drained and dried after washing.

Keep salads in the refrigerator until serving time; then serve them on really cold plates.

Make salads interesting in appearance by color contrast;

interesting in taste by flavor contrast. Use herbs both in the salads and the dressings. (If you are lucky enough to have a garden, especially one with an old-time herb border, you may have at your disposal chives, sage, parsley, mint, tarragon, basil, and rosemary.)

Do not mash or mince the ingredients; dicing or shredding is infinitely preferable.

Blend enough dressing with the salad ingredients, even though some is reserved to use as a garnish.

That dressing, by the way, is just as important as the salad itself. To so many of us, salad dressing means only mayonnaise, French, or boiled dressing. Good as they are, there are innumerable ways of varying these three valuable basic dressings to fit different types of salads.

And a word about flavored vinegars: one of the latest members of the condiment family, herb-flavored or wine-flavored, they add tang and zest to an otherwise bland mild dressing; and last, but not least, mignonette pepper— merely peppercorns freshly ground in your own little pepper mill—but what a difference that fresh grinding makes!

GREEN AND VEGETABLE SALADS

MIXED (TOSSED) GREEN SALADS

Use any desired combination of salad greens—lettuce, watercress, romaine, endive, chicory, dandelion greens, heart leaves of spinach, celery. Wash and pick over carefully, then crisp in refrigerator. Lettuce and romaine should be broken into convenient-sized pieces with fingers, never cut. Combine in salad bowl, adding sliced radishes, diced beets or pimiento or cubed firm tomato for color value, young scallions, minced onion and slivered green pepper for flavor, with or without hard-cooked egg. Mois-

ten generously with French dressing. Mix and toss to
gether and serve immediately.

MIXED RAW VEGETABLE SALADS

Select any preferred variety of vegetables—ripe tomatoes,
celery, green pepper, cucumber, radishes, carrots, heart
leaves of spinach, young onions, tiny cauliflower flowerets,
etc. Prepare according to their individual needs: wash
spinach thoroughly, shred or grate carrots, discard seeds
and connecting fiber of peppers, cut tomatoes into sections, use only the tiniest cauliflower flowerets, etc. Be
sure that all vegetables are thoroughly chilled and crisped,
arrange in salad bowl with due regard for color, and at
serving time moisten generously with French dressing,
tossing the salad ingredients about in it with spoon and
fork that all may be thoroughly coated.

CHEF'S SALAD

It is difficult to give exact directions for a chef's salad.
Ordinarily it consists of a variety of crisped salad greens
such as dandelion greens, tender leaves of spinach, lettuce,
romaine, or escarole, together with shredded green pepper
and slivered young onions plus Julienne strips of chicken,
ham or tongue, and sometimes even a little firm cheese,
usually of the Swiss type. Arrange in large salad bowl; mix
and toss with a good French Dressing which, if desired,
may be reinforced by the addition of crushed hard-cooked
egg.

CHIFFONADE SALAD

Use any preferred plain salad green, shredded lettuce,
shredded cabbage, watercress, endive, etc., or a combina-

tion of greens with either Chiffonade French Dressing or Chiffonade Mayonnaise.

COLE SLAW

Shred cabbage very finely, crisp in ice water, drain thoroughly, season, and serve either with French, Roquefort, Cream, Sour Cream, or Boiled Dressing.

For Jewel Salad, add to Cole Slaw an equal bulk of mixed, highly colored, cooked vegetables, such as peas, diced carrots, and string beans, with minced green pepper or pimiento.

BAKED BEAN SALAD

1 cup baked beans	¼ teaspoon salt
¼ cup diced celery	Dash of pepper
1 teaspoon finely minced onion	Chili Dressing
	Plain or shredded lettuce

Combine all ingredients, chill thoroughly, and serve on plain or shredded lettuce.

POTATO SALAD

3 medium-sized cooked firm potatoes, sliced	2 tablespoons French Dressing
1 teaspoon grated onion	⅓ cup mayonnaise or Boiled Dressing
2 teaspoons minced parsley	
Salt and pepper	

Combine potatoes, onion, parsley, and seasonings, and moisten with French Dressing. Chill and just before serving add mayonnaise or Boiled Dressing, and toss all thoroughly together. Garnish, if desired, with a little additional parsley, sliced radishes, chilled tomato, or hard-cooked egg, and pass additional dressing separately.

HOT POTATO SALAD

3 medium-sized fresh cooked potatoes
1 tablespoon bacon drippings
2 tablespoons minced onion
2 tablespoons water
3 tablespoons vinegar
½ teaspoon sugar
¼ teaspoon salt
Dash of paprika
¼ teaspoon mustard, optional

Slice potatoes while still hot and keep hot while preparing the dressing. For this, heat the bacon drippings and cook onion in it until golden brown. Meanwhile combine and bring to boiling point all remaining ingredients, add to onion and bacon drippings, pour over potatoes, and toss together thoroughly. Serve immediately.

STUFFED TOMATO SALAD

2 firm tomatoes
Salt
⅓ cup cooked seasoned vegetables—lima beans, peas, diced carrots, etc.
⅓ cup diced celery
1 tablespoon minced green pepper
Few drops onion juice
French Dressing
Mayonnaise or Boiled Dressing
Plain or shredded lettuce

Wash, peel, and scoop centers from tomatoes. Sprinkle with salt, invert on plate, and chill. Fill with blended stuffing ingredients moistened with French Dressing, and serve on plain or shredded lettuce, topping with a spoonful of mayonnaise, Horseradish mayonnaise or Boiled Dressing.

Additional stuffings for tomatoes are asparagus tips; cole slaw or a combination of cole slaw and cooked flaked fish; baked beans with celery; chicken with celery; diced cucumber and flaked canned red salmon or tuna fish; flaked crabmeat, fresh or canned with diced celery; cubes of Liederkranz cheese with finely minced parsley, or cottage cheese—either of these last, seasoned with Boiled Dressing or mayonnaise.

To skin tomatoes impale on prongs of fork, plunge into boiling water for a few seconds, then into cold water Pierce skin at blossom end with tip of paring knife and peel.

MEAT AND FISH SALADS

CHICKEN SALAD

1½ cups diced cooked chicken	Mayonnaise or Boiled Dressing
⅓ cup French Dressing	Lettuce
1 cup diced celery	Sliced stuffed olives
½ teaspoon salt	Sliced hard-cooked egg
⅙ teaspoon paprika	

Combine chicken and French Dressing and chill. Add celery, seasonings and, if salad appears dry, a little mayonnaise or Boiled Dressing. Arrange on lettuce, and garnish with additional dressing, sliced olives, and hard-cooked egg.

If celery is not available, substitute finely shredded cabbage and season with celery salt or celery seed.

Other good chicken salad combinations are: equal parts diced chicken and canned pineapple with a few diced ripe olives; equal parts diced chicken, boiled ham, and celery; equal parts diced chicken, celery, canned mushrooms, and a few shredded salted almonds; equal parts diced chicken and orange sections with shredded pecans.

DUCK AND ORANGE SALAD

1 cup cold duck
1 seedless orange
Watercress

¼ cup Mignonette Dressing
Ripe olives

Combine duck, diced, with orange sections, and marinate with dressing. Chill and serve on watercress garnishing with ripe olives.

MINTED LAMB SALAD

1 cup cold lamb, diced
1 cup green peas
1 teaspoon minced mint
1 cup cooked new potatoes, diced, optional

Salt and pepper
3 tablespoons French Dressing
Chicory, watercress, or shredded lettuce

Combine lamb, peas, mint, potatoes if used, and seasonings. Marinate with French Dressing. Chill thoroughly, and serve with garnish of chicory, watercress, or shredded lettuce, passing mayonnaise or Boiled Dressing separately, if desired.

COMBINATION MEAT AND SALAD PLATTERS FOR COMPANY SERVICE—SUPPER, BUFFET, OR SUNDAY NIGHT

1. Slices of chicken (or turkey) flanked by thin slices of boiled ham stuffed with India relish and held together with small rings of green pepper. Potato salad and olives.

2. Separate a large round plate into six sections by means of stalks of stuffed celery or asparagus tips marinated with French Dressing. In two opposite sections, arrange slices of cold lamb; in two more, carrots and peas marinated with French Dressing; in remaining two, Saratoga

potatoes; and in very center a shallow dish containing cranberry sauce.

3. Slices of cold roast beef (rare) garnished with scraped horseradish and dill pickles. Cottage-cheese-stuffed toma-toes and shoestring potatoes.

4. A variety of sausages as bologna, salami, liverwurst, etc. with halved stuffed eggs and heart leaves of lettuce filled with cubed cranberry sauce.

MOLDED SALMON SALAD

1 small can red salmon	1/2 cup mayonnaise
1/2 cup diced celery	Cucumber
Salt and paprika	French Dressing
Few drops onion juice	Watercress
1 teaspoon lemon juice	1 hard-cooked egg, sliced

Pick over salmon, discarding any particles of skin and bone, also oil. Combine with celery, seasonings, flavorings, and mayonnaise; then press into mold or bowl, and chill. Unmold and garnish with overlapping slices of cucumber marinated in French Dressing, watercress, and hard-cooked egg.

SHRIMP SALAD

1 cup shrimps, fresh cooked or canned	Salt and pepper
1 hard-cooked egg	2 tablespoons French Dress-ing
1/3 cup diced celery	Lettuce
1 or 2 minced sweet pickles	Horseradish Mayonnaise

Pick over shrimps, and remove black intestinal vein which runs down center of back. Crush egg; add shrimps with celery, pickles, and seasonings. Moisten with French Dressing, chill, then serve on lettuce garnishing with Horseradish Mayonnaise.

JELLIED AND FROZEN SALADS

QUICK TOMATO ASPIC

1 tablespoon gelatin	Additional seasoning, if
2 cups canned tomato juice	needed

Soften gelatin in ¼ cup of the tomato juice, then dissolve in remaining scalded tomato juice. Season if necessary (tomato juice varies materially in its seasoning content); cool, turn into a mold, and chill.

JELLIED TOMATO CRABMEAT RINGS

Mold tomato aspic in small ring molds, chill, unmold, and fill centers with crabmeat, carefully picked over and blended with one-fourth its bulk Ravigote Mayonnaise or Chili Dressing. Garnish with watercress, chicory, or shredded lettuce.

INDIVIDUAL SUPPER SALADS

1 package lime or lemon gelatin	1 cup cooked green peas
2 cups water	½ cup grated carrot
1 tablespoon lemon juice	Salt and pepper
2 cups diced cold meat— chicken, tongue, veal, lamb, ham	Lettuce or watercress
	Radish roses
	Russian or Thousand Island Dressing

Prepare gelatin according to directions on package, add lemon juice. When almost at setting point fold in meat, peas, carrot, and seasonings. Turn into individual molds; chill, unmold, and garnish with lettuce or watercress and radish roses. Pass Russian or Thousand Island Dressing separately.

FROZEN FRUIT SALAD

1 tablespoon butter, melted	2 tablespoons lemon juice
1 egg yolk	2 cups mixed fruit, cut
1½ tablespoons cornstarch	small
2 tablespoons sugar	½ cup heavy cream,
Dash of salt	whipped
½ cup milk	

Blend butter, egg yolk, cornstarch, sugar, salt, and milk, and cook in double boiler until thick, stirring constantly. Add lemon juice slowly, beating while adding. Chill, then fold in fruit and cream. Pack in a mold, cover, seal and bury in three parts ice to one part salt for four hours. Or freeze in automatic refrigerator. No accompanying dressing is needed.

Suitable fruits are canned pineapple, fresh or canned peaches, pears, apricots, cherries, fresh strawberries.

FRUIT SALADS

AVOCADO SALADS

Chill one medium-sized avocado, divide lengthwise, and remove stone. Cut a very thin slice from under side of each half so that they may rest steadily on salad plates, then pour highly seasoned French Dressing into cavity.

For Avocado and Tomato Salad, marinate slices of peeled avocado and tomato in highly seasoned French Dressing. Then arrange for individual service in alternate slices on romaine.

For Oakland Salad, marinate sections of peeled orange, avocado, and grapefruit in French Fruit Dressing. Then arrange for individual service on romaine in alternate sections (two of each).

To prepare seedless oranges for salads or other service use a sharp stainless knife, remove all rind, white inner skin, and membrane; then separate into sections by cutting down on each side of the dividing membrane, thus releasing fruit without any waste.

ORANGE AND ONION SALAD

Arrange shredded lettuce in salad bowl, placing over it sections of peeled seedless orange. Cover with a thin layer of mild onions which have been peeled, diced, then soaked for two hours in ice water to which a tablespoon each of salt and sugar have been added. Top with further sections of orange, and pass Mayonnaise or French Dressing separately.

Or cut orange into thick slices, onion into thin ones, and arrange sandwich fashion for individual service on shredded lettuce—a slice of onion between each two orange slices. Pour over this a spoonful of French Dressing made with lemon juice.

FRUIT SALAD COMBINATIONS

Of delightful combinations for fruit salads there is almost no end. It should, however, be remembered that crisp fruit or nuts should offset softer fruit; also that it is well always to have a base of citrus fruit, grapefruit, orange, or a combination of the two. Some good blends are:

1. Diced dates, sections of orange, coconut.
2. Red bananas, orange, diced cooked prunes.
3. Orange, banana, pineapple (canned or fresh), seeded grapes.
4. Strawberries and pineapple (fresh or canned).

5. Pineapple, banana, grapefruit with garnish of maraschino cherries for color value.
6. Banana, pear, orange, pistachio nuts.
7. Peaches, cream cheese balls, shredded almonds (plain or toasted).
8. Pineapple (fresh or canned), cream cheese, red cherries.
9. Canned pineapple, pears, preserved ginger.
10. Tangerines, pineapple (fresh or canned), green or red pepper.
11. Cantaloupe, honeydew, and watermelon balls with sections of seedless orange.
12. Sections of orange with fresh mint or coconut.
13. Prunes or dates stuffed with cream or cottage cheese.

COTTAGE CHEESE SALAD

2 slices molded strained cranberry sauce
¼ pound cottage cheese
2 or 3 finely minced mint leaves, optional

Watercress or heart leaves of lettuce
Sour cream or Sour Cream Mayonnaise

Dice cranberry sauce and blend lightly with cottage cheese, adding mint if used. Arrange for individual service on watercress or lettuce, and top with a spoonful of sour cream or Sour Cream Mayonnaise.

SALAD DRESSINGS

FRENCH DRESSING

¾ cup salad oil
¼ cup vinegar or lemon juice

1⅓ teaspoons salt
⅔ teaspoon pepper or paprika

Combine all ingredients and beat or shake until thoroughly emulsified. If a tartar dressing is preferred, slightly increase the amount of vinegar or lemon juice. Obviously a whole cup of French Dressing will not be needed for a salad for two, but it is a good thing to have on hand, and does not spoil if kept in the refrigerator.

For Mineral Oil French Dressing, for the reducing diet substitute mineral oil for salad oil.

For Mignonette Dressing, use half vinegar or lemon juice and half tarragon vinegar, seasoning highly with freshly ground whole pepper.

For Savory French Dressing, add to ½ cup French Dressing, 1 teaspoon prepared mustard, 1 teaspoon Worcestershire sauce, and a few drops tabasco; then shake vigorously.

For Chili Dressing, beat into ½ cup French Dressing, 1 tablespoon tarragon vinegar, and 2 tablespoons chili sauce.

For Roquefort (Blue) Dressing, beat into ½ cup French Dressing, 2 to 3 tablespoons crumbled Roquefort (Blue) cheese.

For Chiffonade Dressing, add to ½ cup French Dressing, 1 tablespoon minced parsley, ½ teaspoon grated onion, 1 minced hard-cooked egg, and 1 tablespoon minced pimiento, with a little additional seasoning.

For Vinaigrette Dressing, add to ½ cup French Dressing (made with half plain and half tarragon vinegar), 1 teaspoon minced parsley, 1 teaspoon minced chives or ½ teaspoon grated onion, and 1 tablespoon each minced green pepper and minced cucumber pickles.

For French Fruit Dressing, beat into ½ cup French Dressing made with lemon juice, 2 tablespoons powdered sugar or 1 tablespoon honey.

MAYONNAISE

Because of the excellence of the commercial product, the making of mayonnaise in the home is almost a lost art. Golden hued, firm in texture, rich in flavor, it is ready for instant service just as it comes from the jar, or as a base for any of the suggested mayonnaise variations. Even so, in case you want to make your own, here is a good recipe:

¼ teaspoon salt	1 egg yolk
⅛ teaspoon paprika	1 cup salad oil
¼ teaspoon dry mustard, optional	2 tablespoons vinegar or lemon juice
1 teaspoon sugar, optional	

Combine dry ingredients in a bowl. Add egg yolk, and mix thoroughly; then work in oil, at first literally a few drops at a time, beating and stirring constantly. When quite thick add slowly 1 tablespoon vinegar or lemon juice; then work in remaining oil which may now be added more rapidly. Add also remaining vinegar or lemon juice.

If mayonnaise should curdle during mixing (which is caused by too rapid addition of the oil), take a fresh egg yolk, beat a little oil into it, then slowly add the curdled dressing. This will almost invariably restore the smoothness.

For Mineral Oil Mayonnaise, for the reducing diet substitute mineral oil for the salad oil and omit sugar.

For Savory Mayonnaise, add to ½ cup Mayonnaise, 1 tablespoon India relish, 1 tablespoon finely diced celery, and 1 tablespoon minced green pepper.

For Horseradish Mayonnaise, add to ½ cup Mayonnaise, 1 teaspoon grated horseradish, and a squeeze of lemon juice.

For Chiffonade Mayonnaise, add to ½ cup Mayonnaise, 2 tablespoons minced green pepper or pimiento, 1 tablespoon chopped sweet pickles, and 1 teaspoon horseradish mustard.

For Green Pepper Mayonnaise, add to ½ cup Mayonnaise, 2 tablespoons minced green pepper, 1 tablespoon minced parsley, ½ teaspoon onion juice, and 1 teaspoon lemon juice.

For Ravigote Mayonnaise, add to ½ cup Mayonnaise, 1½ teaspoons tarragon vinegar, ½ teaspoon each minced parsley, grated onion, and finely minced capers with a dash of cayenne.

For Russian Dressing, add to ½ cup Mayonnaise, ¼ cup chili sauce, ½ teaspoon Worcestershire sauce, 1 tablespoon minced pimiento, 1 teaspoon each minced green pepper, minced chives or grated onion, and minced pickles or capers.

For Thousand Island Dressing, add to Russian Dressing, ½ finely chopped hard-cooked egg, 1 tablespoon chopped stuffed olives, and ¼ cup whipped cream or thick sour cream.

For Whipped Cream or Sour Cream Mayonnaise, fold into ½ cup Mayonnaise (made without mustard), ¼ cup whipped sweet cream or ¼ cup sour cream.

In every instance chill before using.

BOILED SALAD DRESSING

2 tablespoons butter	1 teaspoon dry mustard
1 tablespoon flour	⅔ teaspoon salt
2 eggs	⅓ teaspoon pepper
2 tablespoons sugar	1 cup mild vinegar

Combine all ingredients except vinegar in upper part of double boiler, and cook over hot water until they begin to thicken, stirring and beating while cooking. Gradually add vinegar and continue cooking three minutes. Beat occasionally while cooling.

SOUR CREAM DRESSING

1 teaspoon dry mustard	2 egg yolks
1 teaspoon salt	1 cup sour cream
Pinch of cayenne	2 tablespoons mild vinegar
1 tablespoon sugar	

Combine and blend dry ingredients and egg yolks in upper part of double boiler. Gradually add sour cream, and cook over hot water, stirring constantly until thick, about seven minutes. Remove from fire, cool, and add vinegar slowly. Chill.

HORSERADISH CREAM DRESSING

¾ cup cream, whipped	2 tablespoons lemon juice
1 tablespoon grated horse-radish	Salt and cayenne

Fold horseradish, lemon juice, and seasonings into the cream which should be whipped quite stiff. Chill before using.

HONEY CREAM DRESSING

Heat ½ cup honey to boiling point. While beating, pour slowly onto 2 beaten egg yolks. Cook 1 minute over hot water, stirring constantly. Remove from heat, beat until cool and thick. Add gradually ¼ cup salad oil, ⅓ teaspoon salt and dash of paprika. Beat 2 more minutes. Chill. Just before serving fold in 1½ tablespoons lemon juice and ½ cup heavy cream, whipped.

SALADS FOR COMPANY
LOBSTER SALAD
(8 servings)

4 cups cooked lobster meat, diced	1½ dozen stuffed olives, sliced
2 cups diced celery	1⅓ teaspoons salt
6 hard-cooked eggs, chopped	¼ teaspoon paprika
2 teaspoons capers, minced	1½ cups Mayonnaise

Blend all ingredients. Chill well. Serve on lettuce, plain or shredded, garnishing with additional Mayonnaise and olives. Rock lobster or lobster tails are excellent for this.

FAIRY FRUIT SALAD
(8 servings)

Combine ⅔ cup each, diced peaches, pineapple, orange, apple, banana and celery. Add ¼ cup each, diced candied cherries and coarsely chopped nut meats. Moisten with Honey Cream Dressing (doubled). Chill, serve on lettuce.

PERFECTION SALAD
(8 servings)

2 tablespoons gelatin	1 teaspoon salt
½ cup cold water	1 cup finely shredded cabbage
2 cups boiling water	
¼ cup mild vinegar	2 cups finely diced celery
¼ cup pineapple juice	3 tablespoons diced pimiento or red pepper
½ cup sugar	

Soften gelatin five minutes in cold water. Add boiling water and stir until dissolved. Add vinegar, pineapple juice, sugar and salt. Chill. When almost set, stir in vegetables lightly. Turn into previously wet individual molds and chill. Unmold, garnish with lettuce, Mayonnaise.

See also Potato Salad (page 209), Chicken Salad (page 211), and Quick Tomato Aspic (page 214). Triple each for eight servings.

CHAPTER THIRTEEN

SANDWICHES

The sandwich family is constantly increasing. Not many years ago sandwiches were in demand only at picnics, in the daily lunch box, or as a makeshift for a regular meal. They were hearty sandwiches, generously cut, generously filled, thoroughly satisfying; but with no pretension to attractiveness. Today's sandwich, especially in its party dress, is dainty, small, colorful, and flavorful.

Bread is an all-important factor in the making of sandwiches. It should be of rather close texture, and several hours, but preferably not more than a day, old; the one exception to this rule is rolled sandwiches, which demand the freshest of bread so that it may be tender and pliable. Nor need we limit ourselves to white bread; add variety by using whole wheat, Graham, rye, nut, raisin, or brown bread, and also use crackers and hot biscuits.

Although crusts are frequently left on family and picnic sandwiches, for party service they are always removed; if this decrusting is done before spreading, the crusts are available for many cooking uses, stuffings, crumbs, etc.

Butter comes next on the list of essentials; it should be creamed as for cake making so that it will spread smoothly, evenly, and without waste. Such seasonings as mustard, pepper, and the like may be creamed and spread right with the butter. For Savory Butters for sandwiches, see page 289.

As far as bread is concerned, the most economical shapes

for sandwiches are oblongs, squares, and triangles; but for party use they may be cut into any number of fancy forms, including all of the playing card suits. For even further variety of appearance, inlays are often resorted to; for these, stamp out sections from the upper slices of bread, replacing with bread of a different color. There is no waste because the portion cut from the white bread fits into the brown slice and vice versa. Next time you have a card party use the tiniest cutters of all to make inlays of the various pips for card-shaped-and-sized sandwiches, replacing the cut-out portions with pimiento.

ROLLED SANDWICHES

Use very fresh bread, decrusting before slicing. Spread first with creamed butter, then with any preferred soft filling: deviled ham, crushed hard-cooked egg, cream cheese, any of the fish or meat pastes, all well seasoned and moistened with light cream or mayonnaise. Roll up, fasten with toothpicks, and chill, preferably wrapping in a damp cloth before placing in the refrigerator. Remove picks before serving.

These sandwiches may be brushed lightly with melted butter, then placed in a very hot oven or under the broiler to toast.

Another variety of the rolled sandwich is the one where buttered fresh bread is rolled around a spray of watercress, a short stalk of celery (plain or stuffed), or a tip of cooked asparagus, any of these being first dipped into French Dressing for greater flavor.

PINWHEEL SANDWICHES

Proceed exactly as for rolled sandwiches, except that the bread is to be cut lengthwise of the loaf. Then after roll·

ing and chilling, slice down with a very sharp knife. It is best here to use fillings which will sharply contrast in color with the bread used.

CHECKERBOARD SANDWICHES

Cut an equal number of slices of white and Graham bread about half an inch thick. Remove crusts, butter bread generously, and place five alternate dark and light slices together, having buttered side of top and bottom slices turned inward. Make second group of five slices, reversing order of bread. Now butter and cut off half-inch thick slices from each striped group, placing these together so that the colors of bread again alternate. Wrap in damp cloth, chill, and cut sandwiches into slices just before serving.

RIBBON SANDWICHES

Make as directed for Checkerboard Sandwiches, stopping when the plain ribbon stripes are formed. Wrap, chill as directed, then slice.

TURKEY OR CHICKEN SANDWICH À LA SCHRAFFT

Two whole slices lightly sautéed French toast with filling of minced turkey or chicken reheated in its own gravy. Cranberry sauce garnish.

CHICKEN LIVER SANDWICH

Reserve liver from a roasting chicken. Sauté in butter, then mince finely with a tiny bit of onion and a very slight grating of nutmeg. Moisten with mayonnaise to spreading consistency. Use with or without lettuce on whole wheat bread.

SMOKED SALMON SANDWICH

Arrange on hot buttered toast sliced tomato marinated in French Dressing, top with shredded lettuce also French Dressing marinated, then smoked salmon cut small. Cover with second slice of toast, cut into quarters and garnish with olives.

TOASTED CHEESE SANDWICH

Pass one cup coarsely broken cheese through food chopper with a little minced green pepper or pimiento. Season with a few drops Worcestershire sauce and a dash of mustard. Spread generously between slices of bread and toast very slowly on both sides to allow cheese to melt. Serve immediately.

CLUB SANDWICHES

Three slices buttered white or whole wheat toast, two layers filling.

Chicken, Ham, and Cheese

First layer: lettuce, sliced chicken and ham, sweet pickles. Second layer: Swiss cheese, sliced tomatoes, mayonnaise. Garnish with small whole sweet pickles.

Savory Lobster

First layer: diced lobster meat, minced pimiento, capers, French Dressing. Second layer: chilled sliced tomato, lettuce, mayonnaise. Garnish with bacon curls and stuffed olives.

Egg and Olive

First layer: shredded lettuce, crushed hard-cooked egg blended with mayonnaise and minced ripe olives. Second layer: crisp bacon, chilled sliced tomato dipped into French Dressing. Garnish with whole ripe olives.

Corned Beef and Cole Slaw

First layer: sliced browned corned beef hash (canned), diced fried onions. Second layer: cole slaw with Chili Dressing. Garnish with dill pickles.

Hot Tomato and Bacon

First layer: hot broiled tomato slices topped with Green Pepper Mayonnaise. Second layer: lettuce marinated in French Dressing, diced crisp bacon or broiled ham, and sliced hard-cooked egg.

SALAD SANDWICH ROLLS

Split, then scoop centers from soft rolls—round or long. Fill shells with salmon, lobster, tuna fish, egg, chicken, or chicken and pineapple salad, using plenty of mayonnaise.

For company service, use cream puff or éclair shells in place of the rolls.

BROILED OR BAKED SANDWICHES
(ANY PREFERRED BREAD)

1. Toast bread on one side, spread untoasted side with highly seasoned crabmeat or lobster (canned or fresh) moistened with a little mayonnaise. Top with sliced or diced cheese, and place in hot oven or under broiler until cheese melts.

2. Spread bread with creamed butter and mustard: on

this, place sliced, cooked ham and sprinkle with brown sugar. Top with sliced tomato dipped in French Dressing. Bake in hot oven or broil until piping hot.

3. Arrange seasoned, sliced tomato and chopped, cooked bacon on buttered toast; top with second slice toast; pour spoonful of melted cheese or Welsh Rarebit over, and run under broiler to make piping hot.

SHORTCAKE SANDWICHES

Roll Baking Powder Biscuit Dough rather thin; cut in squares or rounds; bake, split, butter.

Filling	*Garnish*
Shrimp, chicken, or lobster Newburg	Ripe olives Parsley, radish roses
Creamed ham, tongue, chicken, or fish	Watercress, lemon fans Chutney
Broccoli or asparagus tips with Hollandaise Sauce	Pimiento, celery curls Horseradish, mustard
Curried meats, eggs, or fish	pickles
Chicken à la king	
Diced cold roast beef heated in gravy	

AFTERNOON TEA SANDWICHES

Bread for afternoon tea sandwiches should always be cut thin, and decrusted. The sandwiches should be very small and dainty.

Cucumber

White bread with filling of finely minced well-drained cucumber, seasoned with onion juice, lemon juice, and minced parsley.

Peach Cream

Spread white, Graham, or whole wheat bread first with
softened butter, then with cream cheese, next with peach
(or apricot) marmalade. Nuts if you like, but the sandwiches are good without them. Serve either as open or
closed sandwiches.

Date Nut

Thin slices of pound cake or sponge cake with filling
of chopped dates and nuts (in equal proportions), moistened with orange juice.

Cream Cheese, Orange, and Ginger

Add grated orange rind to cream cheese with a few
pieces preserved ginger finely minced, and moisten with a
very little orange juice. Nut bread.

SALAD SANDWICH LOAF

**1 loaf fresh bread,
decrusted
Creamed butter**

**3 cups Chicken, Chicken
and Pineapple, or Mixed
Raw Vegetable Salad**

Cut loaf lengthwise into five slices; discard top irregular
one. Butter middle slices on both sides; top and bottom
slices on lower side only. Spread salad mixture on three
slices, top with last slice. Place in pan, cover with cloth and
put weight on top. Chill. Arrange on platter, garnish with
lettuce, olives and pickles, and slice.

CHAPTER FOURTEEN

DESSERTS—FRUIT, PUDDINGS, AND FROZEN

The dessert course has two objectives: first, to make the meal itself more attractive; second, to complete or round it out so as to provide proper balance. The choice of a dessert therefore for any and every day is a highly important part of the menu-builder's task. If the first courses have been lacking in fuel-value foods—a clear soup and a lean meat or fish with green vegetables, for example—the meal may be rounded out and balanced by the inclusion of a dessert rich in those elements which have been omitted earlier in the meal—a pie, a steamed pudding, or a layer cake with rich filling. With a heavy soup and meat, or a stew with dumplings or potatoes, or a generous New England boiled dinner, a much lighter dessert would be in order. Remember that cold desserts may be properly served when the greater part of the meal has been hot; while hot desserts give the correct temperature balance to cold meals.

FRUIT DESSERTS

STEWED APPLES

3 apples   ½ to ⅔ cup sugar
1 cup water

Pare, core, and cut apples into eighths. Prepare a sirup by boiling together the water and sugar. Cook apple sections, a few at a time, in sirup until tender, lifting them out as soon as done. When all are cooked boil sirup down until thick, then pour over fruit. One-half cup red cinnamon candies may be added to the sirup if desired to give flavor and color, or a little stick cinnamon, a few cloves, or a three-inch strip of lemon rind may also be cooked in the sirup.

HONEYED APPLES

½ cup honey	2 cooking apples
½ cup water	1 tablespoon lemon juice

Bring honey and water together to boiling point in small saucepan. Pare, quarter, and core apples, and cook gently in sirup until clear and tender. Lift out apples, boil sirup down until thick, add lemon juice and pour over fruit. Serve hot or chilled, with or without cream. If preferred, pare, core, and cook apples whole, turning them about in the sirup while cooking.

For Apple Sauces, see Meat Accompaniments, page 177.

BAKED APPLES

Wipe and core apples. Skins may be left on, or apples may be pared halfway down. Place in baking dish, fill cavities from which cores were taken with sugar, a teaspoon of butter, and a dash of cinnamon, or a slight grating of lemon rind. For 4 apples add 1 cup water and bake in moderate oven, 350° F., until tender. The dish may be covered for the first half of the baking, then cover removed. The length of time will depend on the apples, some cooking more quickly than others.

Other stuffings for baked apples are seeded or seedless raisins, pitted dates with a squeeze of lemon juice, nuts and raisins, preserved ginger.

BAKED WINTER PEARS

Pare, halve, and core hard winter pears. Arrange in deep baking dish (a bean pot is good), cover with equal parts water and molasses, and bake in slow oven, 300°-325° F., until pears are tender. Hard winter pears take a long time to bake, so are best prepared when the oven is in use for other baking.

BAKED GINGER PEARS

Pare, halve, and core large firm pears, place in baking dish, and fill hollows from which cores were taken with preserved ginger and a little of the ginger sirup. Pour around pears just enough water to prevent burning, cover, and bake in moderate oven, 350° F., twenty to thirty minutes or until tender. Serve hot or cold, plain or with cream.

HONEY BAKED BANANAS

3 bananas   ⅓ cup water
½ cup honey

Peel and scrape bananas then arrange close together in small baking dish. Pour over them the honey and water which have been boiled together for three minutes. A squeeze of lemon juice may be added, if desired. Cover and bake in moderate oven, 350° F., until bananas are tender, fifteen to twenty minutes.

Peeled whole or halved apples may be prepared in the same manner.

Sprinkle with chopped nut meats if desired.

Dried fruits are an excellent source of minerals and vitamins, especially A, B and $G(B_2)$ while their well known
laxative qualities need no stressing.

STEWED DRIED FRUITS

Modern methods of processing have rendered the old-
time long soaking of dried fruit unnecessary. After rinsing
cover with cold water, bring to boiling point and continue
briskly boiling, adding more water if needed, until fruit
is tender, approximately 35 to 45 minutes. Follow directions on package in each instance. If sugar is needed add
it about 5 minutes before cooking time is completed.

FRUIT COMPOTE

Actually, fruit compote is rather rich stewed fruit prepared by first making a sirup of sugar and water and cooking the fruit in it gently so that each portion retains its
form. One fruit alone, or a blend of two or more, may be
used. Sometimes, however, this name is given to an in-
dividually molded cornstarch or farina served with the
fruit (cooked as indicated) as a sauce.

APRICOT FLUFF

½ cup heavy cream, whipped	⅔ cup diced canned apricots
6 marshmallows, quartered	¼ cup shredded coconut

Chill cream after whipping. Just before serving, fold
all other ingredients lightly into it. If desired, the coconut
may be toasted and sprinkled over the top of the dessert
instead of being stirred into it.

APRICOT WHIP

1 egg white
1 cup sieved cooked apri-
cot pulp

Few drops lemon juice
2 tablespoons powdered
sugar

Beat egg white until very stiff. Add lemon juice, then apricot pulp (measured after pressing through sieve) and sugar gradually, beating constantly. Chill and serve in sherbet glasses topping, if desired, with light cream or boiled custard.

For Prune Whip substitute prune pulp for apricot, beating in 2 tablespoons orange marmalade, if desired.

AMBROSIA

2 small seedless oranges
¼ cup shredded coconut

3 tablespoons powdered
sugar

Peel oranges, remove every particle of skin and connecting fiber; then arrange sections in serving dish in layers with sugar and coconut. Chill very thoroughly before serving.

For Honeyed Ambrosia, substitute 3 tablespoons warmed honey for powdered sugar.

APPLE FRITTERS

Core, pare, and cut two large tart apples into one-third inch thick slices. Sprinkle with lemon juice and sugar, and let stand about half an hour. Dip into fritter batter; then cook in shallow pan in a little hot fat until apples are tender, and fritters golden brown. Drain, sprinkle with sugar, and serve with a liquid sauce.

For Pineapple Fritters, substitute well-drained slices

canned pineapple for apple, and omit the marinating in lemon juice and sugar.

FRITTER BATTER

Scant ½ cup flour
Dash of salt
1 egg
1 teaspoon lemon juice

1 teaspoon melted shortening
About ⅓ cup milk

Sift flour and salt, make a hollow in center, and pour into it the beaten egg yolk, lemon juice, melted shortening, and part of the milk. Beat with back of spoon until perfectly smooth, add remaining milk, and fold in stiffly beaten egg white.

MILK DESSERTS

BOILED CUSTARD

1 cup milk
1 egg
Dash of salt

1½ tablespoons sugar
⅓ teaspoon flavoring

Scald milk, beat egg, salt and sugar; pour milk over gradually, beating while pouring; return to fire and cook over hot water (double boiler) until thick enough to coat the back of the spoon. Cool slightly and add flavoring. Use as a simple dessert or a dessert sauce. Should custard curdle while cooking, place pan containing it in a bowl of cold water and beat vigorously with rotary beater.

For Rich Golden Custard, use 2 egg yolks in place of 1 whole egg.

For Boiled Chocolate Custard, add ½ square (ounce) unsweetened chocolate to milk while heating.

For Mocha Custard, substitute ½ cup strong coffee for

an equal amount of milk and flavor with cinnamon or vanilla, or tie 1 to 2 tablespoons ground coffee in double cheesecloth, and scald with milk.

BAKED CUSTARD

1 egg or 2 egg yolks
1 tablespoon sugar
Dash of salt

1 cup milk, scalded
¼ teaspoon vanilla

Beat egg or egg yolks slightly with sugar and salt; then add scalded milk gradually, beating while adding. Add vanilla, strain into individual custard cups or into one baking dish. Set in pan of hot water and bake in moderate oven, 350° F., until set, about twenty-five minutes. Test by inserting knife blade in center of custard; if it comes out clean custard is done. If desired, sprinkle surface of custard with nutmeg or cinnamon before baking.

For Honey Custard, use 1 tablespoon honey in place of sugar.

For Baked Chocolate Custard, dissolve ½ square (ounce) unsweetened chocolate in the milk while scalding.

RENNET-CUSTARD (JUNKET)

This is a commercial product available either in powdered or tablet form, the former sweetened, the latter requiring the addition of both sweetening and flavoring. It is the simplest of all desserts to prepare provided package directions are exactly followed.

TAPIOCA CREAM

2 tablespoons sugar
Dash of salt
2 tablespoons quick-cook-
  ing tapioca

1 egg
1½ cups milk
¼ teaspoon vanilla

Combine sugar, salt, tapioca, egg yolk, and 2 tablespoons
of the milk. Scald remaining milk in double boiler, add
gradually to first mixture, stirring constantly; return to
double boiler and cook five to eight minutes, still stirring
until thickened. Remove from fire, fold in stiffly beaten
egg white and vanilla, and chill. Serve plain, or with light
cream or custard.

For Fruited Tapioca, stir in after cooking ¼ cup fruit—
pitted diced dates, halved seeded raisins, diced canned,
stewed, or fresh fruit. Nuts or coconut may also be added,
if desired. Or arrange fresh fruit, sliced strawberries,
crushed raspberries, sliced peaches, etc., in sherbet glasses
and pour tapioca cream over.

For Chocolate Tapioca, melt ½ square (ounce) unsweetened chocolate in double boiler with milk, beating
the two thoroughly together before adding tapioca.

Do not overlook the convenience of commercially prepared tapioca puddings, which are sweetened and flavored,
and need only the addition of milk and a very few minutes
cooking, the same being true of the various packaged milk
puddings.

GELATIN DESSERTS

There are two types of gelatin, the plain unflavored in
granulated form, and prepared gelatin to which sugar,
coloring, and flavoring have already been added.

A jelly of whatever type should be firm enough to hold
its form without breaking; yet not be in the least hard nor
stiff. Here is the secret of unmolding: dip the mold into
warm—not hot—water, then invert the serving dish over
the mold and turn both back together. Then slightly lift
one edge of mold from plate to let in the air and shake
sharply. If the jelly does not unmold promptly, either re-

peat the dipping process, or press a cloth wrung out of warm water over the mold for a moment; then shake again.

LEMON JELLY

1 tablespoon gelatin	½ cup sugar
½ cup cold water	Dash of salt
1 cup boiling water	⅓ cup lemon juice

Soften gelatin in cold water, add boiling water, sugar, and salt, and stir until gelatin and sugar are both dissolved. Combine with lemon juice, turn into mold or serving glasses, and chill. Serve plain or with cream, Custard Sauce, or fruit.

For Lemon Whip, prepare Lemon Jelly as directed. When beginning to thicken, beat vigorously with rotary beater until frothy.

For Lemon Sponge (Snow Pudding), follow directions for Lemon Whip adding the stiffly beaten white of one egg while beating with rotary beater. Serve with Custard Sauce.

For Fruited Gelatin, fold into Lemon Jelly when almost at setting point ½ cup fruit—fresh berries, raspberries, strawberries, cherries, etc., or sliced bananas. Canned fruits may also be added, in which case some of the canned fruit sirup may be used as part of the liquid when preparing the Lemon Jelly. As this fruit juice will be sweet, scant slightly the amount of sugar called for in the recipe.

For Orange Jelly, follow directions for Lemon Jelly substituting orange juice for lemon juice, adding also 1 tablespoon lemon juice.

Any of the suggestions for varying Lemon Jelly apply equally to Orange Jelly.

COFFEE JELLY

½ tablespoon gelatin   2 tablespoons sugar
1 cup coffee   ¼ teaspoon vanilla

Soften gelatin in 2 tablespoons of the coffee (cold); dissolve sugar in remaining coffee which should be scalding hot, then add softened gelatin and stir until it is completely dissolved. Cool, add vanilla, turn into two sherbet glasses, and chill. Serve plain, or with Custard Sauce or cream.

APRICOT LIME DESSERT

Prepare Lime Gelatin as directed. Turn into a mold and chill. Unmold, and serve with garnish of halved canned apricots, in each of which has been placed a small cream cheese ball, lightly sprinkled either with paprika or minced fresh mint.

BAVARIAN CREAM

½ tablespoon gelatin   Dash of salt
2 tablespoons cold water   1 egg yolk
½ cup milk   ½ cup heavy cream
2 tablespoons sugar   ½ teaspoon vanilla

Soften gelatin in water. Scald milk with sugar and salt, pour over beaten egg yolk, beating while pouring; then return to double boiler and cook until thickened, about three minutes. Add softened gelatin, stir until dissolved, cool and when almost at setting point fold in the cream whipped and flavored. Turn into serving glasses or a mold, and chill thoroughly.

For Coffee Bavarian, substitute strong coffee for the milk.

For Maple Nut Bavarian, substitute maple sugar for

granulated sugar, adding 2 or 3 drops maple extract with
the vanilla, and 2 tablespoons chopped walnuts or pecans,
when folding in the cream.

PUDDINGS—HOT AND COLD

BREAD OR CABINET PUDDING

2-3 slices buttered day-old
  bread
¼ cup halved seeded raisins
1 egg

1 cup milk
2 tablespoons sugar
Dash of salt

Cut bread, preferably decrusted, into large cubes, and
arrange in baking dish distributing raisins among it. Beat
egg, add milk, sugar, and salt, and pour over bread. Let
stand half an hour, then bake in moderate oven, 350°-
375° F., about twenty-five minutes. Serve hot or cold.

The buttered bread may be spread generously with jam
or jelly (sugar and raisins being omitted), or diced tart
apple or sliced peaches with a little additional sugar may
be substituted for the raisins.

For Black Cap Pudding, sprinkle raisins thickly over
bottom of buttered baking dish instead of distributing
them through the pudding, then follow recipe for Bread
Pudding, unmolding for service..

BROWN BETTY

1½ cups soft bread crumbs
1½ cups peeled, cored,
  diced apples
Scant ½ cup sugar or honey

⅔ teaspoon ground cinna-
  mon or grated rind ½
  lemon
2 tablespoons butter or
  shortening

Arrange in layers in buttered baking dish first one-third
of the crumbs, next one-third of the apples, then one-third
of the sugar or honey to which cinnamon or lemon rind
has been added. Repeat layers twice, having crumbs for top
layer and moistening them with the butter or shortening,
softened. Cover and bake in moderately hot oven, 375° F.,
three-quarters of an hour. Remove cover during last fifteen
minutes of baking to allow crumbs to brown. Serve with
any preferred hot sauce.

For Rhubarb Betty, substitute finely diced rhubarb for
apples and omit cinnamon.

For Peach Betty, substitute peeled, diced peaches for
apples.

DELMONICO APPLE PUDDING

1 cup apple sauce	½ cup crushed macaroons
2 tablespoons finely chopped almonds or nut meats	1 tablespoon melted butter

Place half the apple sauce in buttered baking dish, cover
with half the nuts, then half the macaroons into which
butter has been stirred. Repeat layers and bake in moderate oven, 350° F., fifteen to twenty minutes. Serve hot or
cold with or without light cream or custard.

STEAMED GINGER PUDDING

¾ cup sifted flour	½ cup finely chopped suet
1 teaspoon baking powder	1 egg
¼ teaspoon salt	⅓ cup molasses
1 teaspoon ground ginger	About ⅓ cup milk
¼ cup bread crumbs	

Sift together flour, baking powder, salt, and ginger; add
crumbs and suet and moisten with beaten egg, molasses,

and milk. Turn into greased mold, cover with butter
paper, twisting it under rim of bowl, and steam about one
and a half hours. Serve with Hard or Lemon Sauce.

For Steamed Fig Pudding, add ½ cup dried figs, cut
small.

FRUIT COBBLER

2 tablespoons butter or shortening	1 scant teaspoon baking powder
¼ cup sugar	Dash of salt
1 small egg	About ⅓ cup milk
¾ cup sifted flour	1½ cups juicy stewed fruit

Cream shortening and sugar, add beaten egg, then sifted
dry ingredients alternately with milk. Beat thoroughly,
pour over hot stewed fruit in baking dish. Bake, uncovered, in moderate oven, 350°-375° F., about thirty-five
minutes. Serve with Hard Sauce. Suitable fruits are plums,
apples, apples and blackberries, peaches, rhubarb or cranberries.

OLD-FASHIONED CREAMY RICE PUDDING

¼ cup rice	1 tablespoon butter
Dash of salt	1 quart milk
3 tablespoons sugar	

Wash rice well and put it in a baking dish with salt,
sugar, and butter. Pour milk over and bake in slow oven,
325° F., at least two and a half hours, stirring twice during
the first hour. This pudding is only likely to be made when
a slow oven is needed for other cooking, a casserole dish or
baked beans, for example. Serves four.

COTTAGE PUDDING

3 tablespoons butter or	1 cup sifted flour
shortening	1 teaspoon baking powder
3 tablespoons sugar	1/4 teaspoon salt
1 egg	About 1/3 cup milk

Cream shortening and sugar until very light. Beat and add egg, then sifted dry ingredients alternately with milk. Turn into a well-greased baking dish and bake in moderate oven, 350°-375° F., half an hour. Cut into squares and serve with Chocolate Mint, Butterscotch, or Maple Nut Sauce. If preferred, bake in greased muffin pans for individual service.

APPLE DUMPLINGS BAKED IN SIRUP

Roll Baking Powder Biscuit dough out thin and cut into six-inch squares. Core and peel apples, place one in each square, and fill cavity with sugar plus a dash of cinnamon. Wet edges of dough and draw up over apple. Place close together in greased baking dish, and bake in hot oven, 400° F., about fifteen minutes; after which pour into dish around dumplings a sirup made by cooking together equal parts brown sugar, water, and corn sirup. Continue baking until apples are tender. Serve with a spoonful of the sirup and, if desired, a spoonful of Hard Sauce.

JAM ROLY-POLY

Roll Pastry or Baking Powder Biscuit dough out rather thin, spread generously with jam, moisten edges of dough, then roll mixture up as for Jelly Roll. Place on greased baking sheet, smooth side uppermost, and bake in moderately hot oven, 375°-400° F., twenty to thirty minutes.

Serve sliced with Clear Dessert or Wine Sauce. If desired, cut pastry or biscuit dough into five- or six-inch squares and bake as individual rolls. A very good way to use left-over pastry.

For Apple Roly-poly or Pudding, substitute diced apples with a little sugar and cinnamon for the jam.

CHOCOLATE SOUFFLÉ

⅔ cup milk	2 eggs
1 square (ounce) unsweetened chocolate	5 tablespoons sugar
	3 tablespoons chopped nuts
⅔ cup cake or cookie crumbs	Few grains salt

Scald milk with chocolate, beat until smooth and add crumbs. Stir until milk is absorbed, then add egg yolks mixed with half the sugar and the nuts and salt. Beat egg whites until stiff with remaining sugar, and fold into first mixture. Bake in hot oven, 400° F., twenty to twenty-five minutes.

DESSERT SAUCES

HARD SAUCE

3 tablespoons butter	¼ teaspoon vanilla
½ cup powdered sugar	

Cream butter until very light, gradually adding sugar. Work in vanilla, pile in serving dish and, if desired, grate a little nutmeg over surface. Chill. One to two teaspoons of boiling water may be gradually added to the sauce while beating, this makes for quicker creaming and slightly increases the bulk.

For Fruit Hard Sauce, beat into Hard Sauce while creaming, a few crushed raspberries, or strawberries, or a tablespoon of crushed apricot or peach.

For Brown Sugar Hard Sauce, use brown sugar in place of powdered sugar, and beat in 1 egg yolk, after butter and sugar are creamed.

VANILLA OR CLEAR DESSERT SAUCE

1 tablespoon butter, melted	2 tablespoons sugar
1 tablespoon cornstarch	1/2 teaspoon vanilla
2/3 cup water	

Blend melted butter and cornstarch smoothly together in saucepan, add water and bring to boiling point, stirring constantly. Simmer ten minutes, sweeten and flavor.

For Orange or Lemon Sauce, flavor with grated orange or lemon rind, adding a little orange or lemon juice, and slightly increasing the amount of sugar used.

For Wine or Brandy Sauce, substitute 2 tablespoons white wine or 1 tablespoon brandy for the vanilla.

APRICOT OR PEACH SAUCE

1/4 cup apricot or peach preserves	1 tablespoon sugar
1 teaspoon lemon juice	2 teaspoons cornstarch
1/2 cup boiling water	1 tablespoon cold water
	1 teaspoon butter

Simmer preserves, lemon juice, boiling water, and sugar for five minutes. Thicken with cornstarch rubbed smoothly with the cold water. Cook gently for five minutes and add the butter.

For Foamy Sauce, pour scalding hot Apricot or Peach Sauce slowly over stiffly beaten egg white, beating constantly while combining.

CHOCOLATE SAUCE

1 square (ounce) unsweet-
ened chocolate
3 tablespoons water
¼ cup sugar

Dash of salt
1½ tablespoons butter
Few drops vanilla

Combine chocolate and water, and cook over gentle heat, stirring constantly until blended. Add sugar and salt, and continue cooking until sugar is dissolved, and mixture begins to thicken slightly. Then add butter and vanilla. Serve either hot or cold.

For Chocolate Mint Sauce, substitute ¼ teaspoon peppermint extract or 2 drops oil of mint for the vanilla.

CUSTARD SAUCE

1 tablespoon sugar
1½ teaspoons flour
⅛ teaspoon salt

1 egg yolk
¾ cup milk
¼ teaspoon vanilla

Combine sugar, flour, salt, and egg yolk. Moisten with a little milk; when perfectly smooth, pour over the mixture the remaining milk which has been heated in double boiler. Return to boiler and continue cooking, stirring constantly, until sauce thickens. Cool, and add vanilla.

BUTTERSCOTCH SAUCE

½ cup brown sugar
½ cup corn sirup

½ cup boiling water
2 tablespoons butter

Combine all ingredients in saucepan, place over low heat, stir until sugar is dissolved; then continue cooking until a little dropped into cold water forms a very soft ball (if using a sugar thermometer, 234° F.).

MAPLE NUT SAUCE

½ cup maple sirup   ¼ cup shredded salted pe-
¼ cup light cream   cans or almonds

Boil maple sirup down to half its bulk, then combine
with cream, and add nuts immediately before serving.

WHIPPED CREAM SAUCES

For Maple Cream Sauce, combine ¼ cup heavy cream,
whipped, with 1 tablespoon heavy maple sirup, and add a
dash of salt.

For Molasses Cream Sauce, combine 1 tablespoon molasses with ¼ cup heavy cream, whipped.

For Jam Cream Sauce, combine 2 tablespoons rich jam
(raspberry, peach, or apricot is especially good) with ¼
cup heavy cream, whipped.

SUZETTE SAUCE

¼ cup sugar   2 tablespoons curaçao
Grated rind 1 orange   1 tablespoon brandy
3 drops vanilla   ¼ pound sweet butter

Blend sugar, orange rind and vanilla, and let stand half
an hour. Add curaçao and brandy, stir until well blended;
then beat in, a little at a time, the butter creamed until
very light.

FROZEN DESSERTS

DIRECTIONS FOR FREEZING IN HAND FREEZER

Have ice thoroughly crushed, then mix with rock salt,
using three parts ice to one part salt for ice creams, sherbets, and ices; for frappés use equal parts ice and salt.

Added salt means quicker freezing, but it also means coarser texture.

Pour mixture to be frozen into freezer can, adjust dasher and cover, then pack ice and salt around can. Let stand about five minutes, then turn crank steadily, but slowly at first, increasing the speed as the mixture begins to set. When frozen, remove cover of freezer can, being careful that no particles of ice or salt fall into the can; take out dasher, scrape mixture from it and sides of can, pack down firmly and replace cover, corking dasher opening. Pack in more ice and leave to ripen, first covering freezer with heavy burlap or layers of newspaper.

Rich cream mixtures, mousses, and parfaits, are frozen by packing in a mold, sealing, then burying in equal parts ice and salt for at least three hours. The easiest and simplest method of insuring a perfect seal is by means of a strip of adhesive tape.

FREEZING IN AUTOMATIC REFRIGERATOR

When freezing in an automatic refrigerator such rich combinations as mousses and parfaits need no stirring. Sherbets and water ices, however, must be removed from the freezing chamber and rapidly beaten two or three times during the freezing period to prevent the formation of crystals. The addition of one teaspoon of gelatin to each cup of liquid assures smoother texture, as does also the use of marshmallows, as in the popular marlows. It is always well, when freezing in any automatic refrigerator, to be guided by the directions given by the manufacturer of that particular model. Generally speaking, allow three to four hours for such freezing. Beware of the addition of too much sugar as this retards freezing. Do not fail to set temperature regulator at coldest point.

Do not overlook the value of the various commercial ice cream powders now on the market for both hand freezer and refrigerator use. They make excellent ice cream. Follow directions on package.

The following recipes will average four servings.

RICH VANILLA (PHILADELPHIA) ICE CREAM

1 pint light cream	Dash of salt
½ cup sugar	1 teaspoon vanilla

Combine all ingredients, stirring until sugar is thoroughly dissolved. Freeze, using three parts ice to one part salt, or in automatic refrigerator without stirring.

For Nutted Ice Cream, stir in, when partly frozen, ½ cup very finely chopped pecan or walnut meats, or blanched almonds, or Brazil nuts.

For Macaroon Ice Cream, stir in, when partly frozen, ⅔ cup finely crushed macaroons.

For Strawberry or Raspberry Ice Cream, stir in, when partly frozen, 1 cup sieved sweetened strawberry or raspberry pulp. Vanilla may be omitted.

For Chocolate Ice Cream, melt 1 square (ounce) unsweetened chocolate over hot water, add slowly ⅓ cup hot water, blend, cool, then combine with Rich Vanilla Ice Cream Mixture, and strain into freezer can or refrigerator tray.

RASPBERRY ICE

1 cup fresh raspberry juice	2 cups water
Scant cup sugar	Juice ½ lemon

Crush raspberries thoroughly then press through double cheesecloth to hold back seeds. Boil sugar and water together for five minutes, add raspberry juice and lemon juice. Strain, cool, and freeze by either method.

MILK SHERBET

Juice of 1 orange and 1   2 cups milk
lemon or 1½ lemons   Dash of salt
¾ cup sugar

Strain fruit juice, add sugar, and let stand until this is dissolved. Combine with milk and salt, and freeze by either method. The mixture will appear curdled but this disappears during the freezing process.

PEPPERMINT MOUSSE

¼ pound peppermint stick   1 cup heavy cream, whipped
candy   Dash of salt
½ cup light cream

Break candy into small pieces and dissolve in light cream, if necessary heating in double boiler. Cool, combine with whipped cream and salt, and freeze by either method.

FRESH PEACH OR APRICOT MOUSSE

1 cup fresh peaches or apri-   1 cup heavy cream, whipped
cots   ¼ teaspoon almond ex-
⅓ cup sugar   tract

Peel and cut up fruit, cover with sugar and let stand one hour, then press through sieve and combine with cream and flavoring. Freeze by either method. Other fruit—raspberries, strawberries, or cooked drained dried fruits—may be substituted for the peaches or apricots.

CHANTILLY MOUSSE

1 cup heavy cream	1 teaspoon vanilla
4 tablespoons confectioners' sugar	1/4 cup finely chopped toasted almonds
Few grains salt	1 cup crumbled macaroons

Whip cream until thick, add other ingredients in order given. Freeze by either method.

GRAPENUTS MOUSSE

1/3 cup sugar	1 cup heavy cream, whipped
1/4 cup water	1/2 teaspoon vanilla
2 egg whites, stiffly beaten	1/4 cup grapenuts

Boil sugar and water together until they spin a thread, 230° F. Pour slowly over egg whites, beating constantly, and continue beating until cool, about three minutes. Fold in cream, vanilla, and grapenuts. Freeze by either method.

BUTTERSCOTCH PARFAIT

1/3 cup brown sugar	1 cup heavy cream, whipped
1 tablespoon butter	Dash of salt
1/4 cup water	1 teaspoon vanilla
2 egg yolks	

Melt sugar and butter in saucepan, stirring to prevent burning. Cook one minute, add water, and continue cooking until smooth and sirupy. Now pour slowly over beaten egg yolks and cook very gently until light and fluffy. Chill, fold in whipped cream, salt, and vanilla. Turn into refrigerator tray or individual freezing cups, and freeze in automatic refrigerator without stirring.

FROZEN CUSTARD

1 cup milk
1 tablespoon cornstarch
⅓ cup sugar
Dash of salt

2 egg yolks
1 teaspoon vanilla
½ cup heavy cream,
  whipped

Scald milk in double boiler, pour a little of it over the blended cornstarch, sugar, and salt, stirring constantly, then return to double boiler and cook for five minutes, still stirring. Add beaten egg yolks, and continue cooking and stirring until custard coats spoon. Cool, add vanilla, and fold in whipped cream. Freeze by either method.

For Frozen Cherry Custard, slightly scant sugar, and add one small bottle maraschino cherries, cut small, with their sirup.

For Frozen Coffee Custard substitute strong freshly made coffee for the milk, stirring in ¼ cup finely chopped nut-meats when partly frozen.

FROZEN PUDDING

½ cup milk
10 marshmallows
½ cup heavy cream,
  whipped
½ teaspoon vanilla
¼ cup quartered seeded
  raisins

⅓ cup drained crushed
  pineapple
2 tablespoons maraschino
  cherries, cut small
¼ cup coarsely chopped
  nutmeats

Heat milk and dissolve marshmallows in it, stirring and beating until smooth. Cool, then add stiffly beaten cream, vanilla, fruits, and nuts. Freeze in automatic refrigerator, stirring mixture once after first half hour. Cut into squares for serving.

REFRIGERATOR VANILLA ICE CREAM
(With Sweetened Condensed Milk)

⅔ cup (½ can) sweetened   1½ teaspoons vanilla
  condensed milk   1 cup heavy cream
½ cup water   Dash of salt

Combine condensed milk, water, and vanilla and chill thoroughly. Whip cream until thick but not stiff, add salt, then combine the two mixtures. Turn into refrigerator tray and half freeze. Scrape into bowl, beat until smooth but not melted, replace in tray and complete freezing.

COFFEE MARLOW

⅓ cup ground coffee   1 cup heavy cream, whipped
1 cup milk   ½ teaspoon salt
1 egg   ½ teaspoon vanilla
15 (¼ lb.) marshmallows

Tie coffee loosely in cheesecloth, and scald with milk in upper part of double boiler. Remove coffee, add beaten egg and cook two minutes, stirring constantly. Dissolve marshmallows in this custard, beating with rotary beater to insure smoothness. Cool, then combine with remaining ingredients. Freeze in automatic refrigerator.

CHAPTER FIFTEEN

DESSERTS—PASTRY, CAKE, AND COOKIES

Pastry making is no trick at all in spite of the fact that so many women seem to regard it as a difficult chore. The ingredients are always the same, flour, salt, shortening, and liquid; it is the way they are put together that makes the difference in results. The two really hard and fast rules are: keep the pastry cool until it goes into the oven; handle it as little as possible.

The flour may be either all-purpose or pastry flour. Many cooks feel that all-purpose flour gives a firmer, browner, flakier crust than pastry flour, others prefer the latter, or a blend of the two.

The shortening may be animal or vegetable as preferred, but it should invariably be well chilled. Chop it into the flour with one or two knives, or use a wire pastry blender, or work it in lightly with the fingers, as you prefer.

Use no more liquid than is really necessary. Incidentally, milk gives a prettier brown to the finished pastry than water. Too little water makes a pastry which is hard and dry, too much makes it tough.

The *tenderness* of pastry depends very much upon the kind of flour and the amount of shortening used, while *flakiness* is largely governed by the method of combining the two. Reserving part of the shortening, and rolling it into the pastry after it is moistened, produces a flaky rather than a short crisp crust.

Briefly, to insure pastry perfection:

1. Have all ingredients thoroughly chilled.
2. Make pastry just soft enough to handle easily.
3. Roll lightly, keeping dough smooth and compact in shape.
4. Use only enough flour on board to prevent sticking.
5. Never stretch pastry either on board or onto pie plate.
6. Avoid unnecessary handling.
7. If possible, chill before baking.
8. Good pastry greases its own pan.
9. Bake pastry shells (unfilled crusts) at 425°-450° F. fifteen to twenty minutes; filled pies at 425°-450° F. for first fifteen minutes, after which reduce to 350°-375° F.
10. Bake pastry shells between two pie plates, removing upper one for last few minutes of baking in order to brown.
11. Or bake pastry shells over inverted pie plates or tartlet shells over inverted muffin pans, in which case prick pastry with fork before baking to prevent blistering.
12. For very juicy fillings sprinkle one tablespoon quick-cooking tapioca among filling.
13. Always bake meringue in a cool oven, 325° F., long enough to cook egg whites thoroughly so as to prevent falling.

Pastry for two or three pies may be made at one time and kept in the refrigerator until needed, so that when the oven is in use for other baking it will take but a few minutes to prepare a pie for dinner. Use pastry shells for the

service of hash, creamed beef, fish, or left-over vegetables.
Fragments of pastry may be used in cheese straws or pastry
fingers to serve with salads or simple desserts.

SHORT PASTRY

1½ cups sifted flour   ½ cup shortening
½ teaspoon salt   About ¼ cup ice water

Sift flour and salt, work in shortening and mix to light
dough with water, handling as little as possible. Divide
into two portions, work slightly with fingers to insure
smooth surface, and roll out once to fit pie plate. One
double crust, eight-inch pie.

FLAKY PASTRY

1½ cups sifted flour   ⅔ cup shortening
½ teaspoon salt   About ¼ cup ice water

Sift flour and salt, add shortening and chop with knife
into dry ingredients. Add ice water to form dough, turn
onto floured board and roll pastry out thinly, keeping
edges even and straight. Fold together into three layers,
turn halfway around on board and roll out again, repeating the folding, turning and rolling once or twice more.
Keep pastry cold, chilling between rollings if convenient.
One double crust, eight-inch pie.

BOILING WATER PASTRY

½ cup shortening   Dash of salt
¼ cup boiling water   ¼ teaspoon baking powder
1½ cups flour

Cream shortening in mixing bowl with boiling water.
Sift and add dry ingredients, and blend thoroughly. Chill

before using. One double crust pie, or one single crust and several tartlet shells.

GRATED CHEESE CRUST

Sprinkle two tablespoons grated cheese into top crust before rolling out, or sprinkle cheese over top of pie when almost baked.

APPLE PIE

Pastry
Cooking apples
Sugar

Lemon rind, cinnamon, or
nutmeg

Peel, quarter, core, and cut apples into slices. Line pie plate with pastry, half fill with apples, sprinkling in sugar and flavoring. Cover with more apples, moisten pastry at edge of plate and cover with top crust, pressing edges firmly together. Very juicy apples will require no water, with drier ones a spoonful or two may be added. Make one or two slits in top crust to allow for escape of steam and bake three-quarters to one hour, having oven hot, 425°-450° F., for first fifteen minutes, then reducing to 350°-375° F.

BERRY AND JUICY FRUIT PIES

Line pie plate with pastry, partly fill with picked over, washed berries, rhubarb, etc., to which one tablespoon quick-cooking tapioca has been added. Sweeten, add remaining fruit, moisten edge of pastry, cover with top crust, make one or two slits in this, and bake about three-quarters of an hour, having oven hot, 425°-450° F., for first fifteen minutes, then reducing to 350°-375° F.

CRISSCROSS PIES

Line pie plate with any preferred pastry, fill with cold, cooked, sweetened, well-drained fresh or dried fruit, or with drained canned fruit. Lay strips of pastry crisscross over surface, moistening ends that they may adhere to lower crust. Bake about half an hour, having oven hot, 425°-450° F., for first ten minutes, then reducing to 350°-375° F.

CUSTARD PIE

1½ cups milk	Dash of salt
2 eggs	Pastry
¼ cup sugar	Slight grating nutmeg

Scald milk, then pour over eggs which have been lightly beaten with sugar and salt. Line pie plate with any preferred pastry, brush over with a little beaten egg white (reserved for the purpose), pour custard mixture in, and grate a very little nutmeg over the surface. Bake about half an hour having oven hot, 425°-450° F., for first ten minutes, then reducing to 350° F. Test by inserting a knife blade in center of custard; if it comes out clean pie is done. The egg white helps prevent the custard soaking into the crust.

For Coconut Custard Pie, add ½ cup shredded coconut to custard mixture just before pouring into pastry-lined pie plate.

CRANBERRY MERINGUE PIE

Previously baked small pastry shell	2 tablespoons sugar
Cranberry sauce	½ teaspoon grated orange rind
1 egg white	

Fill pastry shell with cranberry sauce which may be homemade or the commercial type, whole-fruit sauce packed in glass jars. Top with meringue made by beating egg whites until light and frothy, then gradually adding sugar and orange rind, and continuing beating until stiff. Return to cool oven, 325° F., fifteen to twenty minutes to set and delicately color meringue.

LEMON MERINGUE PIE

½ cup sifted pastry flour
¼ cup sugar
¼ teaspoon salt
2 eggs, separated
1½ cups water

Juice of 2 and grated rind
of 1 lemon
4 tablespoons sugar, additional
Previously baked pastry shell

Combine flour, first sugar, and salt in upper part of double boiler. Beat egg yolks until light, add water, and blend with dry ingredients. Place over hot water and cook, stirring constantly, for ten minutes. Remove from fire, add lemon juice and rind, and when cool turn into previously baked pastry shell. Top with meringue made by beating egg whites until stiff with remaining sugar. Place in cool oven, 325° F., to set and delicately color meringue, fifteen to twenty minutes.

HONEY MERINGUE

Honey may be used in place of sugar in making meringue. Beat 2 egg whites until light, add gradually ⅓ cup honey, and continue beating until meringue stands high in peaks, eight to ten minutes. Bake as any meringue.

LEMON CHIFFON PIE

4 egg yolks
2 egg whites
Grated rind and juice
  1 lemon
½ tablespoon flour

¼ cup sugar
1 cup boiling water
Previously baked pastry
  shell

Beat egg yolks until thick and light, add lemon rind and juice. Blend flour and sugar, and stir first mixture into them, gradually add boiling water, and cook in double boiler until thick. Beat egg whites until stiff, and fold into the cooked mixture. Turn into previously baked pastry shell, and just before serving top with whipped cream.

MINCE PIE

Make as a double crust pie using a commercial mince-meat. This comes in two forms, fully prepared ready for use, and dry. For the latter follow directions on package. Either may have a little fruit, lemon juice or rind, brandy or rum added.

PUMPKIN PIE

1½ cups sieved pumpkin,
  fresh cooked or canned
⅔ cup brown sugar
1 teaspoon ground cinna-
  mon
½ teaspoon ground ginger

¼ teaspoon salt
3 eggs
1½ cups milk
½ cup light cream
Pastry

Combine pumpkin, sugar, spices, salt, and egg yolks beaten with milk. Beat egg whites until stiff, fold into pumpkin mixture and finally stir in cream gently. Turn into a deep pie plate lined with any preferred pastry and bake about forty minutes, or until knife blade inserted in filling comes out clean as with a custard pie. Have oven hot, 425°-450° F., for first ten minutes, then reduce to 350° F.

PECAN TARTS

1 tablespoon butter	½ cup dark corn sirup
¼ cup brown sugar	¾ cup broken pecans
1 egg	⅓ teaspoon vanilla
1 tablespoon flour	Pastry
Dash of salt	

Cream butter and sugar, add well-beaten egg, then flour, salt, sirup, nuts, and vanilla. Line small tartlet pans with any preferred pastry, put a spoonful of the filling into each, and bake about thirty minutes having oven hot, 425°-450° F., for first ten minutes, then reducing to 350°-375° F.

If preferred, bake as one pie, increasing baking time to forty-five minutes.

GOLDEN GATE TARTS

1 cup dried apricots	½ cup crushed pineapple
½ cup water	Grated rind 1 orange
2 tablespoons strained honey	Previously baked tartlet shells
¾ cup granulated sugar	

Rinse apricots, and pass through food chopper using medium knife. Combine with water, honey, sugar, and pineapple, bring to a boil and continue cooking slowly ten minutes. Cool, add orange rind. Fill tartlet shells and decorate, if desired, with blanched pistachio nuts or shredded almonds.

CREAM PIE

This is most easily made with one of the many excellent prepared puddings now on the market, of which there are several flavors, that is, vanilla, chocolate, butterscotch. Prepare according to directions on package. When partly cooled, turn into previously baked pastry shell, pie, or tartlets. Chill, and top with whipped cream. With a vanilla filling, put a layer of rich preserve—peach, apricot, pineapple or raspberry—into the bottom of pastry shell before pouring in filling.

CAKE

Cake may be roughly divided into two types, butter and sponge cakes, although actually a rich sponge cake may contain a little butter. Generally speaking, the presence or absence .of shortening in a cake mixture determines the method' of mixing, and the texture and appearance after baking.

There is no such thing as luck in cake making. Behind every successful cake of whatever type, there are half a dozen simple rules, which, if observed, assure success, each of these being of individual importance, for no one of them without the co-operation of the others can result in perfect cake.

Use a reliable standard recipe.
Select good ingredients.
Measure accurately.
Mix thoroughly.
Bake at correct temperature.
Observe proper care after baking.

The Ingredients

Shortening. Any shortening, butter or a substitute, may be used. If allowed to stand at room temperature for a while the shortening will cream more easily, but unless definitely indicated it should never be melted.

Sugar. Except for spice cakes, gingerbreads, and dark fruit cakes, fine-grain granulated sugar is best. With dark cakes, however, brown sugar may often be substituted.

Eggs. With many cakes the whole egg (yolk and white) is beaten together. But with very light cakes, which depend largely upon eggs for their lightness, yolks and whites are beaten separately; the yolks then added to the creamed shortening and sugar; the whites, stiffly beaten, folded in just before baking. Remember that by this last method, the cake may be a little lighter but it is apt to dry out more quickly.

Flour. Cake flour produces a finer grain and texture. If all-purpose flour is used, be sure to use two tablespoons less to each cup than with cake flour. Always sift flour once before measuring, then a second time with other added dry ingredients.

Baking Powder. Use a standard brand, measure carefully, sift with flour for even distribution. Be sure to keep baking powder closely covered between usings.

Making the Cake

First assemble the necessary equipment; prepare cake pans; measure all ingredients carefully; light the oven in time to have it at the right temperature when the cake is ready for baking.

Butter Cake

To make a butter cake first cream the shortening and sugar, whipping and creaming and beating until the resultant mass is light and fluffy. Next beat in eggs (or yolks) gradually, beating after each addition, then add sifted dry ingredients and liquid. Some prefer adding liquid and dry ingredients alternately, say one-third of each at a time, others believe that all may be added at once to the creamed mass, claiming that with one vigorous beating they will be evenly and thoroughly blended. Fruits or nuts must be perfectly dry, and should be added before the flour.

Where a recipe calls for stiffly beaten egg whites, fold these in gently after flour and liquid are all mixed. Do not beat, do not stir, but *fold* the batter gently over and over the egg whites until they are incorporated, yet without destroying their lightness and frothiness. The batter may be beaten hard to insure a smooth grain *before* adding the egg whites, *never afterwards.*

Sponge Cake

In a sponge cake, eggs and sugar are first beaten together until very light, after which the liquid is added, and the well-sifted flour folded into the frothy mixture, just as stiffly beaten egg whites are folded into a butter cake batter, thoroughly but gently.

In true sponge cakes made with many eggs, baking powder is not used, but with the less expensive sponge types a little baking powder is substituted for part of the eggs with excellent results.

Using an Electric Mixer

When using an electric mixer for cake making follow manufacturer's directions. Generally speaking, the shortening is creamed at medium speed, this being increased to high after sugar is added. High speed is also used for incorporating eggs, and low speed for the blending in of sifted dry ingredients and liquids. Avoid over-beating after flour is added, as this makes a close-textured cake. Stiffly beaten egg whites are invariably folded in by hand.

Preparing Cake Pans

Use an unsalted fat for greasing. If a crisp surface is de
sired, dust pans after greasing with flour or fine granulated
sugar. Added protection is given to very rich cakes, and
those needing long slow baking, by lining pans with
greased paper.

Baking the Cake

Place cake as near center of oven as possible; in baking
more than one cake or layer at a time, stagger the positions.
In other words, do not place one cake directly above another, and do not overcrowd the oven, as this makes for
uneven baking.

Failing thermostatic control (or even with it), use a portable oven thermometer and watch your temperatures carefully.

The baking time may be roughly divided into quarters.
During the first, the batter begins to rise; during the second, rising continues and surface begins to brown; during
the third, rising finishes and browning continues; in the
final quarter, baking is completed, the cake slightly shrink-
ing from edges of pan.

Sometimes one sees cakes, particularly layers, with a little
mountain peak right in the center, which makes it almost
impossible to put them together, and frost them evenly
and smoothly. With a stiff batter, the tendency is to rise
more in the center than around the edges; therefore hollow
the batter the tiniest bit in the center of the pan to avoid
this. A very soft batter will find its own level. If necessary,
protect cake from over-browning, by laying a sheet of paper
over it in the oven after it has fully risen.

Test for doneness by inserting a cake tester (slender wire
skewer) in cake, pushing right through to the center then

drawing out gently. If the tester comes out clean, the cake is done; if it is sticky, bake a few minutes longer, then retest.

Care after Baking

Butter Cakes: Place cake in its pan on wire cooling rack, then after a few minutes loosen from sides of pan with spatula and turn out. Tear off lining paper if used, then place cake right side up on rack to cool.

Sponge or Angel Cakes: Cool in the pan, turning pan upside down on cooling rack, and allowing cake to "hang" until cold. Then loosen carefully with spatula and turn out. Once the cake is cold, it should be removed from the pan at once, lest it stick.

BUTTER CAKE

½ cup butter or shortening	2 cups sifted cake flour
1 cup sugar	2 teaspoons baking powder
1 teaspoon flavoring extract	½ teaspoon salt
2 eggs, beaten	¾ cup milk

Cream shortening until very light, gradually adding sugar, and beating until fluffy. Add flavoring, then eggs, one at a time, beating vigorously after each addition. Next add sifted dry ingredients alternately with milk, beating until smooth after each addition. Turn into two greased layer cake pans, spread evenly and bake in moderately hot oven, 375° F., about twenty-five minutes.

For Loaf Cake, bake in one greased loaf pan in moderate oven, 350° F., about fifty minutes.

For Old-Fashioned Nut Cake, add ⅔ cup coarsely chopped hickory or black walnut meats after eggs, use almond extract, and bake as Loaf Cake.

For Cup Cakes, prepare one-half Butter Cake batter and

turn into greased cup cake pans, filling these not more than two-thirds full. Bake in hot oven, 400° F., about fifteen minutes. Frost as desired.

For Marble Cake, stir into one-third Butter Cake batter 1 square (ounce) melted unsweetened chocolate with 2 teaspoons additional milk. Bake as Loaf Cake, alternating in the pan two spoonfuls of white batter with one of chocolate.

For Coffee Spice Cake, add to Butter Cake batter in place of flavoring extract 1 teaspoon ground cinnamon, ½ teaspoon ground nutmeg, and ¼ teaspoon ground cloves. Use strong coffee in place of milk. Bake as Loaf Cake, and top with Chocolate Frosting.

For Boston Cream Pie, spread Custard Cream Filling between Butter Cake layers, and sift powdered sugar generously over the top.

For Washington Pie, spread raspberry jam between Butter Cake layers, and sift powdered sugar generously over the top.

For Mocha Nut Cake, fill and frost Butter Cake layers with Mocha Frosting, and garnish with walnut or pecan halves, or sprinkle chopped nut meats over entire surface.

CHOCOLATE LAYERS

½ cup shortening	2 cups sifted cake flour
1 cup sugar	2 teaspoons baking powder
1 egg	½ teaspoon salt
2 squares (ounces) unsweetened chocolate, melted	¾ cup milk
	1 teaspoon vanilla

Cream shortening, gradually adding sugar. When very light add beaten egg, then melted chocolate; and next the sifted dry ingredients alternately with milk to which vanilla has been added, beating until smooth after each addition.

Bake in two well-greased layer pans in moderate oven, 350° F., about twenty-five minutes.

For Chocolate Marshmallow Cake, put Chocolate Layers together with half recipe for Boiled Frosting, into which eight quartered marshmallows have been beaten. Then cover top and sides of cake with remaining plain frosting.

For Chocolate Peppermint Cake, fill and frost Chocolate Layers with Boiled Frosting, flavored with a few drops peppermint extract. Then trickle 2 squares (ounces) melted unsweetened chocolate, to which 1 tablespoon butter has been added, over top surface of cake, pouring in a thin stream.

COCONUT DEVIL'S FOOD CAKE

1 cup sifted cake flour
1/2 teaspoon baking soda
1/4 cup butter or shortening
1/2 cup brown sugar, firmly packed
2 egg yolks

1 1/2 squares (ounces) unsweetened chocolate, melted
1/2 teaspoon vanilla
1/2 cup milk

Sift flour and baking soda together three times. Cream butter, add sugar gradually, and when light beat in egg yolks. Next add chocolate and vanilla, and finally flour alternately with milk, beating until smooth after each addition. Bake in greased pan in moderate oven, 350° F., twenty-five to thirty minutes. When cold, spread with Coconut Seven Minute Frosting.

ONE EGG CAKE

1/4 cup butter or shortening
1 cup sugar
1 egg
2 cups sifted cake flour

2 teaspoons baking powder
1/4 teaspoon salt
3/4 cup milk
1 teaspoon vanilla

Cream shortening, gradually adding sugar, and continue creaming until light and fluffy. Add well-beaten egg, and when blended the sifted dry ingredients alternately with milk and vanilla, beating until smooth after each addition. Turn into two greased layer cake pans and bake in moderately hot oven, 375° F., about twenty-five minutes. When cool, fill and frost as desired.

This is a good plain cake, but because of the small amount of shortening and egg it will not keep moist as long as richer mixtures.

UPSIDE-DOWN CAKE

For the batter:

1¼ cups sifted cake flour	1 egg, well beaten
1¼ teaspoons baking powder	½ cup milk
	1 teaspoon vanilla
¼ teaspoon salt	¼ cup shortening, melted
¾ cup sugar	

For the topping:

4 tablespoons butter	2 cups fruit
½ cup brown sugar, firmly packed	

Sift together flour, baking powder, and salt, then add sugar. Blend egg, milk, and vanilla, and combine with first mixture. Stir in melted shortening, and beat vigorously about one minute. Melt butter in heavy frying pan or cake pan; sprinkle brown sugar over, and place in oven to soften sugar. Arrange fruit in pan, pour cake batter over, and bake in moderate oven, 350° F., forty-five to fifty minutes. Immediately on taking from oven, loosen cake from sides of pan with spatula, and turn upside down onto plate. Serve plain or with garnish of whipped cream.

Suitable fruits are canned peaches, apricots, pineapple

slices, or drained crushed pineapple; stewed, pitted prunes; diced, uncooked rhubarb; diced, peeled, cored apples.

SPICY LOAF CAKE

1 cup brown sugar
1¼ cups hot coffee or water
1 cup halved seeded raisins
½ cup mixed candied peels, cut small
⅓ cup shortening

⅓ teaspoon salt
1 teaspoon grated nutmeg
1 teaspoon ground cinnamon
About 2 cups sifted flour
4 teaspoons baking powder

Boil sugar, coffee or water, raisins, peels, shortening, salt, and spices together for three minutes. When cool, add flour and baking powder sifted together, and blend thoroughly. Turn into greased loaf pan, and bake in moderate oven, 350° F., about forty-five minutes.

MOLASSES TWO EGG CAKE

½ cup butter or shortening
¼ cup sugar
2 eggs
¾ cup molasses
½ teaspoon vanilla
5 tablespoons milk
2 cups sifted cake flour

1 teaspoon ground cinnamon
½ teaspoon ground ginger
¾ teaspoon baking powder
¾ teaspoon baking soda
¾ teaspoon salt

Cream shortening and sugar, add beaten eggs. Combine molasses, vanilla, and milk, stirring to blend thoroughly. Sift all dry ingredients, then add these and liquids to first mixture, and blend until thoroughly smooth. Bake in greased loaf pan in moderate oven, 350° F., forty-five to fifty-five minutes; or bake in three greased layer pans about twenty-five minutes. When cool, fill with apple sauce and top with molasses-flavored whipped cream. Use promptly.

SUGARLESS SPICE CAKE

2¼ cups sifted cake flour
2¼ teaspoons baking powder
¼ teaspoon salt
1¼ teaspoons ground cinnamon
¼ teaspoon each ground cloves and nutmeg
½ cup butter or shortening
1 teaspoon grated lemon rind
1 cup light corn sirup
2 eggs
½ cup milk
1 teaspoon vanilla

Sift all dry ingredients at least twice. Cream shortening with lemon rind, add sirup gradually, beating well after each addition; then add about one-fourth of the flour and beat in well. Next add eggs, one at a time, again beating; and finally add remaining flour in thirds, alternately with milk and vanilla in halves, beating after each addition. Bake in two greased layer pans in moderately hot oven, 375° F., about thirty minutes. When cool, fill with Prune Filling and top with whipped cream.

APPLE SAUCE CAKE

¼ cup shortening
Scant ½ cup brown sugar
1 egg
1½ cups sifted cake flour
1 teaspoon baking soda
Dash of salt
1 teaspoon ground cinnamon
¼ teaspoon ground cloves
1 cup apple sauce
1 teaspoon grated orange rind
1 cup chopped seeded raisins
½ cup chopped pitted dates
⅔ cup chopped nutmeats, optional

Cream shortening, gradually adding sugar. Beat in egg, then add sifted dry ingredients alternately with apple sauce, into which orange rind has been stirred. Stir in fruits and nuts, if used, and turn into loaf pan well greased or lined with greased paper. Bake in slow oven, 325° F., about one hour.

SPONGE CAKE

5 eggs
Grated rind and juice
  ½ lemon

1 cup sifted sugar
1 cup sifted cake flour
¼ teaspoon salt

Beat egg yolks until thick and lemon colored. Add and blend in lemon rind and juice. Beat egg whites with whisk until stiff enough to hold up in peaks. Gradually add sugar, combine with yolks, and finally fold in gently flour and salt sifted together three times. Bake in ungreased tube pan in slow oven, 325° F., about one hour, and cool before removing from pan. See Care After Baking, page 266.

POTATO FLOUR SPONGE CAKE

4 eggs
¾ cup sugar
2 teaspoons lemon juice

¾ cup sifted potato flour
1 teaspoon baking powder
¼ teaspoon salt

Beat egg yolks until thick and lemon colored, adding sugar gradually while beating. Add lemon juice, then the stiffly beaten egg whites. Sift dry ingredients three times, and fold in very gently. Bake in a greased and floured shallow pan in moderate oven, 350°-360° F., thirty to forty minutes.

SPONGE CUP CAKES

1 egg
½ cup sugar
About 3 tablespoons hot
  water

½ teaspoon vanilla
½ cup sifted cake flour
¾ teaspoon baking powder
Dash of salt

Beat egg yolk and sugar until light. Add hot water, vanilla, and dry ingredients, sifted three times. Fold in stiffly beaten egg white, and bake in greased cup cake pans in moderate oven, 350° F., about twenty minutes. Frost as desired.

JELLY ROLL

3 eggs	1 teaspoon baking powder
1 cup sugar	1/3 teaspoon salt
3 tablespoons cold water	Jelly or jam
1 cup sifted cake flour	

Beat eggs and sugar until very light, add water, then sifted dry ingredients, folding them in very gently. Grease shallow oblong pan of cookie sheet type, then line with greased paper, pour in batter, and spread evenly right to corners. Bake in moderately hot oven, 375°-400° F., about twelve minutes. Invert pan onto cloth sprinkled with sugar, cut off any crisp edges, tear off paper, spread almost to edges with jelly or jam warmed or slightly beaten to soften. Roll up quickly and cool on rack.

GINGERBREAD

2 cups sifted cake flour	1/3 cup shortening
1 teaspoon ground cinna-mon	1/2 cup hot water
	1 egg
1 teaspoon ground ginger	1/2 cup sugar
1 teaspoon baking soda	1/2 cup molasses
1/2 teaspoon salt	

Sift together twice all dry ingredients. Melt shortening in hot water, then add it to egg, which has been beaten until light, with sugar. Add molasses, then blend with dry ingredients. Bake in shallow well-greased pan in moderate oven, 350° F., about thirty minutes. If desired, stir into the batter before baking ½ cup diced apples, dates, raisins, candied fruit rind, or nuts.

Because of the amount of spices used, with their rather predominant flavor, one may select any preferred shortening, butter, lard, cooking oil, or some of those homely fats, bacon, beef, or pork drippings. If sour milk is available, substitute it for the water, adding ¼ teaspoon additional baking soda.

For variety of service, bake Gingerbread in layers, and put together when cold with ice cream; or fill with apple sauce and top with plain or molasses-flavored whipped cream. Or bake as cup cakes, and serve as dessert with Chocolate, Orange, or Lemon Sauce.

Do not overlook the possibilities of the commercial, packaged gingerbreads which need only the addition of liquid. They make rich glossy tender cake which literally melts in one's mouth. They lend themselves to exactly the same variations as home-prepared gingerbread, and by reducing the amount of added liquid they will provide excellent ginger cookies of the drop variety.

DOUGHNUTS ·

2 cups sifted flour	½ cup sugar
1½ teaspoons baking powder	1 egg
½ teaspoon salt	1 scant cup milk
½ teaspoon mixed ground spices—cinnamon, nutmeg, mace	1½ tablespoons melted shortening

Sift flour, baking powder, salt, and spices. Add sugar and mix to light dough with beaten egg, milk, and shortening. Turn onto well-floured board, work with fingers until smooth, roll out about half an inch thick, cut with doughnut cutter and cook, a few at a time, in large heavy iron kettle in deep hot fat, 350°-375° F., turning as soon as they rise to top of fat. Drain on soft paper and sprinkle with powdered sugar. The easiest way to sugar doughnuts is to place a little powdered sugar in a large paper bag, drop in three or four doughnuts, twist the top of the bag to close, then shake gently.

FROSTINGS AND FILLINGS

What makes perfection in a cake frosting? Smoothness of texture, fine flavor, a glossy surface combined with a creamy interior, all easily attained by careful attention to a few simple details.

When putting any frosting on a cake, use a generous amount, spread lightly over the top edge and around the sides using long sweeping strokes of your spatula. Finally, pile more frosting on top, spread this out lightly to the edges, and decorate in ridges or swirls with large spoon. Frequently, the frosting serves as both filling and frosting.

Perhaps the most popular of all frostings is the one known as Seven Minute Frosting. Once having mastered it, almost any variety of cooked frosting is easy.

SEVEN MINUTE FROSTING

1½ cups sugar
2 egg whites
5 tablespoons water

1½ teaspoons light corn
  sirup
1 teaspoon flavoring

Combine in upper vessel of double boiler all ingredients except flavoring. Blend thoroughly with rotary beater, then place over rapidly boiling water, and continue beating for seven minutes or until frosting stands in peaks. Remove from heat, add flavoring, and beat again until frosting forms firm swirls and ridges, when it is ready to spread.

To insure success, remember to use a deep boiler and sturdy rotary beater; keep water in lower vessel boiling steadily; beat constantly with no rest pauses.

BOILED FROSTING

1½ cups sugar
1½ teaspoons light corn
 sirup

⅔ cup boiling water
2 egg whites
1 teaspoon flavoring

Combine sugar, sirup, and water, bring quickly to a boil, stirring only until sugar is dissolved, then continue boiling rapidly until a little dropped into cold water forms a soft ball, 238°-240° F. Pour in a fine stream over the stiffly beaten egg whites, beating constantly. Add flavoring and continue beating (rotary beater) until cool and of spreading consistency, ten to fifteen minutes. As frosting becomes too stiff for beater, substitute a flat wooden spoon.

MARSHMALLOW FROSTING

Fold 1 cup quartered marshmallows into Seven Minute or Boiled Frosting before spreading.

COCONUT FROSTING

After spreading, top Seven Minute or Boiled Frosting generously with shredded coconut.

CHOCOLATE FROSTING

Flavor Seven Minute or Boiled Frosting with vanilla, adding with it 3 squares (ounces) unsweetened chocolate, melted and cooled.

FLUFFY MOCHA FROSTING

⅓ cup butter
4 cups sifted confectioners' sugar
3½ tablespoons cocoa

¼ teaspoon salt
⅓ cup strong coffee
1 teaspoon vanilla

Cream butter until very light, then work into it the sugar, cocoa, and salt sifted together. Add coffee a little at a time until of proper spreading consistency, beating the frosting after each addition. Add vanilla and spread.

UNCOOKED FROSTING

1½ cups confectioners' sugar

Orange or lemon juice, milk or coffee

Use just enough liquid to moisten sugar thoroughly, working until smooth, and pressing any lumps out of sugar with back of spoon. With orange or lemon juice add a little grated rind, with milk or coffee a few drops vanilla.

JELLY FROSTING

½ cup tart jelly
1 unbeaten egg white

⅛ teaspoon salt

Combine all ingredients in a bowl, set over boiling water, and beat with rotary beater until perfectly smooth. Remove from water, and continue beating until stiff enough to stand in peaks. Use immediately.

HONEY MERINGUE FROSTING

Follow recipe for Honey Meringue, page 259. When mixture begins to stiffen, add ½ teaspoon grated orange rind. Remember that long beating is necessary in order to have mixture stand in peaks. The frosting may be tinted, if desired, with vegetable coloring.

The very newest members of the frosting family are the "baked on the cake" type:

LEMON MERINGUE FROSTING

1⅓ cups (1 can) sweet-
    ened condensed milk

1 egg white
2 tablespoons lemon juice

Combine milk and lemon juice, and stir until mixture thickens. Fold in stiffly beaten egg white, spread on freshly baked cake, return to moderate oven, 350° F., and bake ten minutes or until delicately browned. If preferred, place low in the broiler under slow flame.

BAKED FUDGE FROSTING

2 squares (ounces) unsweet-
    ened chocolate
1⅓ cups (1 can) sweetened
    condensed milk

1 tablespoon water
1 cup shredded coconut

Melt chocolate over hot water, add milk, and cook over hot water for five minutes, or until mixture thickens. Add water and half the coconut. Spread on freshly baked cake, sprinkle remaining coconut over surface, and place in moderate oven, 350° F., for about ten minutes, or until coconut is golden brown.

CUSTARD CREAM FILLING

⅓ cup sugar
¼ cup sifted flour
Dash of salt
1 whole egg or 2 egg yolks

1 cup milk, scalded
½ teaspoon vanilla or al-
    mond extract

Blend sugar, flour, and salt, add egg or egg yolks slightly beaten, then pour over them the scalded milk, beating while pouring. Cook over hot water (double boiler) until mixture thickens, about ten minutes, stirring constantly. Add flavoring when partly cooled, and when cold spread between cake layers.

For Chocolate Cream Filling, melt ½ square (ounce) unsweetened chocolate with milk when scalding it, stirring occasionally to blend smoothly.

For Coffee Cream Filling, scald with the milk 3 teaspoons fine ground coffee loosely tied in double cheesecloth.

PRUNE FILLING

3½ tablespoons cornstarch
1 cup prune juice
⅛ teaspoon salt
2 teaspoons lemon juice
1 teaspoon grated orange rind
¾ teaspoon grated lemon rind
2 tablespoons corn sirup
1 cup chopped, pitted, cooked prunes
⅓ cup chopped nutmeats, optional

Put cornstarch in upper part of double boiler, gradually add prune juice, mix smoothly, then add salt, lemon juice, and grated rinds. When blended, cook over direct heat until thickened, stirring constantly. Now add corn sirup and prunes, and continue cooking over boiling water twelve minutes, stirring occasionally. Cool, and add nutmeats, if used.

COOKIES

Cookies may be roughly divided into two classes, the old-fashioned plain or spicy cookies such as we used to find in grandmother's cookie jar, and the more dainty and delicate wafers of the afternoon tea variety. Both types may be subdivided into rolled and cut, dropped, and sliced or refrigerator cookies.

With delicate rich varieties, butter is essential, but for those having pronounced flavor of their own, and for the school lunch or cookie jar type, any preferred shortening may be used.

Generally speaking, all-purpose flour is used in the making of cookies, though cake flour may be substituted, especially for fine-grained delicate cookies.

The smaller and richer the cookie, the hotter the oven may be within reasonable limits. Cookies should be lifted from pans as soon as baked, using a broad-bladed knife or spatula. Cool on wire rack and do not pack away until thoroughly cold. To retain crispness, store in air-tight containers, preferably with waxed paper between the layers.

As cookies keep well if properly stored, it is best to make a good-sized batch, and it gives one a comfortable feeling to have something homemade on hand to offer the unexpected guest.

PLAIN COOKIES

½ cup shortening
1 cup sugar
1 beaten egg
½ cup milk

1 teaspoon any desired flavoring
3 scant cups sifted flour
3 teaspoons baking powder
¼ teaspoon salt

Cream shortening and sugar, add egg, milk, and flavoring, then sifted dry ingredients. Chill, if possible, roll, cut, and bake in moderately hot oven, 375° F., about twelve minutes.

The dough may be divided into two portions, rolling

one plain, and adding to the other ½ cup chopped nuts, quartered raisins, or diced pitted dates.

FILLED COOKIES

Roll Plain Cookie dough out thin, cut into rounds, place on half of them blended chopped nuts and raisins, chopped dates plain or with nuts or coconut, jelly or jam, marmalade or mincemeat. Wet edges slightly, cover with a second round of dough, and press firmly together. Bake in moderately hot oven, 375° F., ten to fifteen minutes.

HERMITS

½ cup shortening
⅔ cup sugar
1 egg
2 tablespoons milk
½ cup quartered seeded raisins
1¾ cups sifted flour

1¾ teaspoons baking powder
¼ teaspoon salt
½ teaspoon ground cinnamon
¼ teaspoon each ground cloves, ground mace, and grated nutmeg

Cream shortening, adding sugar gradually. Add well-beaten egg and milk, stir in raisins, then the sifted dry ingredients. Roll out about one-fourth inch thick on floured board, cut into rounds, and bake on greased baking sheets in moderately hot oven, 375° F., about twelve minutes.

CREAM CHEESE COOKIES

⅓ cup butter
¼ cup sugar
1 egg yolk
2 oz. cream cheese

¼ cup sour cream
1¾ cups sifted flour
1 teaspoon baking powder

Cream butter until light, adding sugar and egg yolk gradually. Work in cheese smoothly, add sour cream and sifted flour and baking powder. Chill, preferably overnight. Roll very thin on floured board, cut as desired, and bake on ungreased cookie sheets in moderate oven, 350°-375° F., about twelve minutes. A rich mellow cookie which keeps well.

HANNA'S GINGERSNAPS

½ cup butter
½ cup sugar
½ cup molasses
½ cup heavy cream
About 2½ cups sifted flour

½ teaspoon baking soda
⅓ teaspoon each ground cloves and cinnamon
¾ teaspoon ground ginger

Cream butter and sugar until light, add molasses and cream, which has been whipped until thick but not stiff. Combine with dry ingredients twice sifted together. Form into a dough and chill, preferably overnight, in refrigerator. Roll out thin on floured board, cut as desired, and bake on greased cookie sheets in moderate oven, 350°-375° F., about twelve minutes.

CHOCOLATE CHIP COOKIES

½ cup shortening
½ cup granulated sugar
¼ cup brown sugar, firmly packed
1 egg
1 cup sifted flour

½ teaspoon salt
½ teaspoon baking soda
1 cup chocolate chips
½ cup chopped nutmeats
1 teaspoon vanilla

Cream shortening, gradually adding sugars, and beating until light and fluffy. Add egg, and, when well blended, gradually the sifted dry ingredients with chocolate, nutmeats, and vanilla, mixing all in thoroughly. Drop from tip of spoon onto greased baking sheets a little distance apart, and bake in moderately hot oven, 375° F., ten to twelve minutes.

JUMBLES

⅓ cup butter	1 to 1¼ cups sifted flour
½ cup sugar	⅓ teaspoon salt
1 egg	1 teaspoon baking powder
Grated rind half a lemon	

Cream butter and sugar, add beaten egg, lemon rind, and sifted dry ingredients. Drop by spoonfuls onto greased baking sheet, and bake in moderately hot oven, 375° F., about ten minutes.

BUTTERSCOTCH COOKIES

½ cup butter or shortening	1½ teaspoons vanilla
1¼ cups brown sugar, firmly packed	2 cups sifted flour
1 egg, well beaten	2 teaspoons baking powder
1 cup finely chopped nut-meats	⅛ teaspoon salt

Cream butter and sugar thoroughly together, adding the sugar a little at a time. Beat in egg, add nuts and vanilla, then the sifted dry ingredients, mixing thoroughly after each addition. Form into a roll and wrap in waxed paper or pack into fancy molds. Chill overnight in refrigerator or until firm enough to slice. Cut into one-eighth-inch slices, and bake on ungreased baking sheets in hot oven, 425° F., six to eight minutes. This dough will keep a week or more in refrigerator.

BROWNIES

⅓ cup butter
1 cup sugar
2 beaten eggs
¾ cup sifted flour
½ teaspoon baking powder

2 squares (ounces) unsweetened chocolate
¾ cup chopped nutmeats
1 teaspoon vanilla

Cream butter and sugar, add eggs, then sifted dry ingredients with chocolate, and finally nutmeats and vanilla.
Blend thoroughly, and spread evenly in greased shallow
pan. Bake in moderate oven, 350° F., about half an hour.
Cut into squares while still warm.

FLAKED CEREAL MACAROONS

½ cup sweetened condensed
milk
½ teaspoon vanilla or
maple flavoring

1½ cups flaked cereal
½ cup shredded coconut

Combine milk and flavoring, then stir in cereal and
coconut lightly so as not to break up the flakes. Drop
from tip of spoon onto greased baking sheet about one
inch apart. Bake in moderate oven, 350° F., twelve to
fifteen minutes, and remove from pan as soon as done.

CHAPTER SIXTEEN

APPETIZERS AND BEVERAGES

For Tomato Juice Cocktail, Clam Juice Cocktail, Vegetable Juice (Health) Cocktail, Sauerkraut Juice Cocktail and Cranberry Juice Cocktail use the prepared canned or bottled commercial juices, adding additional seasoning, or a squeeze of lemon juice, if desired. Certain of these such as tomato and clam or tomato and sauerkraut may be combined in equal portions. Allow ½ cup per portion.

SEA FOOD COCKTAILS

CLAM, OYSTER, LOBSTER, CRABMEAT, SHRIMP, AND FISH

The main ingredient in a sea food cocktail may be either raw or cooked, depending on its nature. Clams and oysters are served raw, usually on the half shell, arranged on a bed of shaved ice, the cocktail sauce in a glass in the center.

Lobster, crabmeat, shrimp, and fish are precooked, and they can be served right in the cocktail sauce; or the main ingredient may be arranged in tiny lettuce cups, the sauce in its own glass, as with clam or oyster cocktails.

All sea food cocktails should be well chilled, and the sauce rather highly seasoned.

Allow 6 clams or oysters or ¼ cup diced lobster, whole shrimps, flaked crabmeat, or fish per portion.

COCKTAIL SAUCE FOR SEA FOOD

I

4 tablespoons tomato catsup   2 drops tabasco
  or chili sauce   Scant teaspoon Worcester-
½ teaspoon celery salt   shire sauce
1 tablespoon lemon juice

Blend ingredients and chill thoroughly.

II

1 teaspoon minced onion   ½ teaspoon tarragon vine-
2 tablespoons chili sauce   gar
2 tablespoons tomato   ½ teaspoon salt or celery
  catsup   salt
2 teaspoons lemon juice   Dash of pepper and cayenne
                              Garlic

Cut garlic clove in half and thoroughly rub small bowl
with the cut surface. Combine all other ingredients in that
bowl, then chill thoroughly.

FRUIT JUICE COCKTAIL

Use any combination of fruit juices, making sure that
at least one is a citrus fruit. A good blend would be:

⅓ cup orange juice   ⅓ cup apricot or peach
⅓ cup canned pineapple   nectar
  juice   Squeeze of lemon juice
                             Sugar, optional

Combine and chill all ingredients; then shake with two
ice cubes, and pour quickly into cocktail glasses. Garnish,
if possible, with minced mint leaves or tiny tips of mint.

AVOCADO AND GRAPEFRUIT COCKTAIL

⅓ cup diced avocado
⅔ cup grapefruit pulp
Powdered sugar

Squeeze of lime or lemon
juice

Peel avocado, remove stone, and dice pulp. Remove all skin and fiber from grapefruit, and break into small pieces. Combine the two fruits, sweeten, add lime or lemon juice, and chill thoroughly. Serve in cocktail glasses garnishing each with a mint cherry.

For Avocado and Orange Cocktail, substitute orange for the grapefruit and maraschino cherries for the mint cherries.

PINEAPPLE MINT COCKTAIL

2 slices canned pineapple,
diced or ½ cup diced
fresh pineapple
Powdered sugar, if fresh
pineapple is used

2 teaspoons finely minced
mint
1 tablespoon orange juice
Sprigs of mint

If using fresh pineapple, peel, remove eyes, dice, sprinkle generously with powdered sugar, and chill. With canned pineapple, dice and chill. Add mint and orange juice, blend thoroughly, and serve in small glasses garnishing with sprigs of fresh mint.

For Orange Mint Cocktail, substitute diced seedless orange for the pineapple.

STRAWBERRY AND PINEAPPLE CUP

½ cup hulled strawberries
½ cup diced fresh pine-
apple

3 tablespoons orange juice
1 tablespoon lemon juice
Powdered sugar

If strawberries are very large they may be sliced or halved. Combine with pineapple, add fruit juices, sugar and chill. (Reserve two perfect strawberries to use as toppings.)

MELON BALL COCKTAIL

½ cup watermelon balls
½ cup honeydew or canta-
  loup balls
6 peeled seeded white
grapes

2 tablespoons grenadine
2 teaspoons lemon juice
Powdered sugar, optional

Combine fruits, add grenadine and lemon juice with sugar if desired, and chill thoroughly before serving.

BROILED GRAPEFRUIT

1 grapefruit

Sugar, honey, corn sirup, or
  molasses

Wash and halve grapefruit, remove all seeds and white skin. Sprinkle generously with sugar, which may be white or brown, or drizzle honey, corn sirup, or molasses over the surface. Broil under low heat until grapefruit is hot and slightly browned, about fifteen minutes.

CANAPÉS

The essentials of good canapés are that they should look appetizing and attractive, and that they taste as good as they look. They *must* be small, just a mouthful, and they should stimulate but not sate the appetite. Except for special occasions, do not fuss with complicated recipes, but make use of whatever your refrigerator and pantry have to offer in the way of bases, spreads, and garnishes, supplementing these, if necessary, with one or two varieties of cheese, sausage, etc.

The Bases

These are many and varied. Bread—white, rye, pumpernickel, and brown—heads the list, always decrusted, cut into small fancy forms (remember that oblongs, triangles, and finger strips cut to the best advantage) and toasted either on one or both sides, or sautéed. Then there are crackers, plain and flavored, also commercial toasts and pastry bases, ready for immediate use. One can even use potato chips or miniature hollowed-out biscuits!

The Garnishes

These are the most important features of any canapé. Among the most popular and practical are: finely minced parsley, watercress, pimiento, green pepper, riced hard-cooked egg yolk, finely chopped egg white, olives (plain or stuffed), tiny pearl onions, pickles, capers, caviar, mayonnaise, radishes—and above all else, imagination and artistry.

Savory Butters for Canapés and Sandwiches

These are just what the name implies, creamed butter made savory and flavorful by the addition of some tangy or piquant ingredient. To each half cup of creamed butter add a dash of cayenne, paprika, or white pepper, with a squeeze of lemon juice, then work in for:

Anchovy Butter

1 teaspoon anchovy paste, or 1 or 2 anchovies mashed and pressed through a sieve.

Horseradish Butter

1 teaspoon freshly grated or prepared horseradish.

Lemon Butter

½ teaspoon grated lemon rind and about 2 teaspoons lemon juice additional.

Mint Butter

1 teaspoon finely minced mint and a little additional lemon juice.

Mustard Butter

1 teaspoon prepared mustard.

Parsley Butter

1½ to 2 teaspoons finely minced parsley with a little additional lemon juice.

Pimiento Butter

1 tablespoon canned pimiento pressed through sieve, with a few drops onion juice, if liked.

Shrimp Butter

1 to 2 tablespoons finely minced canned or fresh-cooked shrimps, with a very slight grating of nutmeg.

Watercress Butter

2 tablespoons finely minced watercress leaves with a few drops onion juice, if liked.

CANAPÉS WITH CRACKER BASE

1. Blend cream cheese and Roquefort (blue) cheese, add a few drops Worcestershire sauce, and spread on crisp

crackers. Remove pimiento from stuffed olives, refill with caviar, top with pearl onions. Place on cheese-spread crackers. Chop pimiento and use as garnish.

2. Use above spread, top with anchovy curl, sprinkle with minced, drained sweet pickle. Garnish with watercress or parsley.

3. Moisten deviled ham with mayonnaise, add a few drops each of lemon juice and Worcestershire sauce. Chill. Spread on crackers and garnish with riced hard-cooked egg yolk and strips of pimiento.

4. Blend sharp cheese spread with a small amount of butter and a few drops lemon juice and Worcestershire sauce. Spread on crackers, garnish with sliced stuffed olives or finely minced chives.

CANAPÉS WITH BREAD BASE

1. Crush sardines to paste in mixing bowl which has been rubbed with a cut clove of garlic. Season, moisten with prepared mustard, lemon juice, and cayenne. Spread on toast base, sprinkle with grated cheese, and brown in hot oven.

2. Spread rounds of thinly cut rye bread generously with mayonnaise, cover with finely minced hard-cooked egg white and sprinkle with onion juice. Top with mounds of caviar and garnish with riced, hard-cooked egg yolk.

3. Season and moisten smoothly mashed liverwurst with lemon juice, Worcestershire sauce, paprika and light cream. Spread generously on toast crescents, and garnish with onion or horseradish.

4. Spread thin rounds of rye or pumpernickel with creamed butter and arrange on each a thin slice of Liederkranz cheese. Top with a slice of Bermuda onion which

has been marinated in French dressing, then drained. Garnish with parsley or watercress.

SUGGESTIONS FOR HORS D'OEUVRE TRAY FOR LIVING ROOM SERVICE

Plan for not more than four hors d'oeuvre, then arrange around them on the tray a variety of canapés with plain or stuffed celery; olives, green, ripe, stuffed, and small pickles.

The following hors d'oeuvre are simple and easily prepared:

ANGELS ON HORSEBACK

Drain and pat dry large oysters, season with salt, pepper, and lemon juice, then roll each in a very thin slice of bacon. Fasten with canapé picks, and bake in hot oven, 450° F., about six minutes. Or sauté until crisp, turning, to brown both sides. Serve very hot.

DEVILS ON HORSEBACK

Cook large meaty prunes without sugar until just tender. When cold remove pits and replace these with stuffed olives. Wrap in bacon, secure with canapé picks, and broil or bake in hot oven, 450° F., until bacon is crisp, about six minutes.

FISH CAKES

Tiny fish cakes, little larger than cherries, fried golden brown and impaled on canapé picks.

SAUSAGES

Miniature cocktail sausages or frankfurters, broiled or baked, then impaled on canapé picks.

CHEESE OLIVES

Large stuffed olives, cut into lengthwise halves, and pressed into the opposite sides of marble-sized balls of seasoned cream cheese.

CURLED CELERY

Cut cleaned celery into two and one-half inch lengths, then with very sharp knife score lengthwise as thinly as possible to within one-half inch of center at both ends. Place in ice water for two or three hours and the cut ends will curl.

STUFFED CELERY

Use tender stalks of crisp celery. Scrape and cut into pieces about three inches long. Wipe dry and stuff as desired, piling the stuffing in or flattening as preferred. The stuffing may be inserted with the flat blade of a small knife or, for a more decorative effect, smooth fillings may be pressed into place by means of a decorating bag and tube. Dust with paprika, finely minced parsley, minced mint or capers, depending on the type of stuffing used. Suggested stuffings:

Equal parts cream cheese and Roquefort (blue), or other cheese, blended and seasoned with a little mayonnaise or cream, salt, and pepper.

Cream cheese moistened and seasoned with a prepared savory sandwich spread.

Mashed liverwurst seasoned and moistened with a few drops chili or Worcestershire sauce and a little cream.

Peanut butter moistened with mayonnaise or Russian dressing.

BEVERAGES

COFFEE

Coffee is so easy to make that it should always be perfect when served. There are, however, a few rules which must be observed:

Use fresh coffee—fresh roasted and fresh ground—unless you prefer a vacuum-packed coffee which keeps its freshness practically indefinitely.

Select the blend you prefer (this varies with different tastes). Be sure that the grind is right for the type of coffee maker employed—drip, percolated, or boiled coffee.

See that the coffee pot is thoroughly, surgically clean, and frequently aired.

Use *enough* coffee. The generally accepted rule is one heaping tablespoon per standard cup. After-dinner coffee, also iced coffee, should always be made double strength.

DRIP COFFEE

Scald pot. Place measured coffee in its compartment, and add freshly boiled measured water. Cover and let stand where the coffee will keep hot, but never boil, until all water has dripped through.

PERCOLATED COFFEE

Measure water (cold or boiling as preferred) into lower compartment of percolator. Set basket in position, put measured coffee in it, cover, place over low heat and percolate, always slowly, ten to fifteen minutes depending on type of percolator used.

BOILED COFFEE

With cold water: Combine measured coffee and water, bring slowly to boiling point, stirring occasionally. Then remove from fire, pour in a very little cold water to settle the grounds, and let stand from three to five minutes.

With boiling water: Combine measured coffee and water, boil up rapidly two or three times, and settle with cold water as directed.

AFTER-DINNER COFFEE (DEMI-TASSE)

Use any preferred method, but double the proportion of coffee to water as after-dinner coffee *must* be strong, fragrant and clear.

CAFÉ AU LAIT

This also must be double strength coffee, blended with an equal proportion of freshly scalded milk, the two being poured into the cup simultaneously from separate pots.

ICED COFFEE

Use double strength coffee (see after-dinner coffee) and pour hot over cracked ice or ice cubes in tall glasses. Serve with plain or whipped cream and sugar.

DECAFFEINATED COFFEE

Decaffeinated coffee is coffee from which most of the caffein has been extracted, and is preferred by many, especially those who find coffee unduly stimulating. Follow directions on container, or prepare according to any of the above methods.

SOLUBLE OR INSTANT COFFEE

This is commercially made by evaporating a very strong coffee infusion. Follow directions on container, or use 1 teaspoon to 1 cup boiling water, stirring until coffee is completely dissolved.

COFFEE SUBSTITUTES

There are any number of coffee substitutes on the market, usually prepared from cereals. These make a pleasing hot beverage for those who do not wish for, or cannot drink, regular coffee. Follow directions on container.

TEA

Use an earthen, china, or glass teapot. Scald, measure the tea into it, allowing ½ to 1 teaspoon for each cup, according to the strength desired, plus one for the pot. Add freshly boiled boiling water, infuse three to five minutes, strain, and serve with or without sugar, cream, or lemon.

Commercial tea bags or tea balls are very convenient for the making of individual cups or pots of tea.

RUSSIAN TEA

Use freshly made tea, pour into tall glasses, each containing a generous teaspoon of raspberry jam. Serve very hot.

ICED TEA

Prepare strong tea (use double the amount of tea suggested for hot tea), pour over cracked ice or ice cubes in tall glasses. Serve plain, or with powdered sugar and a slice of lemon or orange.

COCOA

2 tablespoons cocoa   2 cups milk or water, or a
Sugar   blend of the two

Combine cocoa and sugar, using 1½ teaspoons of the latter for each cup, or more or less according to taste. Add just enough liquid to moisten, and work with back of spoon until perfectly smooth. Then add remaining liquid, bring slowly to boiling point, stirring frequently, and simmer five minutes.

Prepared cocoas, being specially treated, can frequently be made without boiling, merely requiring boiling water or scalded milk to be added to them, mixing smoothly first with a little liquid. But there is no objection to boiling if one so desires.

CHOCOLATE SIRUP

3½ squares (ounces) un-   ½ cup hot water
sweetened chocolate   4 tablespoons sugar
⅔ cup (½ can) sweetened
condensed milk

Melt chocolate over hot water (double boiler), remove from heat, add milk, and blend thoroughly. Then add water slowly, and finally the sugar, still stirring constantly until sugar is dissolved. Keep closely covered in refrigerator. This sirup will keep for a week or ten days and may be used for hot or iced chocolate drinks.

Use 2 tablespoons chocolate sirup to 1 cup milk.

HOT CHOCOLATE

1 square (ounce) unsweet-   4 teaspoons sugar
ened chocolate   Dash of salt
½ cup water   1½ cups milk

Combine chocolate and water in upper part of double boiler, place over direct heat, using low flame, and stir until chocolate is dissolved. Add sugar and salt, and cook four minutes, stirring constantly. Place over boiling water, add milk, then heat just to boiling point, still stirring constantly. Just before serving, beat vigorously with rotary beater until light and frothy.

For Brazilian Chocolate, substitute strong coffee for the water and serve topped with whipped cream.

FROSTED CHOCOLATE

4 tablespoons chocolate
sirup
2 cups chilled milk

2 dippers chocolate or
vanilla ice cream

Combine milk and sirup, blend thoroughly, add ice cream, then shake until light and frothy. Serve in tall glasses.

EGGNOG
(Individual)

1 egg
2 teaspoons sugar
1 cup milk

Few drops vanilla
Dash of nutmeg or cinna-
mon

Beat egg with sugar until very light, add milk and vanilla, and beat again. Pour into tall glass, and dust with nutmeg or cinnamon.

If desired, the egg yolk and white may be beaten separately. In which case, beat the yolk and sugar together, add milk and flavoring, and finally fold in the stiffly beaten white.

Also, if desired, corn sirup or honey may be used in place of sugar.

For Fruited Eggnog, substitute 2 tablespoons grapejuice or orange juice for the vanilla.

For Eggnog with Wine, substitute 2 tablespoons of any desired wine for the vanilla.

SUGAR SIRUP

All cold drinks are smoother and richer if sweetened with sugar sirup instead of plain sugar. For this, boil gently together for five minutes 2 cups sugar and 1 cup water. Cool and store, closely covered, in refrigerator. Use as needed, 1½ to 2 tablespoons to each tall drink. Equal parts corn sirup and sugar may be used in place of all sugar.

LEMONADE
(Individual)

Juice of 1 lemon   1½ to 2 tablespoons sugar
Thin shaving of lemon rind   or sugar sirup
                          ¾ cup water

Combine all ingredients, stirring thoroughly. Pour into tall glasses over cracked ice or ice cube.

For Limeade, substitute fresh lime juice for lemon juice.

For Orangeade, use two-thirds orange juice and one-third lemon juice in place of all lemon juice.

For Raspberry Mintade, simmer 3 sprigs mint with ½ cup boiling water for five minutes. Strain, cool, and add with ½ cup crushed fresh raspberries to double Lemonade recipe. Serve in tall glasses with cracked ice and a sprig of fresh mint in each glass.

CHAPTER SEVENTEEN

COMPANY'S COMING!

(The starred recipes are all in this book.
Double or triple them as necessary.)

One of the nicest things about the new home is entertaining friends. Of course you want to honor your guests
but do make it fun, not hard work. Keep menus reasonably
simple so that you can all have a good time.

Today entertaining is done at any time—morning, noon
or night. Sunday mornings are grand for that informal
meal known as brunch, really a combination breakfast and
lunch, served any time in the late morning. In fact, brunch
is good just for two because it makes Sunday an easy two-
meal day.

SUNDAY MORNING BRUNCHES

Flaked Cereal with Fresh Berries
Eggs Benedict *
Quick Coffee Cake *   Preserves

Orange Juice
Puffed Cereal (optional)
Waffles * with Sausages and Fried Apple Slices
Sirup   Butter

Halved Grapefruit
* Stewed Kidneys with Fried Potatoes
Corn Muffins *   Butter   Jam

Do plan things ahead so you won't be rushed. Have the
dry ingredients for hot breads or muffins ready for moisten-

ing (or use a prepared mix). Completely prepare the kidneys on Saturday so they will need only reheating on Sunday. For fried potatoes cook extra ones with Saturday's dinner. Then they will be ready for slicing. Yes, even the table can be set the night before.

LUNCHES OR SUPPERS

These three menus are interchangeable, just as good for lunch as for supper, although the third one *was* definitely planned for with men in mind.

Clam Juice Cocktail (canned)

Chicken à la King

Green Peas

Olives   Salted Nuts

Pecan Tarts * or Golden Gate Tarts *

Creamed Mushrooms with Broiled Bacon

Hot Biscuits

Chiffonade Salad *

Lemon Meringue Pie *

Hot Onion Soup *

Cold Sliced Ham

Baked Beans *   Brown Bread

Olives   Pickles

Apple Sauce *   Hermits *

CHICKEN À LA KING
(8 servings)

6 tablespoons butter	2 cups milk
¼ pound mushrooms, sliced	3 egg yolks
	⅔ cup cream
1 medium-sized green pepper, minced	3 cups diced cooked chicken
4 tablespoons flour	1 diced pimiento
⅔ teaspoon salt	¼ cup sherry
⅔ teaspoon paprika	Toast

Melt butter and cook mushrooms and green pepper gently in it for five minutes. Add flour, salt and paprika and when smoothly blended, add milk, and bring to boiling point, stirring constantly over low heat. Beat egg yolks slightly, add cream, and stir into sauce with chicken and pimiento. Set over hot but not *actually boiling* water or sauce may curdle. Stir in sherry just before serving and garnish with toast points.

CREAMED MUSHROOMS WITH BACON GARNISH

(8 servings)

2 tablespoons minced onion	3 cups milk
6 tablespoons butter	1 teaspoon salt
2 pounds mushrooms	¼ teaspoon pepper
6 tablespoons flour	1 tablespoon lemon juice
	Broiled bacon

Cook onion in butter for five minutes without browning. Add mushrooms, washed and thickly sliced. Cover and cook gently for ten minutes. Stir in flour, add milk and bring slowly to boiling point, stirring constantly. Then simmer fifteen minutes. Add seasonings and serve on toast. Garnish with bacon. (Cook it on rack in broiling oven under moderate heat until crisp.)

DINNERS

We have deliberately kept away from the overworked broiled steak and fried chicken in our dinners. As planned, these will take a little time to prepare but something savory as well as unexpected will result.

Hungarian Goulash

Celery	Radishes	Sweet-Sour Pickles

Garlic Bread *
Jelly Roll *
Chicken Normandy *

Steamed Rice	Hot Buttered Beets
Oakland Salad *	Salted Crackers

Thick Clam Chowder en Casserole
Mixed (Tossed) Green Salad *
Bread Sticks

Stewed Fruit	Frosted Cup Cakes *

HUNGARIAN GOULASH
(8 servings)

¼ pound salt pork
2 large onions, sliced
1½ pounds top round of beef
½ pound veal cutlet
3 tablespoons flour
1½ teaspoons salt
⅓ teaspoon pepper
1 green pepper, minced

1 bay leaf
4 whole cloves
6 peppercorns
2 cups solid canned tomatoes
1 quart diced potatoes
1 tablespoon minced parsley

Fry pork until fat flows freely. Cook onion in it until golden brown. Add meat, cut into one-inch cubes and rolled in blended flour, salt and pepper. Stir frequently and when meat is lightly browned, add green pepper, spices (tied in cheesecloth), tomatoes and just enough water or tomato juice to cover meat. Simmer one hour, remove spices, add potatoes and more water or tomato juice, if needed to prevent any sticking to pan. Continue cooking, without stirring, until potatoes are tender. Sprinkle parsley over just before serving.

THICK CLAM CHOWDER EN CASSEROLE
(8 servings)

3 pints shucked clams   ¼ pound salt pork, diced
½ cup finely minced   3 cups sliced or diced raw
  onion   potatoes
2 cloves of garlic, finely   Salt
  minced   1 teaspoon pepper
1 large green pepper,   3 cups boiling water
  minced   Buttered crumbs
2 cups canned tomatoes

Pick over clams, chop fine, drain, reserve liquor. Combine onion, garlic, green pepper and tomatoes with half the pork. Fry remaining pork until fat flows freely, transfer to casserole and arrange over it alternate layers of potatoes, clams and vegetable mixture with seasonings. (The amount of salt needed will depend on saltiness of clams.) Pour boiling water and reserved clam liquor over all, top with crumbs, cover and bake in moderate oven, 350° F., about forty-five minutes. This makes a thick chowder and may be eaten with fork instead of soup spoon.

EVENING BUFFET SPREADS

There is no required way to set tables for buffet service. Just arrange the china, silver and napkins and the food attractively so that guests can help themselves with little help from you. Serve hot or cold dishes, as you wish.

Lobster Salad *
Saratoga Potatoes   Hot Rolls
Potato Flour Sponge Cake *
or
Washington Pie *
Jellied Chicken Loaf
Mixed Vegetable Salad *

Hot Rolls
Ice Cream with
Butterscotch Sauce *

Assorted Cold Cuts
Hot Potato Salad *
Rye Bread　　　Dill Pickles
Apple Pie *　　　Cheese

JELLIED CHICKEN LOAF
(8 servings)

1 four-pound fowl, cut up	1 onion
2 teaspoons salt	2 stalks celery
1/4 teaspoon pepper	1 1/2 tablespoons gelatin
1 carrot	1/4 cup cold water

Cook fowl with seasonings and vegetables in water to cover until quite tender. Lift out meat and boil stock down to 3 cups. Strain. Soften gelatin in cold water for five minutes, add to stock, stir until thoroughly dissolved, then cool. Meanwhile, remove skin and bones from fowl, chop meat fine and when stock is cool, add meat to it. As it begins to thicken, turn into a loaf pan previously dipped into cold water. Chill, unmold and garnish with parsley, lettuce or watercress, radish roses, and olives.

CARDINAL PUNCH
(For two tables of bridge)

1 quart cranberry juice or bottled cranberry juice cocktail	1 cup orange juice
	2/3 cup lemon juice
1 cup pineapple juice	1 cup water
	Sugar sirup to sweeten

Combine all ingredients and chill. Pour into glasses over cracked ice or ice cubes.

CHAPTER EIGHTEEN

SPOT REMOVAL

All stains are more easily removed when fresh. The nature of the stain largely determines its treatment. Test any cleaning agent (even water, which spots some fabrics) on an inconspicuous place first. Unsuitable removers might set the stain so as to make eradication impossible.

Candle Wax. Before laundering carefully scrape off sur face wax. Place blotting paper over and under spot and apply warm iron, moving blotting paper as it becomes grease soaked.

Chocolate or Cocoa. If stain does not wash out with soap, stretch fabric over bowl, cover stain with borax, wash with cold water, then, if necessary, pour boiling water through from a height. Or use, on white fabrics only, Javelle water (obtainable from drugstore).

Coffee. Stains on fast-colored cottons and linens usually come out with ordinary laundering. Or stretch fabric over bowl and pour boiling water through from a height. Bleach white fabrics only with Javelle water.

Egg. Wash first in cold water, then in warm water with soap.

Fruit. Most fruit stains (when fresh) can easily be removed by sponging or washing with warm water. Do not use soap. If stain is stubborn, stretch fabric over bowl and

306

pour boiling water through stained area. Or spread lightly with borax, then pour boiling water through. Or bleach white fabrics only with Javelle water.

Grease, including Milk and Cream. Wash in warm water with naphtha soap. Or use blotting paper as for candle wax. To remove traces of stain, bleach with Javelle water.

Ice Cream. Use soap and water or sponge with lukewarm water.

Ink. Moisten with salt and lemon juice, lay in sun, keeping stain constantly moistened. Then wash with soap and water. Or soak fabric in milk for several hours, changing milk as it becomes discolored.

Mildew. Light mildew which has not yet attacked the fabric will often wash out with cold water. Drying in the sun helps to bleach it. Or moisten spots with lemon juice and salt and bleach in sun. Or soak overnight in sour milk or buttermilk and bleach in sun, repeating several times if necessary. Mildew stains are only likely to be removable if treated while very fresh.

Scorches. Slight scorch stains can often be washed out, or may even disappear if fabric is dampened and then hung in sunshine.

Tea. Soak fresh stains in borax solution (1 tsp. borax to 1 pt. water). Then rinse in boiling water. Older stains may be boiled in strong soap suds, or moistened with lemon juice and exposed to sunlight, repeating the process as fabric dries.

Wine. Put thick layer of salt on stain, then pour boiling water through from a height.

CHAPTER NINETEEN

TIPS ON CARVING

Two things are essential to good carving (1) sharp tools and (2) a working knowledge of the anatomy of that which is to be carved. Always *keep guard* of carving fork *up* when carving.

Standing Rib Roast. Place on platter with cut surface up and bone side at front. Insert the fork firmly between ribs. From far outside (fat) edge cut slices $\frac{1}{8}$ to $\frac{1}{4}$ inch thick across grain towards bone. Release slices by cutting close along bone with knife tip.

Rolled Roast. Place on platter with cut sides of meat up and down. Insert fork firmly in side and slice across horizontally from right to left about $\frac{1}{8}$ to $\frac{1}{4}$ inch thick. Remove each tie cord as you come to it.

Roast Leg of Lamb. Place on platter with shank bone to your right and thick meaty part at far side of platter. Insert fork firmly, cut one or two lengthwise slices from surface nearest carver to make base on which meat will rest while carving is done. Turn roast so that it rests on this base and cut in parallel slices ($\frac{1}{4}$ to $\frac{3}{8}$ inch thick) right down from surface to bone. Release slices by slipping knife under them, parallel with bone, and cutting through.

Loin of Lamb or Pork. Cut down between ribs. With lamb each chop with its bone forms a serving. Pork, being richer, is often cut one slice with, the next without a bone.

Baked Half Ham. Place on platter fat side up. Insert knife firmly in solid meat and cut in thin slices from top surface right down to bone. Then run knife parallel to bone to free slices.

Pot Roast. Cut crosswise of grain in even slices somewhat thicker than for rib roast.

Porterhouse or T-Bone Steak. Using small carver remove center and end bones, then cut across the full width of steak so that each serving includes a little tenderloin, also a piece of the larger upper side of steak.

Turkey or Chicken. Place bird on platter with legs toward right. Insert fork firmly in leg then cut through skin around second joint. Pressing against body of bird with flat blade of knife, draw leg toward you using fork as lever. Cut through thigh joint and underside of leg to separate it from body. Remove wing in same manner. Cut thin slices of breast meat, parallel to bone. To reach stuffing, cut through skin crosswise near vent, thus making incision to insert spoon.

Roast Duck. Follow same general method as for chicken, remembering though that the joints are further back than those of chicken, also that the breast meat is thinner so slices should be cut a little broader.

INDEX

Sink, equipment, 4
Snow pudding (lemon sponge), 238
Sole, fillet of, broiling of, 122
Soufflé, definition of, 68
   fish, 157-158
Soups, 108-115
   garnishes and accompaniments
      for, 115-116
Sour milk (buttermilk) biscuits, 81
Sour milk griddle cakes, 88
Spaghetti, 94
   boiled (buttered), 94
   and tomato casserole, 95-96
Spanish (creole) rice, 99
Spanish or creole sauce, 171
Spareribs, 132-133
   baked fresh, 132-133
   barbecued, 133
   broiled, 133
Spice cake, sugarless, 271
Spices, how to use, 66
Spicy loaf cake, 270
Spinach, 200-201
   boiled, 200-201
   molded, 201
   spinach ring, 201
Sponge cake, 264, 266, 272
   potato flour, 272
Sponge cup cakes, 272-273
Spoon bread, 86
Spot removal, 306-307
Squab, broiling of, 121
Squash, 201-202
Staples, buying, 43-45
Steak, 123-125
   broiled, 123
   broiling chart, 121
   hash from, 123
   planked, 123
   porterhouse or T-bone, carving,
      309
   round, baked, Creole, 124
      in casserole, with potato balls,
         124
      stuffed, 124
   steak and kidney pie, 125
Stock, for soups and sauces, 108
   to clarify, 109

Strawberry ice cream, 249
Strawberry and pineapple cup, 287-
   288
Stuffings, 173-176
Succotash, 190
Sugar, 69, 263
Sugar sirup, 299
Sugarless spice cake, 271
Summer squash, buttered, 201
Sunday morning brunches, menus,
   300-301
Suppers or lunches, menus, 301-302
Suprême soup, 115
Suzette sauce, 247
Swedish meat balls, 128
Sweet potatoes, 199-200
   baked, 200
   boiled, 199-200
   mashed, 200
   Southern (candied), 200
Sweetbreads
   to blanch, 141
   broiled, 141-142
   broiling chart, 122
   creamed, 142
   patties, 142
Swiss fondue, 106

TAPIOCA CREAM, 236-237
   chocolate, 237
   fruited, 237
Tartare sauce, 173
Tea, 296, 307
   iced, 296
   Russian, 296
   stain removal, 307
Time and temperature charts
   broiling, 121, 122
   deep fat or French frying, 75
   roasting, 119
   vegetables, 180
Tips and timesavers, 79
Toast, 90-91
Tomato aspic, quick, 214
Tomato and bacon sandwiches, 227
Tomato bisque (cream of tomato
   soup), 112
Tomato clam soup, 115

A CATALOGUE OF
SELECTED DOVER BOOKS
IN ALL FIELDS OF INTEREST

A CATALOGUE OF SELECTED DOVER BOOKS IN ALL FIELDS OF INTEREST

CELESTIAL OBJECTS FOR COMMON TELESCOPES, T. W. Webb. The most used book in amateur astronomy: inestimable aid for locating and identifying nearly 4,000 celestial objects. Edited, updated by Margaret W. Mayall. 77 illustrations. Total of 645pp. 5⅜ x 8½.
20917-2, 20918-0 Pa., Two-vol. set $9.00

HISTORICAL STUDIES IN THE LANGUAGE OF CHEMISTRY, M. P. Crosland. The important part language has played in the development of chemistry from the symbolism of alchemy to the adoption of systematic nomenclature in 1892. ". . . wholeheartedly recommended,"—Science. 15 illustrations. 416pp. of text. 5⅝ x 8¼. 63702-6 Pa. $6.00

BURNHAM'S CELESTIAL HANDBOOK, Robert Burnham, Jr. Thorough, readable guide to the stars beyond our solar system. Exhaustive treatment, fully illustrated. Breakdown is alphabetical by constellation: Andromeda to Cetus in Vol. 1; Chamaeleon to Orion in Vol. 2; and Pavo to Vulpecula in Vol. 3. Hundreds of illustrations. Total of about 2000pp. 6⅛ x 9¼.
23567-X, 23568-8, 23673-0 Pa., Three-vol. set $27.85

THEORY OF WING SECTIONS: INCLUDING A SUMMARY OF AIRFOIL DATA, Ira H. Abbott and A. E. von Doenhoff. Concise compilation of subatomic aerodynamic characteristics of modern NASA wing sections, plus description of theory. 350pp. of tables. 693pp. 5⅜ x 8½.
60586-8 Pa. $8.50

DE RE METALLICA, Georgius Agricola. Translated by Herbert C. Hoover and Lou H. Hoover. The famous Hoover translation of greatest treatise on technological chemistry, engineering, geology, mining of early modern times (1556). All 289 original woodcuts. 638pp. 6¾ x 11.
60006-8 Clothbd. $17.95

THE ORIGIN OF CONTINENTS AND OCEANS, Alfred Wegener. One of the most influential, most controversial books in science, the classic statement for continental drift. Full 1966 translation of Wegener's final (1929) version. 64 illustrations. 246pp. 5⅜ x 8½. 61708-4 Pa. $4.50

THE PRINCIPLES OF PSYCHOLOGY, William James. Famous long course complete, unabridged. Stream of thought, time perception, memory, experimental methods; great work decades ahead of its time. Still valid, useful; read in many classes. 94 figures. Total of 1391pp. 5⅜ x 8½.
20381-6, 20382-4 Pa., Two-vol. set $13.00

THE COMPLETE WOODCUTS OF ALBRECHT DURER, edited by Dr. W. Kurth. 346 in all: "Old Testament," "St. Jerome," "Passion," "Life of Virgin," Apocalypse," many others. Introduction by Campbell Dodgson. 285pp. 8½ x 12¼. 21097-9 Pa. $7.50

DRAWINGS OF ALBRECHT DURER, edited by Heinrich Wolfflin. 81 plates show development from youth to full style. Many favorites; many new. Introduction by Alfred Werner. 96pp. 8⅛ x 11. 22352-3 Pa. $5.00

THE HUMAN FIGURE, Albrecht Dürer. Experiments in various techniques—stereometric, progressive proportional, and others. Also life studies that rank among finest ever done. Complete reprinting of *Dresden Sketchbook*. 170 plates. 355pp. 8⅜ x 11¼. 21042-1 Pa. $7.95

OF THE JUST SHAPING OF LETTERS, Albrecht Dürer. Renaissance artist explains design of Roman majuscules by geometry, also Gothic lower and capitals. Grolier Club edition. 43pp. 7⅞ x 10¾ 21306-4 Pa. $3.00

TEN BOOKS ON ARCHITECTURE, Vitruvius. The most important book ever written on architecture. Early Roman aesthetics, technology, classical orders, site selection, all other aspects. Stands behind everything since. Morgan translation. 331pp. 5⅜ x 8½. 20645-9 Pa. $4.50

THE FOUR BOOKS OF ARCHITECTURE, Andrea Palladio. 16th-century classic responsible for Palladian movement and style. Covers classical architectural remains, Renaissance revivals, classical orders, etc. 1738 Ware English edition. Introduction by A. Placzek. 216 plates. 110pp. of text. 9½ x 12¾. 21308-0 Pa. $10.00

HORIZONS, Norman Bel Geddes. Great industrialist stage designer, "father of streamlining," on application of aesthetics to transportation, amusement, architecture, etc. 1932 prophetic account; function, theory, specific projects. 222 illustrations. 312pp. 7⅞ x 10¾. 23514-9 Pa. $6.95

FRANK LLOYD WRIGHT'S FALLINGWATER, Donald Hoffmann. Full, illustrated story of conception and building of Wright's masterwork at Bear Run, Pa. 100 photographs of site, construction, and details of completed structure. 112pp. 9¼ x 10. 23671-4 Pa. $5.50

THE ELEMENTS OF DRAWING, John Ruskin. Timeless classic by great Viltorian; starts with basic ideas, works through more difficult. Many practical exercises. 48 illustrations. Introduction by Lawrence Campbell. 228pp. 5⅜ x 8½. 22730-8 Pa. $3.75

GIST OF ART, John Sloan. Greatest modern American teacher, Art Students League, offers innumerable hints, instructions, guided comments to help you in painting. Not a formal course. 46 illustrations. Introduction by Helen Sloan. 200pp. 5⅜ x 8½. 23435-5 Pa. $4.00

HOLLYWOOD GLAMOUR PORTRAITS, edited by John Kobal. 145 photos capture the stars from 1926-49, the high point in portrait photography. Gable, Harlow, Bogart, Bacall, Hedy Lamarr, Marlene Dietrich, Robert Montgomery, Marlon Brando, Veronica Lake; 94 stars in all. Full background on photographers, technical aspects, much more. Total of 160pp. 8⅜ x 11¼. 23352-9 Pa. $6.00

THE NEW YORK STAGE: FAMOUS PRODUCTIONS IN PHOTOGRAPHS, edited by Stanley Appelbaum. 148 photographs from Museum of City of New York show 142 plays, 1883-1939. *Peter Pan, The Front Page, Dead End, Our Town,* O'Neill, hundreds of actors and actresses, etc. Full indexes. 154pp. 9½ x 10. 23241-7 Pa. $6.00

DIALOGUES CONCERNING TWO NEW SCIENCES, Galileo Galilei. Encompassing 30 years of experiment and thought, these dialogues deal with geometric demonstrations of fracture of solid bodies, cohesion, leverage, speed of light and sound, pendulums, falling bodies, accelerated motion, etc. 300pp. 5⅜ x 8½. 60099-8 Pa. $4.00

THE GREAT OPERA STARS IN HISTORIC PHOTOGRAPHS, edited by James Camner. 343 portraits from the 1850s to the 1940s: Tamburini, Mario, Caliapin, Jeritza, Melchior, Melba, Patti, Pinza, Schipa, Caruso, Farrar, Steber, Gobbi, and many more—270 performers in all. Index. 199pp. 8⅜ x 11¼. 23575-0 Pa. $7.50

J. S. BACH, Albert Schweitzer. Great full-length study of Bach, life, background to music, music, by foremost modern scholar. Ernest Newman translation. 650 musical examples. Total of 928pp. 5⅜ x 8½. (Available in U.S. only) 21631-4, 21632-2 Pa., Two-vol. set $11.00

COMPLETE PIANO SONATAS, Ludwig van Beethoven. All sonatas in the fine Schenker edition, with fingering, analytical material. One of best modern editions. Total of 615pp. 9 x 12. (Available in U.S. only) 23134-8, 23135-6 Pa., Two-vol. set $15.50

KEYBOARD MUSIC, J. S. Bach. Bach-Gesellschaft edition. For harpsichord, piano, other keyboard instruments. English Suites, French Suites, Six Partitas, Goldberg Variations, Two-Part Inventions, Three-Part Sinfonias. 312pp. 8⅛ x 11. (Available in U.S. only) 22360-4 Pa. $6.95

FOUR SYMPHONIES IN FULL SCORE, Franz Schubert. Schubert's four most popular symphonies: No. 4 in C Minor ("Tragic"); No. 5 in B-flat Major; No. 8 in B Minor ("Unfinished"); No. 9 in C Major ("Great"). Breitkopf & Hartel edition. Study score. 261pp. 9⅜ x 12¼. 23681-1 Pa. $6.50

THE AUTHENTIC GILBERT & SULLIVAN SONGBOOK, W. S. Gilbert, A. S. Sullivan. Largest selection available; 92 songs, uncut, original keys, in piano rendering approved by Sullivan. Favorites and lesser-known fine numbers. Edited with plot synopses by James Spero. 3 illustrations. 399pp. 9 x 12. 23482-7 Pa. $9.95

PRINCIPLES OF ORCHESTRATION, Nikolay Rimsky-Korsakov. Great classical orchestrator provides fundamentals of tonal resonance, progression of parts, voice and orchestra, tutti effects, much else in major document. 330pp. of musical excerpts. 489pp. 6½ x 9¼. 21266-1 Pa. $7.50

TRISTAN UND ISOLDE, Richard Wagner. Full orchestral score with complete instrumentation. Do not confuse with piano reduction. Commentary by Felix Mottl, great Wagnerian conductor and scholar. Study score. 655pp. 8⅛ x 11. 22915-7 Pa. $13.95

REQUIEM IN FULL SCORE, Giuseppe Verdi. Immensely popular with choral groups and music lovers. Republication of edition published by C. F. Peters, Leipzig, n. d. German frontmaker in English translation. Glossary. Text in Latin. Study score. 204pp. 9⅜ x 12¼.
23682-X Pa. $6.00

COMPLETE CHAMBER MUSIC FOR STRINGS, Felix Mendelssohn. All of Mendelssohn's chamber music: Octet, 2 Quintets, 6 Quartets, and Four Pieces for String Quartet. (Nothing with piano is included). Complete works edition (1874-7). Study score. 283 pp. 9⅜ x 12¼.
23679-X Pa. $7.50

POPULAR SONGS OF NINETEENTH-CENTURY AMERICA, edited by Richard Jackson. 64 most important songs: "Old Oaken Bucket," "Arkansas Traveler," "Yellow Rose of Texas," etc. Authentic original sheet music, full introduction and commentaries. 290pp. 9 x 12. 23270-0 Pa. $7.95

COLLECTED PIANO WORKS, Scott Joplin. Edited by Vera Brodsky Lawrence. Practically all of Joplin's piano works—rags, two-steps, marches, waltzes, etc., 51 works in all. Extensive introduction by Rudi Blesh. Total of 345pp. 9 x 12. 23106-2 Pa. $14.95

BASIC PRINCIPLES OF CLASSICAL BALLET, Agrippina Vaganova. Great Russian theoretician, teacher explains methods for teaching classical ballet; incorporates best from French, Italian, Russian schools. 118 illustrations. 175pp. 5⅜ x 8½. 22036-2 Pa. $2.50

CHINESE CHARACTERS, L. Wieger. Rich analysis of 2300 characters according to traditional systems into primitives. Historical-semantic analysis to phonetics (Classical Mandarin) and radicals. 820pp. 6⅛ x 9¼.
21321-8 Pa. $10.00

EGYPTIAN LANGUAGE: EASY LESSONS IN EGYPTIAN HIERO-GLYPHICS, E. A. Wallis Budge. Foremost Egyptologist offers Egyptian grammar, explanation of hieroglyphics, many reading texts, dictionary of symbols. 246pp. 5 x 7½. (Available in U.S. only)
21394-3 Clothbd. $7.50

AN ETYMOLOGICAL DICTIONARY OF MODERN ENGLISH, Ernest Weekley. Richest, fullest work, by foremost British lexicographer. Detailed word histories. Inexhaustible. Do not confuse this with Concise Etymological Dictionary, which is abridged. Total of 856pp. 6½ x 9¼.
21873-2, 21874-0 Pa., Two-vol. set $12.00

CATALOGUE OF DOVER BOOKS

AN AUTOBIOGRAPHY, Margaret Sanger. Exciting personal account of hard-fought battle for woman's right to birth control, against prejudice, church, law. Foremost feminist document. 504pp. 5⅜ x 8½.
20470-7 Pa. $5.50

MY BONDAGE AND MY FREEDOM, Frederick Douglass. Born as a slave, Douglass became outspoken force in antislavery movement. The best of Douglass's autobiographies. Graphic description of slave life. Introduction by P. Foner. 464pp. 5⅜ x 8½. 22457-0 Pa. $5.50

LIVING MY LIFE, Emma Goldman. Candid, no holds barred account by foremost American anarchist: her own life, anarchist movement, famous contemporaries, ideas and their impact. Struggles and confrontations in America, plus deportation to U.S.S.R. Shocking inside account of persecution of anarchists under Lenin. 13 plates. Total of 944pp. 5⅜ x 8½.
22543-7, 22544-5 Pa., Two-vol. set $12.00

LETTERS AND NOTES ON THE MANNERS, CUSTOMS AND CONDITIONS OF THE NORTH AMERICAN INDIANS, George Catlin. Classic account of life among Plains Indians: ceremonies, hunt, warfare, etc. Dover edition reproduces for first time all original paintings. 312 plates. 572pp. of text. 6⅛ x 9¼. 22118-0, 22119-9 Pa.. Two-vol. set $12.00

THE MAYA AND THEIR NEIGHBORS, edited by Clarence L. Hay, others. Synoptic view of Maya civilization in broadest sense, together with Northern, Southern neighbors. Integrates much background, valuable detail not elsewhere. Prepared by greatest scholars: Kroeber, Morley, Thompson, Spinden, Vaillant, many others. Sometimes called Tozzer Memorial Volume. 60 illustrations, linguistic map. 634pp. 5⅜ x 8½.
23510-6 Pa. $10.00

HANDBOOK OF THE INDIANS OF CALIFORNIA, A. L. Kroeber. Foremost American anthropologist offers complete ethnographic study of each group. Monumental classic. 459 illustrations, maps. 995pp. 5⅜ x 8½.
23368-5 Pa. $13.00

SHAKTI AND SHAKTA, Arthur Avalon. First book to give clear, cohesive analysis of Shakta doctrine, Shakta ritual and Kundalini Shakti (yoga). Important work by one of world's foremost students of Shaktic and Tantric thought. 732pp. 5⅜ x 8½. (Available in U.S. only)
23645-5 Pa. $7.95

AN INTRODUCTION TO THE STUDY OF THE MAYA HIEROGLYPHS, Syvanus Griswold Morley. Classic study by one of the truly great figures in hieroglyph research. Still the best introduction for the student for reading Maya hieroglyphs. New introduction by J. Eric S. Thompson. 117 illustrations. 284pp. 5⅜ x 8½. 23108-9 Pa. $4.00

A STUDY OF MAYA ART, Herbert J. Spinden. Landmark classic interprets Maya symbolism, estimates styles, covers ceramics, architecture, murals, stone carvings as artforms. Still a basic book in area. New introduction by J. Eric Thompson. Over 750 illustrations. 341pp. 8⅜ x 11¼.
21235-1 Pa. $6.95

YUCATAN BEFORE AND AFTER THE CONQUEST, Diego de Landa. First English translation of basic book in Maya studies, the only significant account of Yucatan written in the early post-Conquest era. Translated by distinguished Maya scholar William Gates. Appendices, introduction, 4 maps and over 120 illustrations added by translator. 162pp. 5⅜ x 8½.
23622-6 Pa. $3.00

THE MALAY ARCHIPELAGO, Alfred R. Wallace. Spirited travel account by one of founders of modern biology. Touches on zoology, botany, ethnography, geography, and geology. 62 illustrations, maps. 515pp. 5⅜ x 8½.
20187-2 Pa. $6.95

THE DISCOVERY OF THE TOMB OF TUTANKHAMEN, Howard Carter, A. C. Mace. Accompany Carter in the thrill of discovery, as ruined passage suddenly reveals unique, untouched, fabulously rich tomb. Fascinating account, with 106 illustrations. New introduction by J. M. White. Total of 382pp. 5⅜ x 8½. (Available in U.S. only)   23500-9 Pa. $4.00

THE WORLD'S GREATEST SPEECHES, edited by Lewis Copeland and Lawrence W. Lamm. Vast collection of 278 speeches from Greeks up to present. Powerful and effective models; unique look at history. Revised to 1970. Indices. 842pp. 5⅜ x 8½.   20468-5 Pa. $8.95

THE 100 GREATEST ADVERTISEMENTS, Julian Watkins. The priceless ingredient; His master's voice; 99 44/100% pure; over 100 others. How they were written, their impact, etc. Remarkable record. 130 illustrations. 233pp. 7⅞ x 10 3/5.   20540-1 Pa. $5.95

CRUICKSHANK PRINTS FOR HAND COLORING, George Cruickshank. 18 illustrations, one side of a page, on fine-quality paper suitable for watercolors. Caricatures of people in society (c. 1820) full of trenchant wit. Very large format. 32pp. 11 x 16.   23684-6 Pa. $5.00

THIRTY-TWO COLOR POSTCARDS OF TWENTIETH-CENTURY AMERICAN ART, Whitney Museum of American Art. Reproduced in full color in postcard form are 31 art works and one shot of the museum. Calder, Hopper, Rauschenberg, others. Detachable. 16pp. 8¼ x 11.
23629-3 Pa. $3.00

MUSIC OF THE SPHERES: THE MATERIAL UNIVERSE FROM ATOM TO QUASAR SIMPLY EXPLAINED, Guy Murchie. Planets, stars, geology, atoms, radiation, relativity, quantum theory, light, antimatter, similar topics. 319 figures. 664pp. 5⅜ x 8½.
21809-0, 21810-4 Pa., Two-vol. set $11.00

EINSTEIN'S THEORY OF RELATIVITY, Max Born. Finest semi-technical account; covers Einstein, Lorentz, Minkowski, and others, with much detail, much explanation of ideas and math not readily available elsewhere on this level. For student, non-specialist. 376pp. 5⅜ x 8½.
60769-0 Pa. $4.50

THE CURVES OF LIFE, Theodore A. Cook. Examination of shells, leaves, horns, human body, art, etc., in "*the* classic reference on how the golden ratio applies to spirals and helices in nature . . . ."—Martin Gardner. 426 illustrations. Total of 512pp. 5⅜ x 8½.   23701-X Pa. $5.95

AN ILLUSTRATED FLORA OF THE NORTHERN UNITED STATES AND CANADA, Nathaniel L. Britton, Addison Brown. Encyclopedic work covers 4666 species, ferns on up. Everything. Full botanical information, illustration for each. This earlier edition is preferred by many to more recent revisions. 1913 edition. Over 4000 illustrations, total of 2087pp. 6⅛ x 9¼.   22642-5, 22643-3, 22644-1 Pa., Three-vol. set $25.50

MANUAL OF THE GRASSES OF THE UNITED STATES, A. S. Hitchcock, U.S. Dept. of Agriculture. The basic study of American grasses, both indigenous and escapes, cultivated and wild. Over 1400 species. Full descriptions, information. Over 1100 maps, illustrations. Total of 1051pp. 5⅜ x 8½.   22717-0, 22718-9 Pa., Two-vol. set $15.00

THE CACTACEAE,, Nathaniel L. Britton, John N. Rose. Exhaustive, definitive. Every cactus in the world. Full botanical descriptions. Thorough statement of nomenclatures, habitat, detailed finding keys. The one book needed by every cactus enthusiast. Over 1275 illustrations. Total of 1080pp. 8 x 10¼.   21191-6, 21192-4 Clothbd., Two-vol. set $35.00

AMERICAN MEDICINAL PLANTS, Charles F. Millspaugh. Full descriptions, 180 plants covered: history; physical description; methods of preparation with all chemical constituents extracted; all claimed curative or adverse effects. 180 full-page plates. Classification table. 804pp. 6½ x 9¼.   23034-1 Pa. $12.95

A MODERN HERBAL, Margaret Grieve. Much the fullest, most exact, most useful compilation of herbal material. Gigantic alphabetical encyclopedia, from aconite to zedoary, gives botanical information, medical properties, folklore, economic uses, and much else. Indispensable to serious reader. 161 illustrations. 888pp. 6½ x 9¼. (Available in U.S. only)   22798-7, 22799-5 Pa., Two-vol. set $13.00

THE HERBAL or GENERAL HISTORY OF PLANTS, John Gerard. The 1633 edition revised and enlarged by Thomas Johnson. Containing almost 2850 plant descriptions and 2705 superb illustrations, Gerard's *Herbal* is a monumental work, the book all modern English herbals are derived from, the one herbal every serious enthusiast should have in its entirety. Original editions are worth perhaps $750. 1678pp. 8½ x 12¼.   23147-X Clothbd. $50.00

MANUAL OF THE TREES OF NORTH AMERICA, Charles S. Sargent. The basic survey of every native tree and tree-like shrub, 717 species in all. Extremely full descriptions, information on habitat, growth, locales, economics, etc. Necessary to every serious tree lover. Over 100 finding keys. 783 illustrations. Total of 986pp. 5⅜ x 8½.   20277-1, 20278-X Pa., Two-vol. set $11.00

AMERICAN BIRD ENGRAVINGS, Alexander Wilson et al. All 76 plates. from Wilson's *American Ornithology* (1808-14), most important ornithological work before Audubon, plus 27 plates from the supplement (1825-33) by Charles Bonaparte. Over 250 birds portrayed. 8 plates also reproduced in full color. 111pp. 9⅜ x 12½. 23195-X Pa. $6.00

CRUICKSHANK'S PHOTOGRAPHS OF BIRDS OF AMERICA, Allan D. Cruickshank. Great ornithologist, photographer presents 177 closeups, groupings, panoramas, flightings, etc., of about 150 different birds. Expanded *Wings in the Wilderness.* Introduction by Helen G. Cruickshank. 191pp. 8¼ x 11. 23497-5 Pa. $6.00

AMERICAN WILDLIFE AND PLANTS, A. C. Martin, et al. Describes food habits of more than 1000 species of mammals, birds, fish. Special treatment of important food plants. Over 300 illustrations. 500pp. 5⅜ x 8½. 20793-5 Pa. $4.95

THE PEOPLE CALLED SHAKERS, Edward D. Andrews. Lifetime of research, definitive study of Shakers: origins, beliefs, practices, dances, social organization, furniture and crafts, impact on 19th-century USA, present heritage. Indispensable to student of American history, collector. 33 illustrations. 351pp. 5⅜ x 8½. 21081-2 Pa. $4.50

OLD NEW YORK IN EARLY PHOTOGRAPHS, Mary Black. New York City as it was in 1853-1901, through 196 wonderful photographs from N.-Y. Historical Society. Great Blizzard, Lincoln's funeral procession, great buildings. 228pp. 9 x 12. 22907-6 Pa. $8.95

MR. LINCOLN'S CAMERA MAN: MATHEW BRADY, Roy Meredith. Over 300 Brady photos reproduced directly from original negatives, photos. Jackson, Webster, Grant, Lee, Carnegie, Barnum; Lincoln; Battle Smoke, Death of Rebel Sniper, Atlanta Just After Capture. Lively commentary. 368pp. 8⅜ x 11¼. 23021-X Pa. $8.95

TRAVELS OF WILLIAM BARTRAM, William Bartram. From 1773-8, Bartram explored Northern Florida, Georgia, Carolinas, and reported on wild life, plants, Indians, early settlers. Basic account for period, entertaining reading. Edited by Mark Van Doren. 13 illustrations. 141pp. 5⅜ x 8½. 20013-2 Pa. $5.00

THE GENTLEMAN AND CABINET MAKER'S DIRECTOR, Thomas Chippendale. Full reprint, 1762 style book, most influential of all time; chairs, tables, sofas, mirrors, cabinets, etc. 200 plates, plus 24 photographs of surviving pieces. 249pp. 9⅞ x 12¾. 21601-2 Pa. $7.95

AMERICAN CARRIAGES, SLEIGHS, SULKIES AND CARTS, edited by Don H. Berkebile. 168 Victorian illustrations from catalogues, trade journals, fully captioned. Useful for artists. Author is Assoc. Curator, Div. of Transportation of Smithsonian Institution. 168pp. 8½ x 9½. 23328-6 Pa. $5.00

HISTORY OF BACTERIOLOGY, William Bulloch. The only comprehensive history of bacteriology from the beginnings through the 19th century. Special emphasis is given to biography-Leeuwenhoek, etc. Brief accounts of 350 bacteriologists form a separate section. No clearer, fuller study, suitable to scientists and general readers, has yet been written. 52 illustrations. 448pp. 5⅝ x 8¼. 23761-3 Pa. $6.50

THE COMPLETE NONSENSE OF EDWARD LEAR, Edward Lear. All nonsense limericks, zany alphabets, Owl and Pussycat, songs, nonsense botany, etc., illustrated by Lear. Total of 321pp. 5⅜ x 8½. (Available in U.S. only) 20167-8 Pa. $3.95

INGENIOUS MATHEMATICAL PROBLEMS AND METHODS, Louis A. Graham. Sophisticated material from Graham *Dial*, applied and pure; stresses solution methods. Logic, number theory, networks, inversions, etc. 237pp. 5⅜ x 8½. 20545-2 Pa. $4.50

BEST MATHEMATICAL PUZZLES OF SAM LOYD, edited by Martin Gardner. Bizarre, original, whimsical puzzles by America's greatest puzzler. From fabulously rare *Cyclopedia*, including famous 14-15 puzzles, the Horse of a Different Color, 115 more. Elementary math. 150 illustrations. 167pp. 5⅜ x 8½. 20498-7 Pa. $2.75

THE BASIS OF COMBINATION IN CHESS, J. du Mont. Easy-to-follow, instructive book on elements of combination play, with chapters on each piece and every powerful combination team—two knights, bishop and knight, rook and bishop, etc. 250 diagrams. 218pp. 5⅜ x 8½. (Available in U.S. only) 23644-7 Pa. $3.50

MODERN CHESS STRATEGY, Ludek Pachman. The use of the queen, the active king, exchanges, pawn play, the center, weak squares, etc. Section on rook alone worth price of the book. Stress on the moderns. Often considered the most important book on strategy. 314pp. 5⅜ x 8½. 20290-9 Pa. $4.50

LASKER'S MANUAL OF CHESS, Dr. Emanuel Lasker. Great world champion offers very thorough coverage of all aspects of chess. Combinations, position play, openings, end game, aesthetics of chess, philosophy of struggle, much more. Filled with analyzed games. 390pp. 5⅜ x 8½. 20640-8 Pa. $5.00

500 MASTER GAMES OF CHESS, S. Tartakower, J. du Mont. Vast collection of great chess games from 1798-1938, with much material nowhere else readily available. Fully annoted, arranged by opening for easier study. 664pp. 5⅜ x 8½. 23208-5 Pa. $7.50

A GUIDE TO CHESS ENDINGS, Dr. Max Euwe, David Hooper. One of the finest modern works on chess endings. Thorough analysis of the most frequently encountered endings by former world champion. 331 examples, each with diagram. 248pp. 5⅜ x 8½. 23332-4 Pa. $3.75

SECOND PIATIGORSKY CUP, edited by Isaac Kashdan. One of the greatest tournament books ever produced in the English language. All 90 games of the 1966 tournament, annotated by players, most annotated by both players. Features Petrosian, Spassky, Fischer, Larsen, six others. 228pp. 5⅜ x 8½.   23572-6 Pa. $3.50

ENCYCLOPEDIA OF CARD TRICKS, revised and edited by Jean Hugard. How to perform over 600 card tricks, devised by the world's greatest magicians: impromptus, spelling tricks, key cards, using special packs, much, much more. Additional chapter on card technique. 66 illustrations. 402pp. 5⅜ x 8½. (Available in U.S. only)   21252-1 Pa. $4.95

MAGIC: STAGE ILLUSIONS, SPECIAL EFFECTS AND TRICK PHO-TOGRAPHY, Albert A. Hopkins, Henry R. Evans. One of the great classics; fullest, most authorative explanation of vanishing lady, levitations, scores of other great stage effects. Also small magic, automata, stunts. 446 illus-trations. 556pp. 5⅜ x 8½.   23344-8 Pa. $6.95

THE SECRETS OF HOUDINI, J. C. Cannell. Classic study of Houdini's incredible magic, exposing closely-kept professional secrets and revealing, in general terms, the whole art of stage magic. 67 illustrations. 279pp. 5⅜ x 8½.   22913-0 Pa. $4.00

HOFFMANN'S MODERN MAGIC, Professor Hoffmann. One of the best, and best-known, magicians' manuals of the past century. Hundreds of tricks from card tricks and simple sleight of hand to elaborate illusions involving construction of complicated machinery. 332 illustrations. 563pp. 5⅜ x 8½.   23623-4 Pa. $6.00

MADAME PRUNIER'S FISH COOKERY BOOK, Mme. S. B. Prunier. More than 1000 recipes from world famous Prunier's of Paris and London, specially adapted here for American kitchen. Grilled tournedos with anchovy butter, Lobster a la Bordelaise, Prunier's prized desserts, more. Glossary. 340pp. 5⅜ x 8½. (Available in U.S. only)   22679-4 Pa. $3.00

FRENCH COUNTRY COOKING FOR AMERICANS, Louis Diat. 500 easy-to-make, authentic provincial recipes compiled by former head chef at New York's Fitz-Carlton Hotel: onion soup, lamb stew, potato pie, more. 309pp. 5⅜ x 8½.   23665-X Pa. $3.95

SAUCES, FRENCH AND FAMOUS, Louis Diat. Complete book gives over 200 specific recipes: bechamel, Bordelaise, hollandaise, Cumberland, apri-cot, etc. Author was one of this century's finest chefs, originator of vichyssoise and many other dishes. Index. 156pp. 5⅜ x 8.
                                                         23663-3 Pa. $2.75

TOLL HOUSE TRIED AND TRUE RECIPES, Ruth Graves Wakefield. Authentic recipes from the famous Mass. restaurant: popovers, veal and ham loaf, Toll House baked beans, chocolate cake crumb pudding, much more. Many helpful hints. Nearly 700 recipes. Index. 376pp. 5⅜ x 8½.
                                                         23560-2 Pa. $4.50

THE PHILOSOPHY OF HISTORY, Georg W. Hegel. Great classic of Western thought develops concept that history is not chance but a rational process, the evolution of freedom. 457pp. 5⅜ x 8½.   20112-0 Pa. $4.50

LANGUAGE, TRUTH AND LOGIC, Alfred J. Ayer. Famous, clear introduction to Vienna, Cambridge schools of Logical Positivism. Role of philosophy, elimination of metaphysics, nature of analysis, etc. 160pp. 5⅜ x 8½. (Available in U.S. only)   20010-8 Pa. $2.00

A PREFACE TO LOGIC, Morris R. Cohen. Great City College teacher in renowned, easily followed exposition of formal logic, probability, values, logic and world order and similar topics; no previous background needed. 209pp. 5⅜ x 8½.   23517-3 Pa. $3.50

REASON AND NATURE, Morris R. Cohen. Brilliant analysis of reason and its multitudinous ramifications by charismatic teacher. Interdisciplinary, synthesizing work widely praised when it first appeared in 1931. Second (1953) edition. Indexes. 496pp. 5⅜ x 8½.   23633-1 Pa. $6.50

AN ESSAY CONCERNING HUMAN UNDERSTANDING, John Locke. The only complete edition of enormously important classic, with authoritative editorial material by A. C. Fraser. Total of 1176pp. 5⅜ x 8½.
    20530-4, 20531-2 Pa., Two-vol. set $16.00

HANDBOOK OF MATHEMATICAL FUNCTIONS WITH FORMULAS, GRAPHS, AND MATHEMATICAL TABLES, edited by Milton Abramowitz and Irene A. Stegun. Vast compendium: 29 sets of tables, some to as high as 20 places. 1,046pp. 8 x 10½.   61272-4 Pa. $14.95

MATHEMATICS FOR THE PHYSICAL SCIENCES, Herbert S. Wilf. Highly acclaimed work offers clear presentations of vector spaces and matrices, orthogonal functions, roots of polynomial equations, conformal mapping, calculus of variations, etc. Knowledge of theory of functions of real and complex variables is assumed. Exercises and solutions. Index. 284pp. 5⅝ x 8¼.   63635-6 Pa. $5.00

THE PRINCIPLE OF RELATIVITY, Albert Einstein et al. Eleven most important original papers on special and general theories. Seven by Einstein, two by Lorentz, one each by Minkowski and Weyl. All translated, unabridged. 216pp. 5⅜ x 8½.   60081-5 Pa. $3.50

THERMODYNAMICS, Enrico Fermi. A classic of modern science. Clear, organized treatment of systems, first and second laws, entropy, thermodynamic potentials, gaseous reactions, dilute solutions, entropy constant. No math beyond calculus required. Problems. 160pp. 5⅜ x 8½.
    60361-X Pa. $3.00

ELEMENTARY MECHANICS OF FLUIDS, Hunter Rouse. Classic undergraduate text widely considered to be far better than many later books. Ranges from fluid velocity and acceleration to role of compressibility in fluid motion. Numerous examples, questions, problems. 224 illustrations. 376pp. 5⅝ x 8¼.   63699-2 Pa. $5.00

THE COMPLETE BOOK OF DOLL MAKING AND COLLECTING, Catherine Christopher. Instructions, patterns for dozens of dolls, from rag doll on up to elaborate, historically accurate figures. Mould faces, sew clothing, make doll houses, etc. Also collecting information. Many illustrations. 288pp. 6 x 9. 22066-4 Pa. $4.50

THE DAGUERREOTYPE IN AMERICA, Beaumont Newhall. Wonderful portraits, 1850's townscapes, landscapes; full text plus 104 photographs. The basic book. Enlarged 1976 edition. 272pp. 8¼ x 11¼. 23322-7 Pa. $7.95

CRAFTSMAN HOMES, Gustav Stickley. 296 architectural drawings, floor plans, and photographs illustrate 40 different kinds of "Mission-style" homes from The Craftsman (1901-16), voice of American style of simplicity and organic harmony. Thorough coverage of Craftsman idea in text and picture, now collector's item. 224pp. 8⅛ x 11. 23791-5 Pa. $6.00

PEWTER-WORKING: INSTRUCTIONS AND PROJECTS, Burl N. Osborn. & Gordon O. Wilber. Introduction to pewter-working for amateur craftsman. History and characteristics of pewter; tools, materials, step-by-step instructions. Photos, line drawings, diagrams. Total of 160pp. 7⅞ x 10¾. 23786-9 Pa. $3.50

THE GREAT CHICAGO FIRE, edited by David Lowe. 10 dramatic, eye-witness accounts of the 1871 disaster, including one of the aftermath and rebuilding, plus 70 contemporary photographs and illustrations of the ruins—courthouse, Palmer House, Great Central Depot, etc. Introduction by David Lowe. 87pp. 8¼ x 11. 23771-0 Pa. $4.00

SILHOUETTES: A PICTORIAL ARCHIVE OF VARIED ILLUSTRATIONS, edited by Carol Belanger Grafton. Over 600 silhouettes from the 18th to 20th centuries include profiles and full figures of men and women, children, birds and animals, groups and scenes, nature, ships, an alphabet. Dozens of uses for commercial artists and craftspeople. 144pp. 8⅜ x 11¼. 23781-8 Pa. $4.50

ANIMALS: 1,419 COPYRIGHT-FREE ILLUSTRATIONS OF MAMMALS, BIRDS, FISH, INSECTS, ETC., edited by Jim Harter. Clear wood engravings present, in extremely lifelike poses, over 1,000 species of animals. One of the most extensive copyright-free pictorial sourcebooks of its kind. Captions. Index. 284pp. 9 x 12. 23766-4 Pa. $8.95

INDIAN DESIGNS FROM ANCIENT ECUADOR, Frederick W. Shaffer. 282 original designs by pre-Columbian Indians of Ecuador (500-1500 A.D.). Designs include people, mammals, birds, reptiles, fish, plants, heads, geometric designs. Use as is or alter for advertising, textiles, leathercraft, etc. Introduction. 95pp. 8¾ x 11¼. 23764-8 Pa. $3.50

SZIGETI ON THE VIOLIN, Joseph Szigeti. Genial, loosely structured tour by premier violinist, featuring a pleasant mixture of reminiscenes, insights into great music and musicians, innumerable tips for practicing violinists. 385 musical passages. 256pp. 5⅝ x 8¼. 23763-X Pa. $4.00

DRAWINGS OF WILLIAM BLAKE, William Blake. 92 plates from Book of Job, *Divine Comedy, Paradise Lost,* visionary heads, mythological figures, Laocoon, etc. Selection, introduction, commentary by Sir Geoffrey Keynes. 178pp. 8⅛ x 11. 22303-5 Pa. $4.00

ENGRAVINGS OF HOGARTH, William Hogarth. 101 of Hogarth's greatest works: *Rake's Progress, Harlot's Progress, Illustrations for Hudibras, Before and After, Beer Street and Gin Lane,* many more. Full commentary. 256pp. 11 x 13¾. 22479-1 Pa. $12.95

DAUMIER: 120 GREAT LITHOGRAPHS, Honore Daumier. Wide-ranging collection of lithographs by the greatest caricaturist of the 19th century. Concentrates on eternally popular series on lawyers, on married life, on liberated women, etc. Selection, introduction, and notes on plates by Charles F. Ramus. Total of 158pp. 9⅜ x 12¼. 23512-2 Pa. $6.00

DRAWINGS OF MUCHA, Alphonse Maria Mucha. Work reveals draftsman of highest caliber: studies for famous posters and paintings, renderings for book illustrations and ads, etc. 70 works, 9 in color; including 6 items not drawings. Introduction. List of illustrations. 72pp. 9⅜ x 12¼. (Available in U.S. only) 23672-2 Pa. $4.00

GIOVANNI BATTISTA PIRANESI: DRAWINGS IN THE PIERPONT MORGAN LIBRARY, Giovanni Battista Piranesi. For first time ever all of Morgan Library's collection, world's largest. 167 illustrations of rare Piranesi drawings—archeological, architectural, decorative and visionary. Essay, detailed list of drawings, chronology, captions. Edited by Felice Stampfle. 144pp. 9⅜ x 12¼. 23714-1 Pa. $7.50

NEW YORK ETCHINGS (1905-1949), John Sloan. All of important American artist's N.Y. life etchings. 67 works include some of his best art; also lively historical record—Greenwich Village, tenement scenes. Edited by Sloan's widow. Introduction and captions. 79pp. 8⅜ x 11¼. 23651-X Pa. $4.00

CHINESE PAINTING AND CALLIGRAPHY: A PICTORIAL SURVEY, Wan-go Weng. 69 fine examples from John M. Crawford's matchless private collection: landscapes, birds, flowers, human figures, etc., plus calligraphy. Every basic form included: hanging scrolls, handscrolls, album leaves, fans, etc. 109 illustrations. Introduction. Captions. 192pp. 8⅞ x 11¾. 23707-9 Pa. $7.95

DRAWINGS OF REMBRANDT, edited by Seymour Slive. Updated Lippmann, Hofstede de Groot edition, with definitive scholarly apparatus. All portraits, biblical sketches, landscapes, nudes, Oriental figures, classical studies, together with selection of work by followers. 550 illustrations. Total of 630pp. 9⅛ x 12¼. 21485-0, 21486-9 Pa., Two-vol. set $15.00

THE DISASTERS OF WAR, Francisco Goya. 83 etchings record horrors of Napoleonic wars in Spain and war in general. Reprint of 1st edition, plus 3 additional plates. Introduction by Philip Hofer. 97pp. 9⅜ x 8¼. 21872-4 Pa. $4.00

GEOMETRY, RELATIVITY AND THE FOURTH DIMENSION, Rudolf Rucker. Exposition of fourth dimension, means of visualization, concepts of relativity as Flatland characters continue adventures. Popular, easily followed yet accurate, profound. 141 illustrations. 133pp. 5⅜ x 8½.
23400-2 Pa. $2.75

THE ORIGIN OF LIFE, A. I. Oparin. Modern classic in biochemistry, the first rigorous examination of possible evolution of life from nitrocarbon compounds. Non-technical, easily followed. Total of 295pp. 5⅜ x 8½.
60213-3 Pa. $4.00

PLANETS, STARS AND GALAXIES, A. E. Fanning. Comprehensive introductory survey: the sun, solar system, stars, galaxies, universe, cosmology; quasars, radio stars, etc. 24pp. of photographs. 189pp. 5⅜ x 8½. (Available in U.S. only)
21680-2 Pa. $3.75

THE THIRTEEN BOOKS OF EUCLID'S ELEMENTS, translated with introduction and commentary by Sir Thomas L. Heath. Definitive edition. Textual and linguistic notes, mathematical analysis, 2500 years of critical commentary. Do not confuse with abridged school editions. Total of 1414pp. 5⅜ x 8½.
60088-2, 60089-0, 60090-4 Pa., Three-vol. set $18.50

Prices subject to change without notice.

Available at your book dealer or write for free catalogue to Dept. GI, Dover Publications, Inc., 31 East Second Street, Mineola, N.Y. 11501. Dover publishes more than 175 books each year on science, elementary and advanced mathematics, biology, music, art, literary history, social sciences and other areas.